King Herod's Dream

Figure 1.
The site of ancient Caesarea, looking northwest. In the left center, the Crusader fortifications are visible and beyond them the modern jetty that rests on top of the southern breakwater of Herod's harbor. North of the harbor, the eddies it created cut away the beach, forming the north bay. To the upper right, the line of the Byzantine wall can be seen curving between the ancient city and a modern development of villas. Just inside the Byzantine wall, in the site's southeastern quarter, lay the circus, or hippodrome, the large rectangle visible at the lower right. To the extreme left, Kibbutz Sdot Yam.
PICTORIAL ARCHIVE
(Near Eastern History) Est.

King Herod's Dream

Caesarea on the Sea

KENNETH G. HOLUM
University of Maryland

ROBERT L. HOHLFELDER
University of Colorado

ROBERT J. BULL
Drew University

AVNER RABAN
Haifa University

General Editors
Kenneth G. Holum
Robert L. Hohlfelder

Editor for Architecture
Robert L. Vann

Consulting Editor
Roberta Blender Maltese

W. W. NORTON & COMPANY
New York *London*

Published simultaneously in Canada by Penguin Books Canada Ltd., 2801 John Street, Markham, Ontario L3R 1B4.
Printed in Hong Kong.

The text of this book is composed in Stempel Garamond.
The composition is by the Sarabande Press,
Manufacturing by South China Printing Co.,
and the book was designed by Homans Design, Inc.

Published on the occasion of an exhibition organized by the Smithsonian Institution Traveling Exhibition Service in cooperation with the Department of Antiquities and Museums of the State of Israel, the Caesarea Ancient Harbour Excavation Project, the Joint Expedition to Caesarea Maritima, and the University of Maryland Center for Archaeology.

Itinerary 1988–90: Evans Gallery, The Smithsonian Institution, Washington, D.C.; Natural History Museum of Los Angeles, Los Angeles, California; Denver Museum of Natural History, Denver, Colorado; Science Museum of Minnesota, St. Paul, Minnesota; Boston Museum of Science, Boston, Massachusetts, and the Canadian Museum of Civilization, Ottawa, Ontario, Canada.

Major support for the exhibition came from the National Endowment for the Humanities, the Smithsonian Institution Special Exhibition Fund, and the University of Maryland. El Al Israel Airlines provided transportation assistance.

First Edition

Library of Congress Cataloging-in-Publication Data

King Herod's dream : Caesarea on the sea / Kenneth G. Holum . . .
[et al.] ; general editors, Kenneth G. Holum, Robert L. Hohlfelder;
editor for architecture, Robert L. Vann; consulting editor,
Roberta Blender Maltese.
p. cm.
Bibliography: p.
Includes index.
1. Caesarea (Israel)—History. 2. Caesarea (Israel)—Antiquities.
3. Excavations (Archaeology)—Israel—Caesarea. 4. Herod I, King of
Judea, 73-4 B.C. 5. Israel—Antiquities. I. Holum, Kenneth G.
DS110.C13K56 1988
933—dc19 87-28316

ISBN 0-393-02493-8

W. W. Norton & Company, Inc., 500 Fifth Avenue, New York, N. Y. 10110
W. W. Norton & Company Ltd., 37 Great Russell Street, London WC1B 3NU
1 2 3 4 5 6 7 8 9 0

To the Caesarea volunteers

Contents

PREFACE 5

ACKNOWLEDGMENTS 6

CHAPTER 1: Introduction: Archaeologists and a City 11

CHAPTER 2: The Search for Strato's Tower 25

CHAPTER 3: King Herod's City 55

CHAPTER 4: The Daughter of Edom: Caesarea in the Roman Period 107

CHAPTER 5: The Advent of Christianity:
Caesarea in the Byzantine Period 155

CHAPTER 6: Caesarea Under Muslim Rule:
"A Beautiful City . . . on the Greek Sea" 201

CHAPTER 7: Caesarea Under Crusader Rule:
A European City in the Holy Land 217

EPILOGUE: Desolation and Development 237

BIBLIOGRAPHY 242

INDEX 245

Preface

This book, the story of archaeologists and a city, represents a congruence of favorable circumstances. Two archaeological expeditions to Caesarea Maritima, a coastal site in Israel, agreed to make their work accessible to the public through a museum exhibition called "King Herod's Dream." One of them, the Joint Expedition to Caesarea Maritima (JECM), had been excavating the land site there since 1972, and the other, the Caesarea Ancient Harbour Excavation Project (CAHEP), was organized in 1980 to explore ancient Caesarea's magnificent port. Archaeologists at the University of Maryland took on the task of producing the exhibition and were soon joined, as full partners, by the Israel Department of Antiquities and Museums (IDAM) and the Smithsonian Institution's Traveling Exhibition Service (SITES). The National Endowment for the Humanities assisted with a large grant to underwrite part of the cost, and distinguished natural history museums in major cities agreed to include the exhibition in their programs.

King Herod's Dream tells the story of an important archaeological site that has been too little known. The book's photographs and drawings—assembled for the exhibition from a wide variety of sources and at considerable expense—tell much about Caesarea even without words. To enliven and complete the story, we have added the voices of ancient writers that speak in literary texts and inscriptions. Our own interpretations have made this into a book of history.

We hope that readers will share our fascination with the science of archaeology and with Caesarea. It is an entrancing place, worth visiting for pleasure, where the blue Mediterranean's wide, sandy beaches and exotic vegetation embrace imposing ancient ruins and statuary. But, as this book hopes to show, Caesarea is much more. This beautiful seaside resort in Israel is proving to be a brimming repository, filled with insights about the human past.

Acknowledgments

We acknowledge that this story, and the exhibition "King Herod's Dream," originated with many others. Five years ago, William Hornyak, past director of the University of Maryland's Center for Archaeology, first proposed joining the work of CAHEP and JECM in the same exhibition. The members of the center set the project in motion, while Gerald Tyson, Kent Cartwright, and, more recently, Deborah Read of the University's College of Arts and Humanities took on the daunting task of managing it and raising funds. Robert G. Smith, vice-president for university relations, has also been a constant source of encouragement. Mary Ann Watkins, College of Arts and Humanities, kept track of schedules, Patricia Honey and Darlene King, History Department, of the project's correspondence and accounts.

Making incohate plans into an exhibition was the task of the Smithsonian Institution. The Smithsonian has had a long-standing interest in archaeology and a commitment to translating scholarly research into public programs. Without the national museum's institutional commitment and resources from its Special Exhibition Fund, this exhibition—the first to survey both land-based and underwater archaeology of a single site—would not have been possible. We are grateful to the Smithsonian's assistant secretary for museums, Tom L. Freudenheim, for his support of the project.

Within the Smithsonian, SITES took the lead in creating "King Herod's Dream." Anne R. Gossett, project director for SITES, brought the capacities of a seasoned museum professional to the task of turning academic research into an actual exhibition. Exhibition assistant Joan MacKeith cheerfully worked on coordination of this complex project. Lee Williams, registrar, and assistants Carol Farra and Barbara Irwin handled transportation of and safeguarding the artifacts. Myriam

Springuel developed interpretive and educational programming. Public information efforts were imaginatively presented by Deborah Bennett, and Andrea P. Stevens supervised publication of the brochure and poster for the exhibition. Linda Bell, assistant director for administration, and Allegra Wright have dealt efficiently with the financial elements of the project.

The Smithsonian Office of Exhibits Central (OEC), under the direction of Karen Fort and Walter Sorrell, collaborated closely with SITES, undertaking the task of editing, designing, and fabricating the exhibition. The clarity of the exhibition text resulted from the skillful editing of Rosemary Regan. Designer Mary Dillon created a handsome environment for the presentation of the artifacts. The details of exhibit construction were carried out by Ken Clevinger and members of the fabrication unit, as well as James "Buddy" Speight and the graphics department. A special word of thanks must go to the many talented men and women of the OEC model shop, under the direction of Ben Snouffer, who worked diligently to create extraordinarily accurate models to enhance the exhibition.

Others who helped make the exhibition "King Herod's Dream" a reality were videographer Larry Klein and cameraman Mark Traver, responsible for the videos, and Timothy Kearns and Shorieh Talaat, who created additional models. The American Friends of the National Maritime Museum, Haifa, graciously contributed the Herodian harbor model. The National Geographic Society and Richard Cleave of the Pictorial Archive, Jerusalem, provided beautiful photographs and artwork.

The following museums and collections provided both assistance and materials for the exhibition and this book: In Israel—The Caesarea Museum, Kibbutz Sdot Yam; the Center for Maritime Studies, University of Haifa, Haifa; the Institute of Archaeology, The Hebrew University, Jerusalem; the Israel Department of Antiquities and Museums (IDAM), Jerusalem; the Israel Museum, Jerusalem; the Museum of Ancient Art, Haifa; Museum Ha'aretz, Tel Aviv; The National Maritime Museum, Haifa; and in the United States—the Drew University Institute for Archaeological Research (DIAR), Madison, N.J.; Dumbarton Oaks, Washington, D.C.; Private Collection, Baltimore, Md.; the Walters Art Gallery, Baltimore, Md.

A wider group of talented and devoted people contributed both to the exhibition and this book. Aaron Levin, staff photographer for the project, created luminous images of Caesarea and its objects. Robert L. Vann, who codirects CAHEP and once served as staff architect for JECM, supervised the drawing of the plans and perspectives. Ann Guida of DIAR and Zaraza Friedmann of the Center for Maritime Studies, Haifa, spent many hours assembling illustrations and data. Celia Gray typed much of the manuscript. Marsha L. Rozenblit read the first drafts with a critical eye, suggested countless improvements, and then unstintingly read them again. Roberta Blender Maltese's skill and patience in correcting and editing a complicated manuscript brought it to the press. James L. Mairs, senior editor, Patty Peltekos, copy editor, Katy Homans, designer, Amy Silin, editorial assistant, and others on the staff of W. W. Norton & Company made the manuscript and illustrations into a volume worthy of one of America's most distinguished publishing houses.

On the Israeli side, Avi Eitan, director of IDAM, heads the list of the authors' colleagues who made this project a rewarding international partnership. "King Herod's Dream" would never have been realized without his strong backing at an early stage and his arrangements to have Israel contribute generously to the exhibition from its archaeological treasures. Ruth Peled, also of IDAM, and Avshi Zemer, director of the Museum of Ancient Art, Haifa, served effectively as our Israeli curators. Many of Israel's most highly regarded archaeologists and museum professionals—especially Ayala Sussmann, Joseph Ringel, Yoram Tsafrir, Yael Israeli, Maud Spaer, Naama Brosh, Ehud Netzer, Avraham Negev, Iren Levitt, Varda Sussman, Lee I. Levin, Raya Zommer, and Gideon Foerster—offered advice and helped us locate appropriate objects and photographs. Aharon Wegman belongs in a class by himself. A member of Kibbutz Sdot Yam, he has worked with or advised every archaeological expedition that has excavated at Caesarea. As director of the Caesarea museum he presides over a small but exquisite collection of the most important archaeological objects from the site. His knowledge of Caesarea makes him an invaluable resource for students of its antiquities, not least for those who have attempted to recreate "King Herod's Dream."

This book, and the exhibition that it mirrors, render tribute to a far larger group of men and women: those who have excavated at Caesarea with JECM or CAHEP. The story is really theirs. The authors recognize especially Edgar Krentz, JECM's associate director, Olin Storvick, supervisor of JECM's field G, and Vivian Bull, registrar and conservator, and archaeologists Marie Spiro, Kenneth Vine, Robert Wiemken, Jeffrey Blakely, James Boyce, Willard Hamrick, and John McCray. From CAHEP it is scholars of the caliber of John Oleson, codirector of the expedition from 1980 to 1985; Elisha Linder, the pioneer of underwater archaeology in Israel; Steven Sidebotham, Thomas Hillard, William Murray, Michael Fitzgerald, Ruthi Gertwagen, Andrew Sherwood, Paul Davis; and Robert Stieglitz, codirector since 1986, who have amassed the knowledge in this book. These must stand for a host of skilled people—field and area supervisors, dive technicians and camp managers, photographers and draftsmen, ceramicists and numismatists, epigraphers and osteologists, registrars and conservators, geologists, botanists, and chemists—whose work this book reflects.

Above all, however, it is a group of extraordinary men and women from all walks of life who have made both this book and the exhibition "King Herod's Dream" a reality. They are the volunteers who found time for archaeology in their busy lives and came to Caesarea to dig. For four, five, or six weeks they labored from early morning under the hot sun or in the sea. They were unpaid and supported their participation with their own resources. After a first grueling season, many returned for a second season, or a third, or a fourth. Archaeology is a labor of love, and these were amateurs in the best sense. It is to them that we dedicate this book, with gratitude and appreciation.

K.G.H.
R.L.H.
R.J.B.
A.R.

Caesarea
July 1987

CHAPTER I

Introduction: Archaeologists and a City

On a hot summer day in 1972 at Caesarea, an ancient city on the Mediterranean coast of Israel, archaeologists of the Joint Expedition to Caesarea Maritima (JECM) uncovered a woman in marble (fig. 2). Whom the broken statue might represent – an empress, perhaps a goddess – excited and intrigued the excavators. Subsequently the team found other fragments, and today the statue – reassembled, although still lacking her head, arms, and much of her right leg – stands just over life-size in the foyer of the Caesarea Museum (fig. 3). There she greets visitors to the antiquities collection lovingly assembled by the members of the adjacent kibbutz, Sdot Yam. Visitors to the museum also wonder, "Who is this woman?"

Figure 2. Archaeologists of the Joint Expedition to Caesarea Maritima (JECM) uncover large fragment of a marble statue.
JECM photo.

Caesarea Maritima was founded late in the first century B.C.E.* by Herod the Great, king of Judaea. Notorious for his ambition as well as his cruelty, this man brought fabulous building projects to completion – palaces, temples, and even entire cities. One of the cities was Caesarea, which grew, after his death, into one of the largest urban centers in the ancient world. Today it is an archaeological site so rich that every bite of the archaeologist's trowel into the soil turns up a potsherd or other artifact. The marble woman, however, was no ordinary find. Wearing a short dress that leaves her right breast bare and a cloak that falls on her left shoulder and right thigh, she carries, over her right shoulder and across her chest, a sword belt with a short ceremonial sword in its scabbard. Her right foot rests on the prow of a ship. To her left, a much smaller half-figure, male and also headless, appears to have gazed upward toward the woman as if appealing to her. This figure wears a harness over his upper body, suitable for attachment to a hawser for towing.

*B.C.E. = "before the Common Era," C.E. = "Common Era."

Figure 3.
Statue of the Caesarea Tyche, the god Sebastos to the right. Marble, height 1.52 m. Israel Department of Antiquities and Museums (IDAM) collection, on display in the Caesarea Museum.
Aaron Levin photo.

Although the archaeologists had liberated the marble woman from the soil, and she now stood in the museum, they had neither come to the end of their adventure nor discharged all of their professional responsibilities. *Archaeology*, from the Greek word *archaeologia*, means literally "the science of old things." As a science, it labors not only to uncover the material remains of the past but to make sense of them. Thus the archaeologists next had to interpret the marble statue. This process involved estimating the date the statue was made, "reconstructing" it in their mind's eye by supplying its missing features, identifying whom it represented, and ultimately explaining its significance in antiquity.

Figure 4. Coin of the Empress Faustina the Younger, 161–180 C.E. Bronze, diameter 2.3 cm. On the coin's reverse, pictured here, image of the Caesarea Tyche. The legend gives the city's official name: COL(onia) (PRIM)a FL(avia) AVG(usta) CAESAREA. Minted at Caesarea, now in the Caesarea Museum. Danny Friedman photo.

Dating the statue proved to be easy enough. Numismatists had long known that bronze coins had been minted at Caesarea with a figure exactly like the marble woman struck on their reverse, or "tails" (fig. 4). The portraits of Roman emperors of the first, second, and third centuries on the obverse – "heads" – of the coins made it fair to assume that the statue came from the same period. Specialists in Roman sculpture confirmed the assumption but could give a more exact date: some time before the middle of the second century C.E. The sculptor's drill marks that are a characteristic of later sculpture are absent on the marble woman, so she probably dates to early in the second century, the work of an unknown sculptor.

The miniature image on the coins also helped in the reconstruction of the statue. The image on the specimen in figure 4 corresponds to the one on the marble statue except that it is intact. In the miniature's left hand – missing on the marble statue – the woman holds the steering oar of a ship whose counterbalance extends from her torso. (The counterbalance was a device that permitted easy manipulation of the oar from the deck of a ship.) In her raised right hand she holds the bust of the emperor. The figure on the coins wears the so-called mural crown – which is shaped like the battlements of a city – as, presumably, did the marble woman.

Some of these features are faint on the coin because of its minute scale. In order to create a precise reconstruction, the archaeologists studied another object, a bronze cup, perhaps produced at Caesarea, that is now on display in Paris at the Louvre Museum (fig. 5). The exterior of the cup is decorated with various scenes executed in the incrustation technique: figures and background elements are enameled or outlined with silver or copper wire inserted into grooves in the surface of the metal. Details and the letters of inscriptions are incised into the surface of the metal. The cup dates to the fourth century C.E.

There is an image of a woman in one of the scenes on the Caesarea Cup that closely resembles both the woman on the Caesarea coin and the marble woman (fig. 6). She wears the same costume, including the mural crown and the sword belt slung

Figure 5.
The Caesarea Cup, decorated with scenes from the mythical founding of Caesarea. Second quarter of the fourth century. Bronze with silver and enamel decoration, height 8.2 cm, diameter 20.2 cm. Cabinet des Médailles, Paris.
Photo by Service photographique de la Réunion des musées nationaux.

across her chest, and she holds a bust of the emperor in her right hand. In her left hand, however, she holds a scepter, or perhaps a lance, not a steering oar. At her lower right side, the same half-figure appears, straining against his harness. The ship's prow is missing from the cup, which suggests that artists of the period had some freedom in selecting detail.

Thus the coins and the Caesarea Cup enabled the archaeologists to reconstruct the damaged marble woman. It was the cup, however, that provided conclusive evidence, a Latin inscription identifying the woman: the Latin reads *genio colonia(e)*, "To the genius of the colony." In classical Greek, the lingua franca in the Caesarea region when the statue was created, the equivalent expression would be "To the *tyche* of the colony." *Tyche* means "luck" or "good fortune." The female figure in the marble statue and on the coins was Caesarea's Tyche, or good fortune.

The cup contains additional visual information about the identity of the marble woman in the Caesarea Museum. Two figures stand to her left: a youth carrying a box for incense used in sacrifices and a veiled man sprinkling a sacrificial offering from a small pan into the flames of an altar. (The surface of the cup is damaged, so the altar is barely visible.) Certainly the disproportionally large female figure to the right of the sacrificer and the altar, now established as Caesarea's Tyche, must represent a great and powerful goddess. To the ancient Greeks and Romans, only immortals were worthy of sacrifice.

Figure 6.
Detail of Caesarea Cup (cf. fig. 5). Scene of sacrifice before statue of the Caesarea Tyche. The inscription Ge/ni/o *is visible to the left of the large female figure and the sacrificial altar and* co/lo/ni/a(e) *to the right of the figure.*
Photo by Service photographique de la Réunion des musées nationaux.

Comparing the details on the Caesarea marble woman with those on the cup and the coins also explains the importance of their Tyche to the ancient inhabitants of Caesarea. This Tyche, with her bare right breast and weapons, was identified by the city's inhabitants with an Amazon, one of a mythical race of warrior women. Her attributes convinced the people of Caesarea that she could protect them, as did the city's battlements, and that the security she brought would permit them to prosper. By wearing the city's battlements as her crown, Caesarea's Tyche actually embodied the city. For the city's ancient inhabitants, this doughty female figure genuinely *was* Caesarea, the human city's immortal double who dwelled with the gods and goddesses. By offering sacrifice to her, they enhanced their security and well-being.

That one's city was a bare-breasted woman to whom one could sacrifice to keep the streets safe and bring greater profits might seem at first to be a primitive notion, far removed from modern concepts of theology, business, and civics. But even we inhabitants of modern metropolises think of our cities as having personalities. Consider "The Big Apple." On the national level citizens of the United States think of Uncle Sam, and older generations may remember singing to the spirit of their country personified as a woman: "O Columbia, the Gem of the Ocean."

The difference is that we do not believe that we have transformed our cities into actual living individuals. That was a habit of the ancients, who similarly transformed the intoxicating power of the grape into Dionysus or Bacchus, female beauty and sexuality into Aphrodite or Venus, and manliness and skill at arms into Ares or Mars. We do not cast offerings on an altar fire in order to ingratiate ourselves with our city. We do "sacrifice" for our city's well-being – by supporting community organizations, for example – and often follow the fortunes of our hometown football team with an intensity that approaches worship.

Below the marble woman and to the right appears the diminuitive half-figure. A creature from the sea, he wears only a skirt of leaves, and he strains against a harness looped over his left shoulder. Because the marble woman embodied Caesarea, it was reasonable to identify this sea creature as Sebastos, the personification of the great harbor King Herod built. If the Tyche appeared to the people of her city to have the attributes of an Amazon, Sebastos could easily have seemed like one of the rugged stevedores who towed ships to their berths along the harbor's quays. Hence his marble figure is fitted with a harness that could be attached to a hawser. Human stevedores wearing this harness, men of low rank but vast importance to the city's economy, must have been a familiar sight in the harbor neighborhood.

Caesarea's Tyche was a great goddess, and Sebastos was a god, albeit a distinctly minor one. His attitude in his marble incarnation expresses the relationship between the two deities, for he gazes up at the Tyche in adoration, expecting her to protect him as well as the city. The appearance of Sebastos with the Tyche stresses how critical the harbor was to the city it served. To the ancient inhabitants of Caesarea, the linkage between city and harbor was intimate and enduring.

Archaeologists uncover the material evidence of the past – in this case the marble statue of a woman. By making sense of what they have found, especially by drawing reasonable conclusions from parallel evidence, they cast a bright light on the past, revealing eternal human thoughts and actions. This single archaeological episode, the discovery and interpretation of the Caesarea Tyche, is a paradigm of archaeology.

The pages that follow tell the story of two teams of archaeologists and of Caesarea Maritima, the city they are excavating, in terms of the science of archaeology – the methodology archaeologists use to excavate and interpret a site's material evidence – and of the history revealed.

The two teams whose story is the subject of this book operate at Caesarea in separate spheres, on land and beneath the sea. Since 1971 the Joint Expedition to Caesarea Maritima (JECM), a consortium of as many as twenty-two colleges, seminaries, and universities in the United States and Canada, has been exploring the land site. It has directed its efforts to obtaining as clear a picture as possible not merely of individual ruins that happen to have survived, but of the entire ancient city and its development through the centuries. The other team, the Caesarea Ancient Harbour Excavation Project (CAHEP), is also a consortium of a number of universities. In 1980 archaeologists from the United States and Canada joined forces with colleagues in Israel who had been working at Caesarea since 1976 to form CAHEP. Together they have developed new strategies for exploring the remains of ancient harbors that they have used to reveal the history of Caesarea's port facilities, especially King Herod's technological breakthrough, the majestic harbor Sebastos.

Expeditions to Caesarea began in the eighteenth and nineteenth centuries, following the awakening of European interest in the Middle East and specifically the Holy Land. Among the travelers and geographers who came to Caesarea were the British explorers, lieutenants C. R. Conder and H. H. Kitchener, who, after a six-day visit to the site in 1873, published the first scientific account (fig. 7). Actual excavation was slow in coming, because generations of archaeologists devoted themselves to more prominent biblical sites. It was not until 1951, after agricultural workers uncovered a porphyry statue in what is now known as the Byzantine esplanade, that Shmuel Yeivin, then director of the Israel Department of Antiquities, conducted a sustained archaeological exploration there.

The flurry of activity that began in the late 1950s and 1960s did not abate. In 1959 the Missione Archeologica Italiana conducted the first of six seasons of excavation, directed by A. Calderini and later by L. Crema and A. Frova. The Mission excavated several of Caesarea's most important ancient buildings: the aqueduct, the north wall, and the theater. In 1960 Avraham Negev, of the Hebrew University of Jerusalem, began work on behalf of the Israeli National Parks Authority, assisted by Gideon Foerster of the same university and Aharon Wegman of Kibbutz Sdot Yam. In several campaigns these archaeologists excavated and restored the impressive Crusader fortifications and explored many of the ruins within them. During the same period an American and Israeli team, directed by Edwin A. Link, first examined the harbor using divers (1960), and Michael Avi-Yonah, also of the Hebrew University, completed work on the remains of a synagogue located north of the Crusader fortifications (1962). More recently, while CAHEP and JECM have pursued their respective goals, still another Hebrew University team, directed by Dan Bahat, Ehud Netzer, and Lee Levine, excavated an important Byzantine building in the northern part of the Crusader fortifications and explored what Netzer calls the promontory palace, perhaps a residence of Herod the Great, to the west of the theater (1975–76, 1979). Despite all of this effort, however, only a small part of Caesarea has been explored, so that the history remains incomplete.

This unfinished story, which has already involved so many participants, is

Figure 7.
Site map of Caesarea from C. R. Conder and H. H. Kitchener, Survey of Western Palestine *(1882). The maps and written accounts that early travelers and explorers published preserve valuable archaeological information. For example, the Conder and Kitchener map includes a Crusader church on the coast that has since disappeared into the sea.*

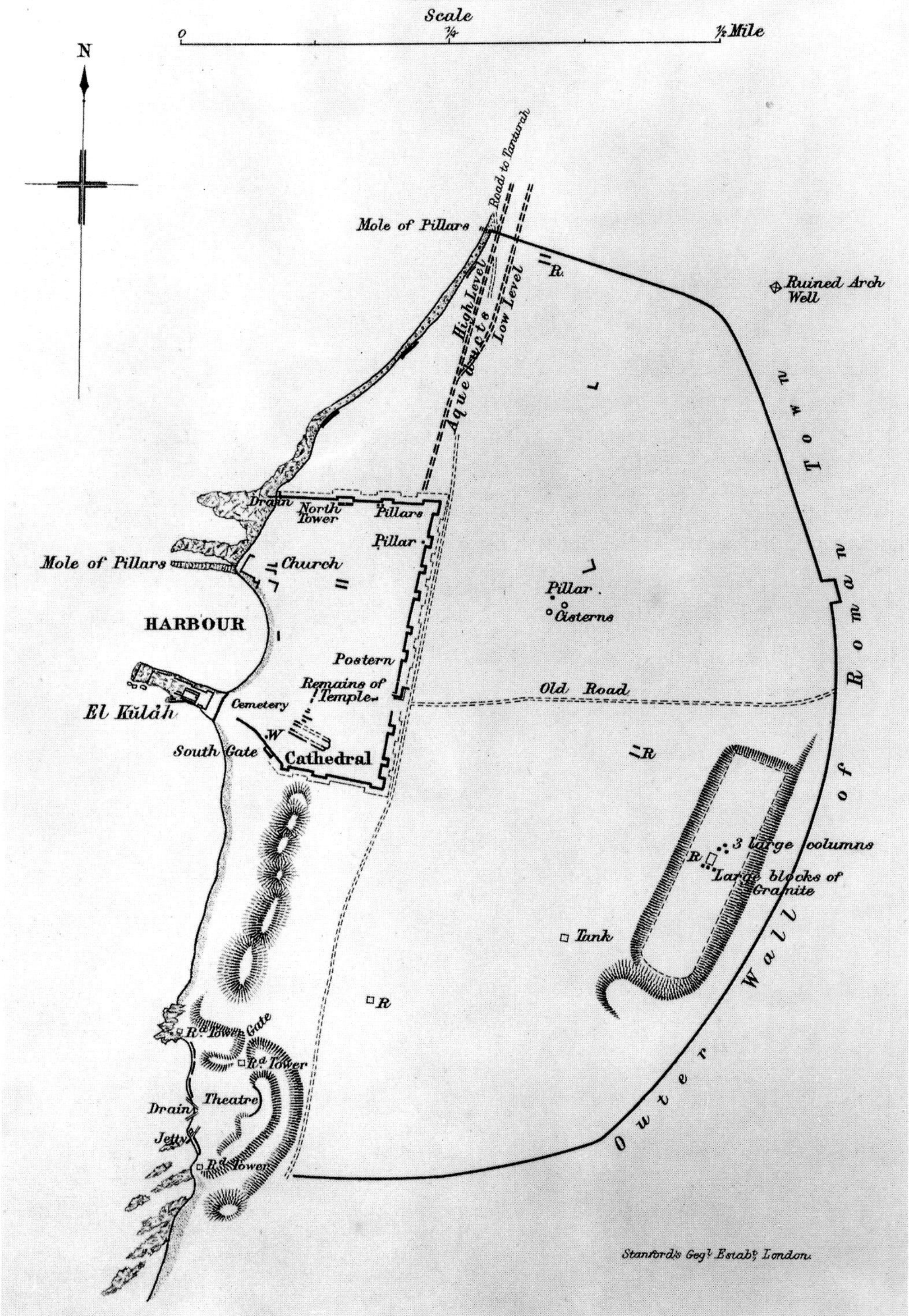

strikingly human and social. Archaeology is a humanist discipline that takes scholars out of cloistered libraries and labs. It is a public activity that attracts widespread attention and that has both an official and a political dimension. In Israel archaeological remains by law belong to the people – a piece of their cultural heritage. The Israel Department of Antiquities and Museums (IDAM), a government agency, protects and develops that heritage. CAHEP and JECM, like all teams working in Israel, secured their dig license from IDAM and are responsible to IDAM for conducting their excavation properly. In addition, CAHEP and JECM receive the endorsement of the American Schools of Oriental Research (ASOR), the association of scholars in the United States and Canada that promotes archaeological research in the Middle East and sets high professional standards.

The archaeologists featured in this story are, first of all, the directors of the excavating teams and their staff members. Among the latter, some lead field teams as field or area supervisors, while others are experts in various aspects of archaeology such as ceramics, numismatics, and ancient glass and jewelry; or in corollary disciplines, such as physical anthropology, architecture, botany, zoology, and art history; or have special skills like photography, surveying, conservation of artifacts, and drafting. The discussion of fieldwork featured in this book also includes the phenomenon on which it depends, the phenomenon known to archaeology in Israel and around the world as the dig volunteer.

To date about 3,500 volunteers have excavated at Caesarea with the two expeditions (fig. 8). From seventeen to seventy, they have come from the United States, Israel, Canada, Great Britain, Australia, and Japan. Many have been students at one of the universities that sponsor the excavation of Caesarea, but nearly as many have simply responded to ads in archaeological magazines or heard about the dig from a friend. Caesarea's volunteers have represented an amazing variety of vocations: schoolteachers, a pilot, medical doctors, an oil company president, housewives, architects, an art gallery assistant, journalists, a Trappist monk, lawyers, and carpenters among them. Of the students, relatively few have been majors in archaeology or even in a related field. As a group they have been amateurs in the loftiest sense, people who do something because they love it.

Enthusiasm at a dig is mandatory because an archaeologist's day begins at 4:15 A.M. or so, early enough to allow a team to get into the field by first light. There is a quick "first breakfast" before leaving for the trenches. Three hours of hard work follow, filling *guffahs* – rubber baskets – with the soil removed from the trenches, sifting, and lifting heavy rocks. Some tasks are more delicate, like drawing top plans, recording finds in a field notebook, or patiently using a small paintbrush or

Figure 8.
Volunteers from the Caesarea Ancient Harbour Excavation Project (CAHEP) at work, excavating beneath the sea.
Harry Wadsworth photo.

wooden spatula to remove the soil from around a skeleton. After a substantial "second breakfast," the team works three or four more hours as the sun reaches higher into the sky and the thermometer approaches 100° F. Exhaustion and lunch are followed by early afternoon naps, but there is always time for a swim in the sparkling Mediterranean that is only a few steps away. After four in the afternoon, volunteers put in two hours or more of work in camp – mostly washing pottery to prepare it for the daily pottery reading, and the cleaning, preservation, and registration of objects. After an early dinner, a staff member or visiting specialist may lecture – it is an educational project, after all.

Volunteers who work with CAHEP as divers have somewhat shorter hours but do equally demanding work. They ride to work on a Zodiac boat, an outboard-powered inflatable dinghy, at about 6:00 A.M. They begin work a little later because the bright morning sunlight must first penetrate the water to illuminate its depths. For the divers the problem is not heat but extreme cold. Water temperatures along Caesarea's coast hover around 70–75° F during the summer. Even in a wetsuit, the hardiest archaeologist can only stay in the water a few hours a day because of the loss of body heat and energy. Most CAHEP divers complete daily only two or three dives of one hour each, with a rest period in between. Then they put in additional hours maintaining equipment and interpreting and recording what they have found, just like their land counterparts.

The teams live in tourist or guest quarters near Kibbutz Sdot Yam. The excavation is sponsored by universities, private foundations like the National Geographic Society, and government agencies like the National Endowment for the Humanities in the United States and the Canadian Social Sciences and Humanities Research Council, but still each volunteer must contribute the cost of accommodations, plus a bit more to defray dig expenses. The volunteers are awakened before dawn, are subjected to hard labor for hours in the frigid water or hot sun – and pay for it. Amazingly, the majority of volunteers not only consider their money well-spent but come back the next summer for more. Some say that archaeology is like a disease. Its cure is expensive, and one usually suffers repeated attacks.

The willingness of volunteers to shoulder so much of the burden, both financial and physical, of conducting archaeological research has something to do with the social setting of a dig. It resembles a summer camp for adults, one where more tons of earth are moved by hand than one could imagine possible.

Volunteers also are fascinated with the process of archaeology and with the archaeologist's techniques, which can be mastered easily enough: laying out a square, manipulating an air lift or a trowel, recording finds with a camera or drafting pen, all under the guidance of an area supervisor. How these methods work out in practice is intriguing because archaeology is full of surprises. The typical archaeological trench, under water or on land, resembles a giant three-dimensional puzzle put together from hundreds of smaller puzzles, each of which must be unraveled to make sense of the whole. The volunteer takes part in a team effort to solve the puzzle.

Above all, the volunteer shares in the excitement of discovery. Supervised fieldwork enables people who have no special training or previous experience to contribute to our understanding of the past and of how human societies work. When a volunteer notices the thumbprint of a potter preserved in the fired clay of an ancient jar handle and places his thumb on top of it, the past suddenly becomes very close and very personal. It is an act of affirmation, of continuity with our predecessors on this earth.

While the nearness of the past confronts us at any archaeological site, volunteers find the past especially familiar at Caesarea – what must have been the excitement, financial rewards, convenience, high standard of living, noise, pressure, and hazards in a major urban center. Moreover, Caesarea's inhabitants witnessed events that engage us because they are part of our heritage: in this city currents flowed that joined to form European and American urban culture.

A brief synopsis of Caesarea's history will make this point. The site, located about 50 kilometers north of modern Tel Aviv – ancient Joppa (fig. 31), was undeveloped until about the second quarter of the fourth century B.C.E., when the king of the Phoenician city of Sidon (now in Lebanon) founded a settlement. In Greek the king's name was Strato, and the Greeks called his settlement Strato's Tower. Through much of its three-hundred-year history it was a trading station with a well-developed harbor, but little more. Although archaeologists have mounted spirited efforts to find Strato's Tower, the results are controversial. What we do know is that by the end of the first century B.C.E., Strato's Tower had fallen into sufficient decay that Herod could build a new city there.

Herod the Great, king of Judaea from 40 to 4 B.C.E., was a master builder. He left behind the fortress of Masada, the winter palace at Jericho, and the Temple of the Jews in Jerusalem, but none surpassed Caesarea Maritima in scale or cultural importance. In only thirteen years (22–10/9 B.C.E.) Herod's architects and engineers laid out streets on an up-to-date grid plan and designed magnificent temples, theaters, and public squares – the typical components of a classical Mediterranean city. Thousands of workmen, both slaves and paid laborers, worked on marble public buildings, an elaborate sewer system, and an aqueduct to nearby Mount Carmel that fed the city's fountains. Their most impressive project, however, was a vast harbor complex, far larger than the harbor of Strato's Tower. Engineers and workmen, using concrete poured under water, created a harbor that was a marvel of technology and design, with docks, warehouses, breakwaters, a lighthouse, and six colossal bronze statues to guard the entrance and welcome seafarers seeking haven.

Herod dedicated the harbor and the city to the first Roman emperor, Caesar Augustus, revealing his own ambition to be known as a faithful client of Rome and its ruler. The name *Caesarea* came from the family name of the Caesars; *Sebastos*, the harbor's special name, is the Greek translation of Augustus. But Herod wanted more from his grandiose project. What better way to establish himself as a great king and to ensure his posthumous fame than to found a city that would prosper far into the future? That was Herod's dream.

Caesarea Maritima, the city of Herod and Caesar, did prosper – for over twelve hundred years. As its people enjoyed the amenities that Herod had provided, they witnessed and took part in major events of history. Pontius Pilate, who executed

Christ, had his headquarters at Caesarea, the capital of the Roman province of Judaea. Saint Paul was imprisoned there, and the Jewish revolt against Rome that ended with the destruction of the Jerusalem Temple broke out there in 66 C.E. Caesarea, protected by its Tyche as well as many other pagan gods and goddesses, not only was the home of one of the first Christian communities, but later of learned rabbis whose teachings appear in the Talmud. At the end of antiquity, Muslim Arabs conquered Caesarea (640/641 C.E.), and later still Crusader knights took it (1101) and built a European city in the Holy Land. Finally, at the end of the thirteenth century, Caesarea's inhabitants abandoned her. In the centuries that followed, much of the city, by then in ruins, slipped gradually beneath advancing sand dunes, where it lay until the arrival of modern archaeologists and developers.

Caesarea is a place of great physical beauty, whose vistas are best conveyed in aerial photographs (fig. 1). To the north of the site twin aqueduct lines approach the city, paralleling the sparkling sea, and to the south lie the buildings of Kibbutz Sdot Yam. On the northeastern and eastern sides, the semicircular line of the Byzantine fortifications can be traced both in the photograph and on the ground, just to the west of a modern development of luxury villas. On the coast the jetties of a small harbor emerge from the sea, built in part on top of the ruins of ancient Sebastos, and just inland from the harbor the fortifications of the Crusader city form a monumental rectangle along the coast. The Herodian-Roman theater (fig. 51) lies off the photograph to the left, but the Byzantine esplanade is clearly visible to the east of the Crusader fortifications, as is the hippodrome, or chariot racetrack, in the foreground, hard against the Byzantine wall. The small oval of green inside the same wall far to the north represents the ruins of the ancient amphitheater, where beasts and gladiators once killed each other and defenseless Jews and Christians.

In the pages that follow we will witness Caesarea's rich history and learn to recognize its surviving monuments. The book's chapters correspond to the site's major archaeological phases. In each chapter the twin themes of field archaeology and the history of urbanism at Caesarea are entwined, so the reader can share with Caesarea's volunteers and professional excavators the adventure of archaeology.

CHAPTER 2

The Search for Strato's Tower

"In the city, time becomes visible," wrote urbanologist Lewis Mumford. "Buildings," he continued, "and monuments and public ways, more open than the written record, more subject to the gaze of many men than the scattered artifacts of the countryside, leave an imprint upon [our] minds."* Cities are a record of the values and accomplishments of their builders and inhabitants and, without words, echo a culture. They have the power to transmit culture from generation to generation.

Figure 9. Area supervisor and JECM volunteers excavating field G, area 8, against the outside face of Caesarea's north wall. Looking south, wall to right. Date of the wall disputed: late Hellenistic (ca. 125 B.C.E.) or Herodian (22-10/9 B.C.E.). JECM photo.

Mumford also recognized that cities give birth to culture and sustain it. Indeed, their chief function is to "convert power into form, energy into culture, dead matter into the living symbols of art, biological reproduction into social creativity."** Among social organisms only the city – not the village or, at the opposite extreme, the nation-state – vibrates with the intense and varied life needed to promote business, art and music, and technological development. Its noise and crowding are virtues. Even sporting events and religious ceremonies express group enthusiasm best in the presence of the large numbers of people that congregate in the city. It is true that those who "convert . . . energy into culture" flee now and then into the countryside to camp, ski, or buy produce in a country market, or spend a week or two at a beach. But they do return to the city. Sometimes city people even move permanently to the suburbs or the country, but most often they too maintain close urban ties, driving to the city to work or to attend the theater. They read newspapers published in the city, and the television signal they receive speaks for the city. These people confirm Mumford's sense that the city creates, sustains, and transmits culture, and that our modern culture is essentially urban.

*Lewis Mumford, *The Culture of Cities* (New York: Harcourt Brace Jovanovich, Inc., 1970), p. 4.

**——— *The City in History* (New York: Harcourt, Brace & World, Inc., 1961), p. 571.

Aristotle, in his *Politics* (1253a3), wrote some famous words that have been translated "man is by nature a political animal." The translation is incorrect. If the Greek sage had expressed himself in English, he would have written "a human being is the type of creature that dwells in cities," or "to be fully human a person must live in a city." Aristotle expressed a common Greek prejudice against life on farms and in villages, and against "barbarians" (non-Greeks) who did not have cities of the Greek type. He shared the general view of the ancient Greeks and Romans that only in an urban setting could they enjoy such refinements as economic prosperity and leisure, a good education, competitive sports, music, painting, and sculpture; philosophy, literature, and the theater. Mediterranean culture, to which Caesarea belonged, was, like our own, a culture of cities, and Aristotle believed, like Mumford, that the city created, sustained, and transmitted culture.

Of course urbanism long preceded even the Greeks and Romans, going back, some scholars believe, as far as the Neolithic Age, about ten thousand years ago. By the beginning of the Bronze Age, about five thousand years later, cities in the Near East had already emerged as the principal creators and transmitters of culture. In one important respect, however, this ancient urbanism – the Greek and Roman as well as the Near Eastern variety – differed from its modern counterpart. The impetus to create and expand cities came not from developers, private individuals intent on making a profit, but from the state. Fostering urbanism was originally the task of kings and other rulers.

There is, for example, the case of Gilgamesh, a semimythical king of the city Uruk (biblical Erech) in ancient Iraq and hero of the long cuneiform poem *The Epic of Gilgamesh*. Gilgamesh was responsible for Uruk's most famous monuments, its mighty fortifications and the lofty shrine of the god Anu and his daughter Ishtar:

Of ramparted Uruk the wall he built,
*Of hallowed Eanna, the pure sanctuary.**

Similarly, in about 950 B.C.E., David, king of Israel, conquered Jerusalem, refortified it, and built an altar there for sacrifices to the Lord. In effect, David founded a new city, naming it, after himself, the City of David (2 Sam. 5:7, 9). But the greatest city builder of all was the Macedonian conqueror Alexander the Great. He founded Alexandria in Egypt, which became one of the largest and most prosperous cities in the ancient world. After defeating the Persian king Darius in 331 B.C.E., he marched with his army all the way to India, creating additional Alexandrias along the way. (One source, the biographer Plutarch, credits him with a total of seventy.) Alex-

*Trans. E. A. Speiser in *The Ancient Near East, An Anthology of Texts and Pictures*, ed. James B. Pritchard (Princeton: Princeton University Press, 1958), p. 40.

ander's successors, the Seleucid kings of Syria, and to a lesser degree the Ptolemies of Egypt, continued the practice, naming numerous cities after themselves and members of their families throughout the Near East. In fact, in no period of the human past have rulers devoted greater energy to founding cities than during the Hellenistic Age, the three centuries that elapsed between the death of Alexander in 323 B.C.E. and the time of the first Roman emperor, Caesar Augustus.

Why ancient rulers built cities usually is not stated explicitly in the texts that relate their exploits. In David's case it is significant that a refortified Jerusalem became a military strongpoint, well positioned to control both the northern and southern parts of his domains. Many of Alexander's cities served a similar strategic purpose. Founding a city would also create a body of prosperous citizens who would not only be loyal to the ruler responsible for their prosperity but would pay taxes or tribute to his treasury. On the other hand, Alexander and the Seleucid kings appear to have built cities specifically to transplant Greek culture, importing colonists from the Greek homeland to form the populations. They too believed that the city creates and sustains culture, and that promoting Greek culture strengthened their own hold on power. Above all, however, the founding of cities contributed to a ruler's fame and therefore to his ability to rule effectively. No act attested more effectively to a king's superhuman wisdom and resourcefulness than founding a successful city, which is why rulers typically named their new foundations after themselves.

The First Settlement

Long before Herod's time, another king, Strato of Sidon, had founded a settlement or town in the same geographical position as Caesarea. Sidon, located on the coast about 120 kilometers to the north of Caesarea, belonged to the Phoenicians, a seafaring and trading people that founded many cities as trading posts and colonies along the Levantine coast and in the western Mediterranean. If historians are right, the Strato in question ruled Sidon in the fourth century B.C.E. Whether Strato named the new settlement for himself or not, it came to be known by his name, Strato's Tower.

Strato most likely founded this settlement for the usual reasons: to increase his wealth, power, and fame. But he also had more specific motives. Because Strato's Tower was located on the busy maritime trade route between Egypt and Phoenicia, it offered drinking water, shelter, food, and storage facilities to merchantmen and their crews sailing the coast to and from Sidon. The word "tower" may refer to a

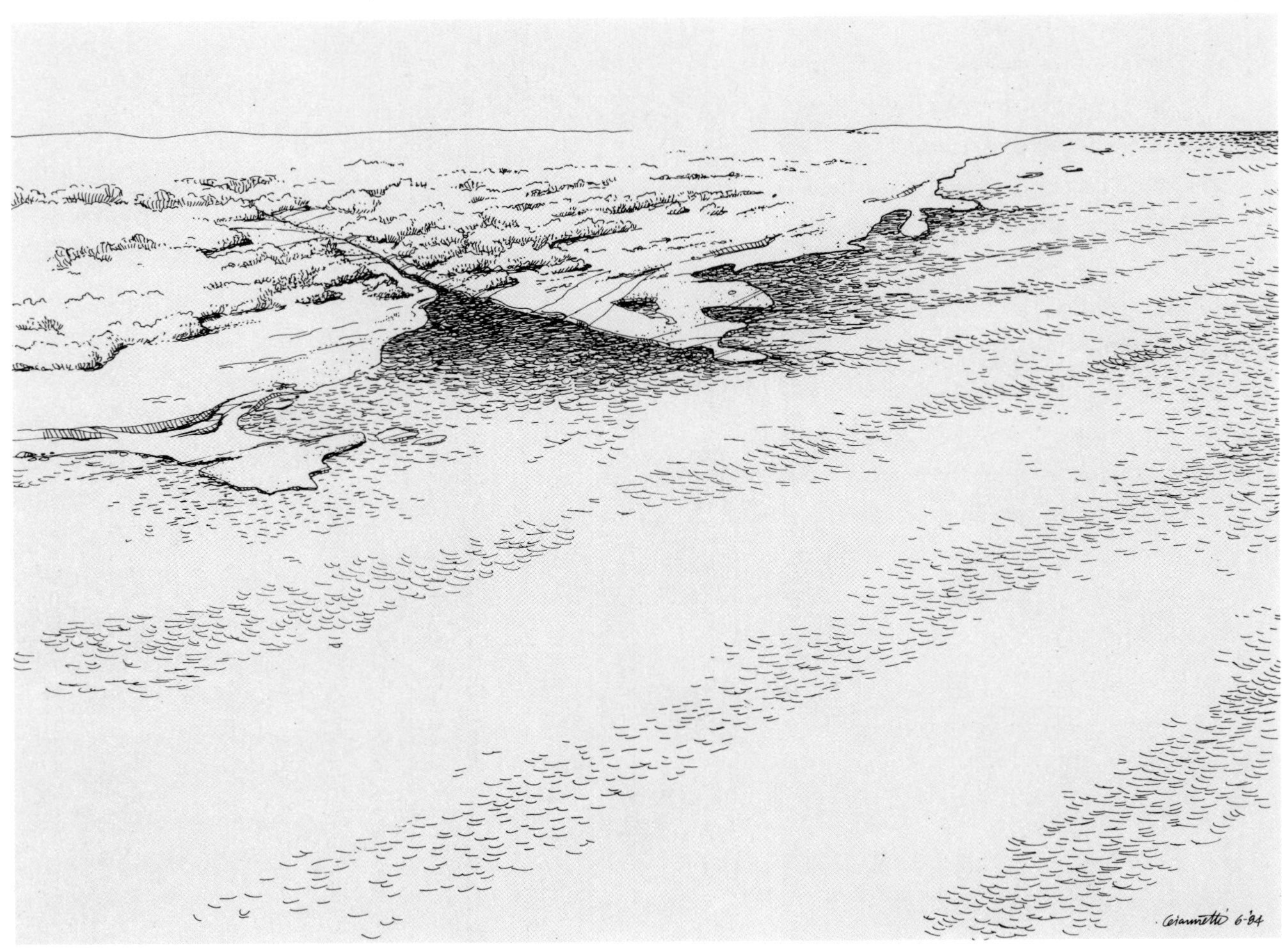

Figure 10.
Site of Caesarea looking southeast, prehistoric configuration.
Stephen Giannetti drawing.

fortification or a tower on the site that guided steersmen. If so, the tower is most likely to have stood on the promontory that Herod the Great subsequently incorporated into the southern breakwater of his harbor's outer basin (fig. 11). It is one of the highest points along this part of the coast and as such is well suited for a lighthouse or fortification. To the north of the promontory and in its lee, protected from prevailing southwest winds and a dangerous coastal current, a modest harbor existed where once, in prehistoric times, a small stream had flowed into the sea (fig. 10). Nearby lay the dwellings and modest public buildings of the town.

At least one other roadstead and perhaps some habitations may have existed in the vicinity even before the foundation of Strato's Tower. In the south bay, south of the promontory, CAHEP archaeologists found a stone anchor from the Late Bronze

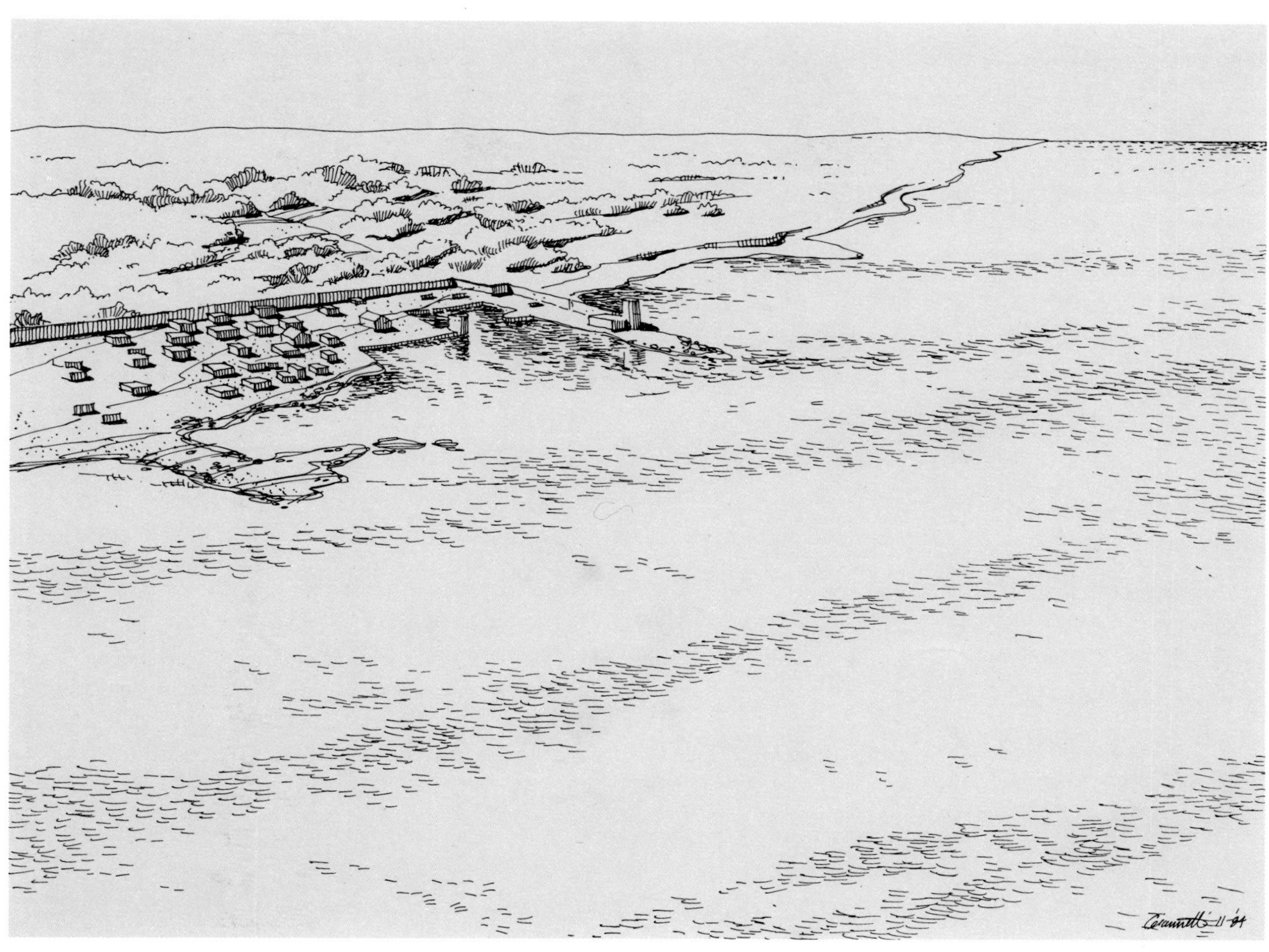

Figure 11.
Strato's Tower at the end of the second century B.C.E. Artist's conception of the settlement that preceded Caesarea on the same site.
Stephen Giannetti drawing.

Age (ca. 1200 B.C.E., fig. 12). The site's topography, combined with this archaeological evidence, suggests, then, that coastal traders had been using the location of Strato's Tower as an anchorage for some time.

The region's topography, geology, and climate also influenced the building of Strato's Tower (cf. fig. 42). Sandy beaches line the coast there, and a kilometer or so behind them a north–south ridge of calcareous sandstone breaks only for a short distance. In antiquity this ridge was quarried by the builders of Strato's Tower for their stone; the sandstone, easily worked but destructible, has been used throughout the centuries there for general building purposes. About 4.0 kilometers north of the site, the Crocodile River – so named for the crocodiles that infested its waters and banks until the mid-nineteenth century – flows into the sea through a break in

Figure 12. Stone anchor found by CAHEP in Caesarea's south bay. From ca. 1200 B.C.E. or later. Height 38.0 cm. IDAM collection, at the Center for Maritime Studies, Haifa.
Robert Hohlfelder photo.

the sandstone ridge. The river marks the northern limit of the Plain of Sharon, a low-lying region of fertile soil that extends inside the sandstone ridge toward the east and southeast as far as the limestone hills of Samaria, about 15 kilometers away, and southward all the way to Tel Aviv (ancient Joppa).

Today the area is one of the richer agricultural regions in the Mediterranean world, as it was in antiquity. Although much of the Levant receives low precipitation, rainfall in the Plain of Sharon has always been more than adequate. Forests once covered parts of it, and the farmers who tilled its soil produced bountiful crops of wheat, citrus fruits, and grapes. The harbor of Strato's Tower provided convenient access to foreign markets for those products. By developing it King Strato probably expected to make a healthy profit himself and to benefit his subjects, the seafarers and traders of Sidon.

In the third century B.C.E., when the entire country was under the control of the Ptolemies, the Macedonian kings of Egypt, an episode occurred that confirms the importance both of the harbor of Strato's Tower and of the agricultural products that flowed from it. An Egyptian named Zeno arrived at Strato's Tower with a large entourage in 259 B.C.E. We know of this mission from a discovery made in Egypt of a papyrus, the Zeno document, which preserves the earliest mention of Strato's Tower and of the site we know as Caesarea. Zeno worked for Apollonius, the rich and powerful finance minister of King Ptolemy Philadelphus. His mission, apparently, was to inspect both Apollonius's and royal estates in the country and otherwise to further the financial interests of his master and the king. After completing his work at Strato's Tower, Zeno continued overland to Jerusalem, Jericho, and other cities in the region. The port of Strato's Tower offered appropriate facilities for beginning such a high-level mission, and the economic possibilities of its hinterland were great enough to appeal even to the lord of the fabulously wealthy Nile Valley.

Apart from the Zeno papyrus and what archaeologists can gather from the site's topography, virtually nothing is known for certain about urbanism at Caesarea's future site until late in the second century B.C.E. Our account here of the controversial search for Strato's Tower requires some understanding of how archaeologists excavate and date ancient remains. The question is, "How would the archaeologists recognize Strato's Tower?" It is therefore appropriate to turn from urbanism to this book's other theme, archaeological fieldwork.

Fundamentals of Stratigraphic Archaeology

Stratigraphic archaeology is the technique of excavating a site layer by layer (by *strata*) in order to date and study its levels of occupation. Human beings occupying a site in successive periods leave behind the debris of daily life and architectural ruins. In each case the next occupants level the ruins and build on them, which creates stratification at a site – another discernible layer, or *stratum*.

Utilizing stratigraphy as an excavation technique goes back to the early days of archaeology in the nineteenth century. For example, Heinrich Schliemann (d. 1890) employed a primitive version of it when he excavated Hissarlik (ancient Troy) on the northwestern coast of Turkey. Schliemann was able to distinguish seven cities that succeeded one another on the site. He dated one of the layers of Troy II, the second city built on the site, to the time of Homer's hero Priam, because of the magnificent treasure of golden vessels he found in it. He believed that only a great king like Priam could have possessed such a treasure. Unfortunately Schliemann's technique was rudimentary, so he missed the city's actual date by more than one thousand years. Scholars now date the city of the Trojan War to the thirteenth century B.C.E.

In the century since Schliemann, the discipline of archaeology has matured. Using techniques that are constantly being refined, archaeologists now can date layers at sites like Troy and Caesarea to within half a century. These advances have changed archaeology fundamentally. In Schliemann's time archaeologists differed only a little from treasure hunters. Their goal was to recover objects that were

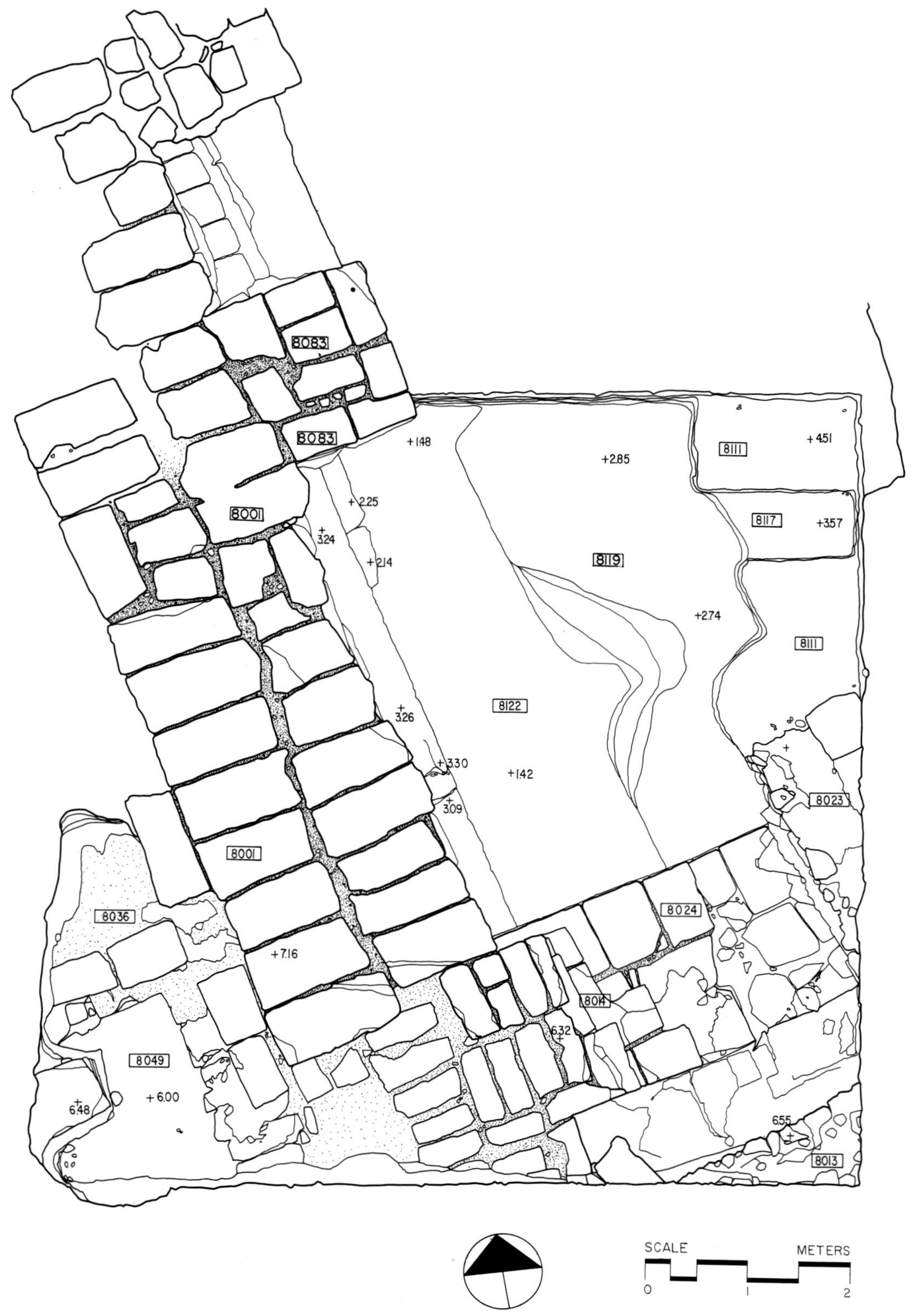

Figure 13.
Top plan of JECM field G, area 8. Drawing of the trench from above. The Hellenistic or Herodian wall crosses the trench from upper left (northwest) to lower right (southeast). Four-digit numbers in rectangles are locus numbers.
JECM drawing.

valuable and beautiful in themselves, rather than to *understand* them and the culture from which they came. Today, in principle, archaeologists value broken pieces of pottery and other paraphernalia of everyday life equally with objects of precious metals and exquisite craftsmanship, because all contribute to the reconstruction of a culture. Profound understanding of cultures first became possible with accurate dating, which enabled archaeologists to *compare* finds from one site with finds from another from the same period.

There is no one technique of stratigraphic archaeology. The one that JECM uses at Caesarea is not the only one used in Israel and surrounding countries, and its principles are not applicable in every case. Often a specific trench requires modified excavation techniques. Although archaeologists, like other scientists, do disagree about field techniques and their application, JECM's methods are widespread and gathering increasing influence. For our purposes here, they and JECM's trench G.8, field G, area 8 (figs. 9 and 13), are the model.

JECM's approach is an adaptation of the Wheeler-Kenyon method, named for two distinguished twentieth-century British archaeologists. Sir Mortimer Wheeler (d. 1976) excavated principally at Roman sites in Britain and at early historic sites in India. His pupil, Dame Kathleen Kenyon (d. 1978), brought his methods to the Holy Land, employing them in excavations at Jericho and Jerusalem. The system Wheeler utilized consists of laying out a grid on a site and then excavating in the squares on the grid. Between adjacent squares, Wheeler left narrow strips, or balks, unexcavated. In Wheeler's method the vertical face of the balk is exposed within the excavated square. The trench's stratification can be "read" on that vertical face (also called a balk). In order to interpret a trench's stratigraphy, the vertical face is photographed and drawn (fig. 14).

American archaeologists have also left their imprint on the version of stratigraphic archaeology practiced by JECM. George Ernest Wright adopted the Wheeler-Kenyon method when he excavated Tell Balatah (biblical Shechem) in the 1960s. But Wright emphasized as well the variety of corollary specialities that an archaeologist must master – ceramics, geology, physical anthropology, palaeobotany, palaeozoology, and ancient texts, for example. For him an archaeologist resembled a renaissance man. The drawing of a top plan was the contribution to field techniques of Paul W. Lapp, Wright's colleague. A top plan is a bird's-eye view of an excavated square in which every feature found in the square is drawn to scale (fig. 13). A top plan and a balk drawing enable the archaeologist to locate in three dimensions any artifact – indeed any feature – excavated in a square.

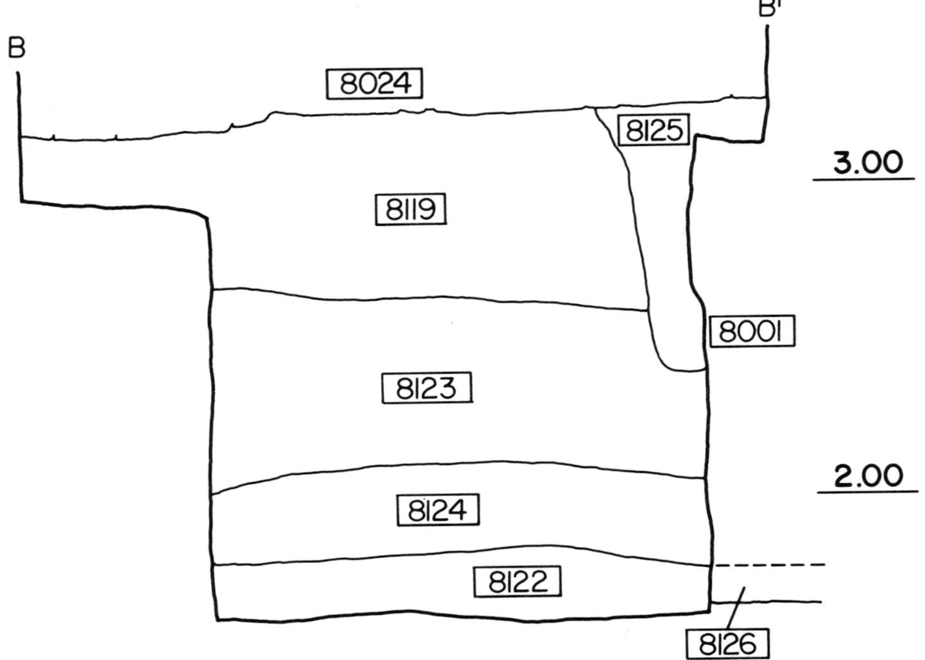

Figure 14.
Temporary south balk of JECM field G, area 8. Drawing of a vertical face reserved within the trench to permit study of its stratification.
JECM drawing.

Digging in squares on a grid, reserving balks, and drawing balks and top plans characterize JECM's work at Caesarea, but they are only part of the team's approach. Also essential are five key concepts: sampling, site survey, control, ceramic analysis, and reporting.

When JECM began work at Caesarea in 1971, it developed a strategy for exploring the entire site in order to learn how the city had developed from the beginning to the end of urbanism. The archaeologists did not anticipate that they would, or could, excavate the site completely – a project that would take a team like JECM several hundred years. Instead, the JECM leadership decided to sample the site of Caesarea. Sampling is a timesaving technique, implying as it does that a lot can be learned from a minimum of excavation.

After the decision to sample, the JECM archaeologists undertook an elaborate site survey to direct them to where they should excavate. In the broadest sense, a survey actually begins in the library with ancient texts that mention the city to be excavated. This helps the archaeologists trace the city's history and even locate and identify its major buildings. The Zeno papyrus, for example, casts a bright light on Strato's Tower, and the works of the first century C.E. author Flavius Josephus help explain the plan of the city and the design of the harbor in King Herod's time. Also important are the published reports of a site's earlier excavators and IDAM's files,

which contain information on chance finds made at Caesarea over the years. Conversations with members of Kibbutz Sdot Yam who have first-hand knowledge of the site from working the land for many years were especially useful to the excavators in deciding where to dig.

Figure 15.
Infrared photograph of JECM field B from the air. Heat emitted by plants produces deep red in the photograph. Zones of lighter coloration in an open field indicate ancient ruins beneath ground level.
JECM photo.

A site survey, in a strict sense, uses aerial photography to develop a contour map of the site and reveal the remains of large structures that may not be visible at ground level. By using this technique earlier researchers discovered Caesarea's amphitheater (fig. 52) and the line of the Byzantine city wall (fig. 1). JECM effectively employed an advancement of the technique – aerial infrared photography (fig. 15). Infrared film registers the heat emitted by living plants. Because dense

Figure 16.
JECM site map showing areas (trenches) excavated between 1971 and 1984.
JECM drawing.

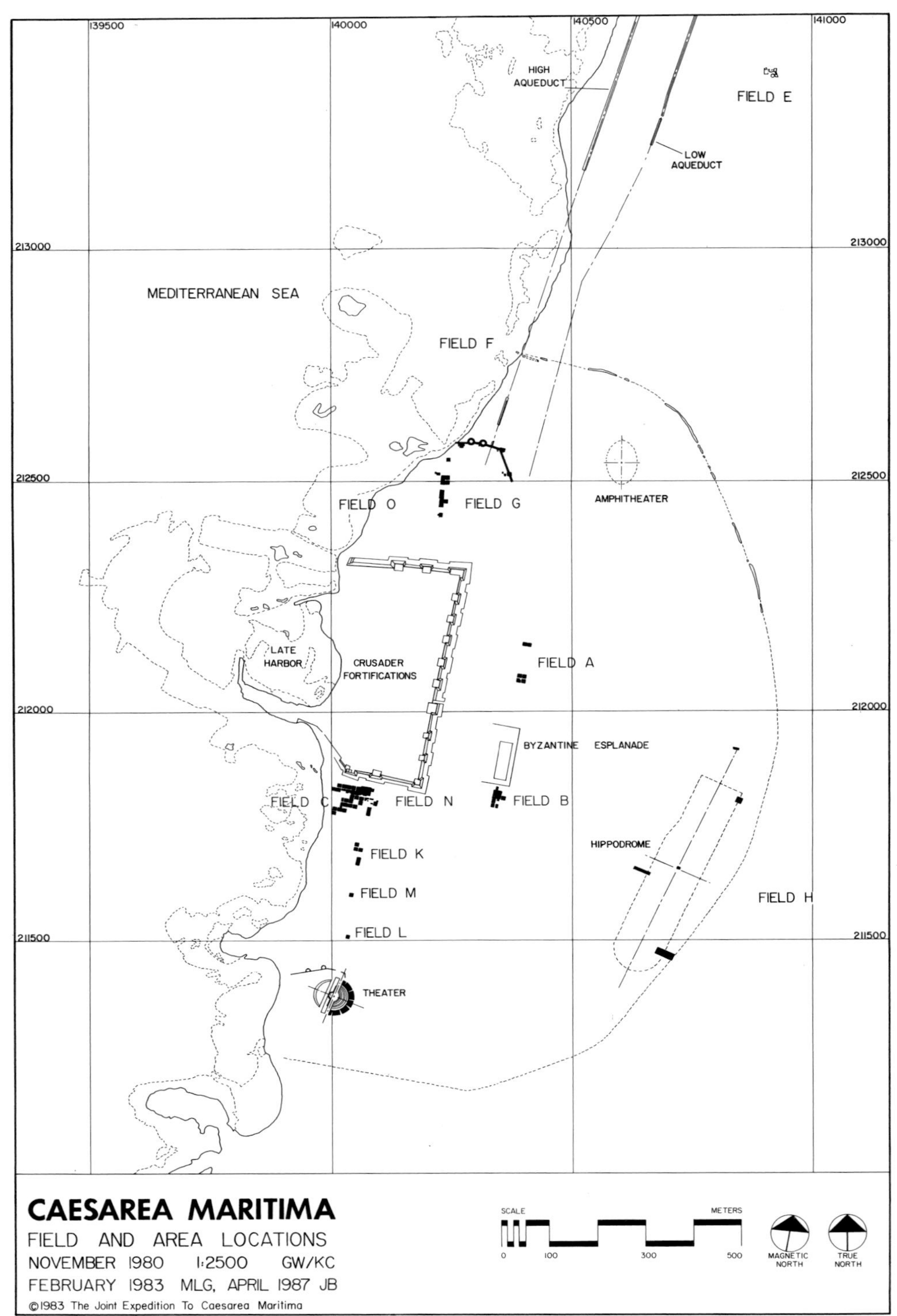

plant growth depends on the amount of water available, and masses of subsurface stone hinder moisture from reaching root systems, infrared photographs enabled JECM to "see" ancient structures below ground level and subsequently place its trenches accordingly.

The final element in JECM's survey was to walk around the site and examine every ancient ruin protruding above the surface, every visible concentration of ancient building stone, and every unusual topographical formation. A surveyor with a transit level recorded the most important surface finds on a site map (fig. 16), to expedite reasonable judgments about where the team might profitably excavate. Archaeologists try never to dig blind.

It is at this point in the procedure that a team's system for proper control, including record-keeping, comes into play. Maintaining control is the archaeologists' solution to the dilemma that, as they dig, they destroy evidence – the exact location and position of movable artifacts and other objects and their relationship to fixed structures. Knowing the exact position of an artifact or object is critical to interpreting a site's stratification.

For proper control, and to facilitate managing the excavation process, JECM's surveyors laid a hypothetical grid of 10 by 10 meter squares over all of Caesarea's terrain. Parts of Caesarea that the site survey found to be the most worthy of exploration are designated fields, each the responsibility of a field supervisor, one of the expedition's most senior archaeologists. So far, JECM has identified sixteen fields (fig. 16). Grid squares excavated within each field are called *areas*, and an experienced archaeologist, an area supervisor, takes charge of each. Areas of 10 by 10 meters proved to be most practical for an area supervisor to control, and for eight to ten volunteers to excavate, in one or two digging sessions of five weeks each. To date, JECM has worked in 117 areas (fig. 16).

Control also influences the actual digging of an area or square, including the choice of tools. In rare cases at Caesarea, when several meters of sterile sand or soil are removed – that is, sand without any pottery or other ancient remains in it – heavy mechanical equipment like a backhoe or even a bulldozer is used, rather than squander the time and labor of the volunteers. A mason's trowel with a pointed four-inch blade is the most commonly used tool on a dig because it allows the required precision (fig. 17). In some situations, however, a more delicate tool, like a paintbrush, may be necessary. A hoe is used to remove large quantities of soil.

Precision is essential because the excavator wants to remove the soil layer by layer in exactly the reverse of the order in which it was deposited. Every trace of one layer must be removed before proceeding to the next, so that material from one

Figure 17.
JECM volunteer excavating with the trowel. The rubber basket is called a guffah. *Plastic buckets receive potsherds.*
JECM photo.

occupation level does not contaminate material from another. Hence the volunteer wielding the trowel and the area supervisor must be attentive to the slightest variation in the soil being removed: to changes in color, compaction, particle size, and in the material the soil contains, such as broken pottery and ashes. Any of these changes could signal a new layer or a new locus.

In JECM's use of stratigraphic archaeology, the *locus* (pl. *loci*) is the smallest and most important unit of control. In digging through sand or soil, any volume of material that has consistent characteristics or is contained within a structure or the limits of a square is designated a separate locus. Archaeologists study each soil locus in an attempt to group it with others deposited during the same time period. A number of soil loci will make up a layer, or stratum. Any built feature or deposit within a square is also called a locus – a wall, an oven (*tabun*), a cache of pottery, a row of stones, a mosaic pavement – and is isolated, studied, and assigned to a stratum.

No element is more important to proper control than recording, and the basis of recording is the locus number. Each field is assigned a letter, each area within a field is assigned an Arabic number (one or two digits), and each locus within an area is assigned another Arabic number (one to three digits). Because computers are involved in processing this information, these numbers are expressed together: e.g., C.25009, locus 9 within area 25 of field C. Such numbers are employed to keep track of virtually everything. The locus number appears on the balk drawings and the top plans, for example, so that each locus can be easily located in space (figs. 13 and 14), and each object found in a soil locus, or in the spaces between building stones, is identified by locus number. Above all, for each locus the area supervisor, or a volunteer to whom this task is assigned, prepares a locus sheet. It specifies the exact location of the locus, gives a detailed physical description of it, and lists every artifact and other material found in it. The area supervisor also keeps a field diary and other records, but the locus sheets are a dig's fundamental documentation.

The first objective of ceramic analysis is to provide a date for the contents of each locus. Indeed, archaeologists can learn much more than dates from pots and other ceramic (fired clay) objects, but pottery's utility for dating is the principal reason so much attention is devoted to ceramic analysis. Other dating methods are available for organic matter – the carbon 14 method, for example. The residual isotope carbon 14 in an organic sample can be measured in a laboratory. Because carbon 14 decays at a known rate, the date of a sample can be estimated. Unfortunately, because of soil conditions at Caesarea, a great deal of organic matter has not survived. In addition, because the procedure is expensive and accurate only

Figure 18.
JECM pottery reading. Experts examine the sherds in each bucket to estimate the dates represented. "Indicator" or "diagnostic" sherds, mostly rims and bases, are saved for further study.
Paul Saivetz photo.

within hundreds of years, it is not used often at a site that is only 2,400 years old. Dendrochronology is another dating technique in which the sequences of tree rings in wood samples are compared with sequences of known dates. The technique is used infrequently at Caesarea because wood samples of sufficient size hardly ever survive.

Inscriptions on stone or in other materials are a precious and rare find at any excavation. At Caesarea inscriptions sometimes help date floors, walls, and other structures. Ancient bronze coins turn up much more frequently, but they can date a locus only to a period after a coin was struck (e.g., fig. 20). In addition, the archaeologist cannot tell how long a coin circulated before it was lost.

For the archaeologist's purposes, then, ceramic material has the triple advantages of being permanent, ubiquitous, and datable. Ceramic vessels were the equivalent of packaging in antiquity. Huge numbers of pots, plates, and cups were used, not only for cooking and tableware, but whenever a container was needed. Their modern counterparts are paper and plastic bags, wooden and cardboard boxes, glass bottles, and buckets. Oil lamps, the functional equivalent of the modern light bulb, also were usually ceramic. Once it has been fired in a kiln, the fabric of pottery is virtually indestructible – so that although lamps and pots are breakable, under normal conditions neither searing heat, permanent immersion in water, nor chemicals in the soil will destroy a sherd. Many sherds have distinct qualities that enable a trained archaeologist to date them to within half a century.

Because it is so important to date each locus, excavators record each artifact in it and list each on the locus sheet. The pottery gets special treatment. The sherds from a locus are deposited in one or more pottery buckets tagged with the locus number. At the end of the day the pottery in the buckets is washed and scrubbed with brushes, then bagged and allowed to dry overnight. The next day the director, field and area supervisors, ceramics specialists, and interested volunteers gather for a pottery "reading" (fig. 18). The experts examine the sherds in each bucket, touching and even tasting them, even listening to them. (Some sherds emit a characteristic metallic tone when struck.)

After the pottery has been read and the results recorded in a notebook, many sherds (those lacking characteristics for dating) end up on the discard pile – or in the volunteers' private collections. A large number, however, are selected for registration, especially "indicator" or "diagnostic" sherds like rims and bases, the fragments most useful for dating (fig. 19). The volunteers use India ink to mark each sherd with its locus number and other identification before it is sent to the archaeological laboratory to be studied further, drawn, and photographed. Sherds from the same

Figure 19.
Group of "indicator" or "diagnostic" sherds from JECM areas G.7, 8, and 9. All are bowl rims. The piece on the upper left is an example of a fine tableware manufactured in the eastern Mediterranean region in the first century B.C.E. The other three pieces represent eastern Mediterranean Megarian Ware from the second century B.C.E. For a complete Megarian Ware bowl, see fig. 21. The sherds are now at the Drew University Institute of Archaeological Research (DIAR).
Aaron Levin photo.

vessel are saved in the hope that the vessel can be restored, completely or in part. Today archaeological expeditions save their pottery in storerooms. Because our knowledge of ceramics is expanding rapidly, sherds of types that are undatable or only approximately dated today may one day benefit from being restudied. JECM preserves its pottery in a repository at Drew University in New Jersey.

The last of the concepts crucial for understanding JECM methods is reporting. To fulfill the purpose of stratigraphic archaeology, to contribute to our understanding of the human past, reports of what the archaeologists find are disseminated.

During the excavation, area supervisors record the results of the daily pottery reading on the locus sheets before beginning the complicated task of analyzing the results and writing their weekly area reports. This step contributes to the archaeologists being able to clarify their goals and strategy and to tighten their research format. At the end of a season, each of the area and field supervisors prepares a concluding report, which the director, in collaboration with the other senior archaeologists, includes in a report to the Israel Department of Antiquities and Museums (IDAM). This report is not discretionary: it is one of the conditions under which a license to excavate is granted. The director or a senior staff member from JECM or CAHEP normally reports a season's results orally at the annual meeting of the American Schools of Oriental Research, the scholarly organization that coordinates and evaluates American archaeological research in Israel and neighboring countries. Ultimately, the director and his associates publish preliminary reports and specialized studies in scientific archaeological journals; final reports in book form, normally issued after a number of seasons of excavation or when the expedition concludes its work; and sometimes popular articles and books.

When archaeologists follow these or equivalent procedures, it is theoretically possible for them to date most of their finds with reasonable accuracy and to interpret material remains by using comparable evidence from other sites. In that way some consensus among colleagues becomes possible. Frequently, however, too few potsherds appear in trenches or those unearthed are difficult to date. It is also true that, in some situations, it is impossible to excavate stratigraphically because layers either do not exist or they cannot be distinguished. As a result controversy often stalks the archaeologist, and advances occur when archaeologists propose an ingenious hypothesis before the evidence normally needed is in. This is the case with CAHEP's search for Strato's Tower.

From Trading Station to Walled City

Figure 20. Bronze coin of Ptolemy V, king of Egypt 204–198 B.C.E., found in JECM's area G.7. On the obverse, pictured here, an image of the Egyptian god Zeus-Ammon. Diameter 1.8 cm. IDAM collection, at DIAR.
Aaron Levin photo.

Early excavations at Caesarea confirmed that there had been a town on the site before the time of Herod, but thus far the evidence has been sparse. Two excavators, Avi-Yonah and Negev, reported finding concentrations of Hellenistic pottery – that is, sherds from the three centuries that preceded the founding of Caesarea – in the vicinity north of the Crusader fortifications (fig. 16). This pottery consisted partly of sherds from second-century Megarian bowls (fig. 21) and handles of the amphoras (wine jars) typical of those from Rhodes and other Aegean islands. In addition, both Avi-Yonah and Negev found in their trenches what they considered to be the foundations of houses from the Hellenistic period. JECM, which has excavated twenty areas in this sector (its field G), has not identified Hellenistic buildings there but has recorded what the archaeologists call "material culture remains": coins, pottery sherds, lamps, and glass from the Hellenistic period (figs. 19–23). This material culture includes the earliest potsherd yet uncovered at Caesarea, a fragment from the rim of a *cyma kantheros*, a large, two-handled wine cup manufactured in Greece in the fourth century B.C.E. The discovery of this single sherd seems to prove that human occupation of the site dates to the time of Strato of

Figure 21.
Ceramic bowl of Megarian Ware, once thought to have been manufactured at Megara in Greece, with red slip and molded decoration. Height 5.7 cm, diameter 12.2 cm. Found at Zikhron Ya'akov near Caesarea, now in the Museum of Ancient Art, Haifa.
Aaron Levin photo.

Figure 22.
Glass bowl from the second or first century B.C.E. Sherds of such bowls, among the earliest mass-produced glass tableware, help identify late Hellenistic levels at Caesarea. Height 9.4 cm, diameter 14.6 cm. Provenance unknown, now in the Israel Museum, Clare Rothschild bequest.
Photo David Harris, Israel Museum.

Figure 23.
Group of Hellenistic oil lamps typical of Caesarea. Sherds of lamps at left and center, with the side lug, occur in levels from the second and early first centuries C.E., those of lamp at right, without the lug, from slightly later contexts. Lengths 8.0–11.5 cm. Provenances unknown, now at DIAR.
Aaron Levin photo.

Sidon. It is also possible, but less likely, that the sherd came from an heirloom vessel, from an antique cup that had been in the possession of one of the town's later inhabitants.

What remains elusive is enough information from excavation to determine the size and importance of Strato's Tower at any time in its existence. Was the settlement several small neighborhoods or villages in close proximity to one another, or did it evolve into a genuine city with a wall, developed port facilities, and other major buildings characteristic of an urban center? If so, when were the fortifications constructed, and can they be identified with any of the remains that various teams have excavated at Caesarea? A spirited debate is being held between CAHEP and JECM over these questions.

A clue to the answer to one of these questions appears in the ancient literary record. At some point in its history, Strato's Tower definitely had a wall. In the collection of Jewish legal texts called the *Tosefta* (Shevi'it 4.11) a debate is recorded among the ancient rabbis on the boundaries of the Holy Land. According to this text, the boundaries extended up to "the city wall of Strato's Tower."

Finding where this wall was is the challenge. Of the teams that have excavated at Caesarea, only CAHEP has addressed the task, in connection with its search for the harbor facilities of Strato's Tower. The evidence is clear and convincing that Strato's Tower had two harbors, one to the north and one to the south. To the north of the Crusader fortifications, not far from where Negev and Avi-Yonah found concentrations of Hellenistic pottery and Hellenistic houses, CAHEP discovered a section of loading quay in its area J (fig. 24). Built of large stone blocks and oriented east–west, the structure resembled loading quays of Phoenician design found in Israel at Atlit and Akko north of Caesarea, and hence probably came from the Hellenistic period. The proximity of the sea – most of the quay was actually submerged – made dating by stratigraphic means impossible, but a trench opened on land next to the quay produced the largest quantity of Hellenistic pottery yet discovered at Caesarea, with dates that span the third and second centuries B.C.E. This pottery suggests commercial or industrial activity near the quay in the Hellenistic period and the consequent formation of a dump. There is little doubt that the quay belonged to Strato's Tower and that it formed the southern flank of a small harbor basin, probably enclosed, in the typical Hellenistic fashion, by quays and a sea wall (fig. 24).

In the southwestern quarter of what was once Crusader Caesarea, a massive artificial platform, formed in part by a row of ancient vaulted chambers, dominates the eastern side of a rectangular open space around which are grouped today restaurants and shops that cater to tourists (fig. 54). The ruins of a Crusader

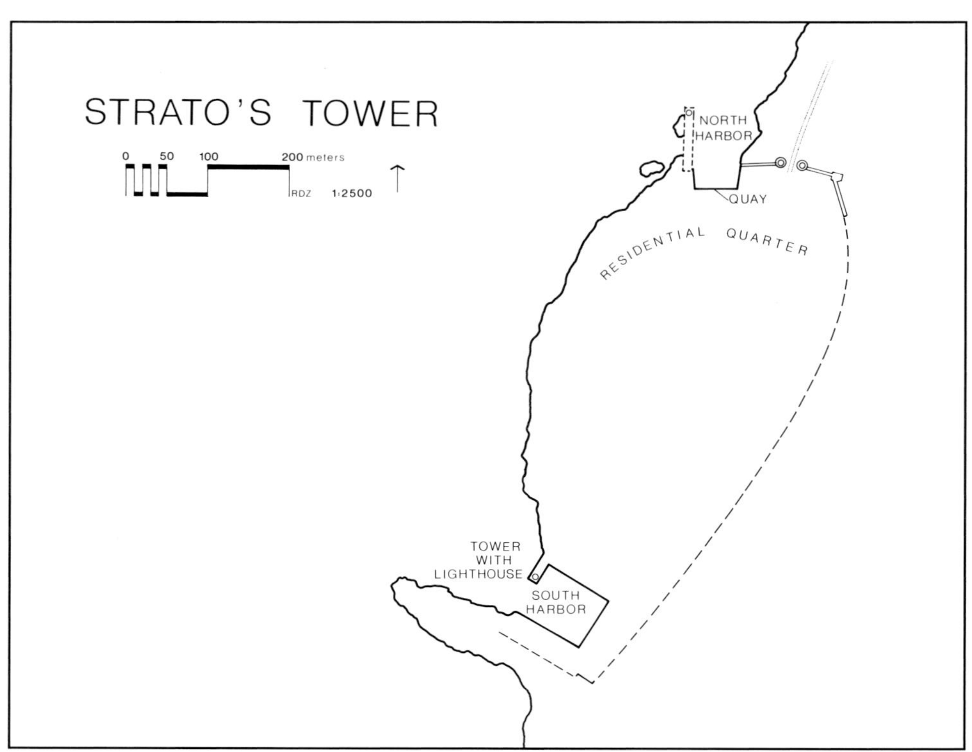

Figure 24. Hypothetical plan of Strato's Tower ca. 125–100 B.C.E.
Robin Ziek drawing.

cathedral stand on top of the platform, where, at the end of the first century B.C.E., King Herod built his great temple to Roma and Augustus (see chapter 3). In the early 1960s, Negev exposed a perplexing array of ancient walls, pavements, and cisterns in front of the vaults, mostly from the Byzantine and Muslim periods. He identified a massive stone structure there as the eastern quay of King Herod's harbor and concluded that in Herod's day the harbor had included the open space to the west of the platform, which is now dry land.

CAHEP archaeologists have now proved this hypothesis and taken it a step farther by discovering evidence that an enclosed harbor had occupied the open space in front of the platform even in the time of Strato's Tower. In its trenches I1 and I2, CAHEP excavated along the Herodian quay, exposing a stone wall (clearly earlier than the Herodian structures) that formed the eastern limit of the enclosed harbor (fig. 26). Near the top of this wall, the archaeologists found a mooring stone set into the wall and pierced horizontally to receive mooring lines. About half a meter below the mooring stone, about 20 to 30 centimeters above the present mean sea level, sea action had worn an abrasion notch (a horizontal cavity) into the stone wall – which indicates that the relative level of the sea has dropped perhaps 30 centimeters since

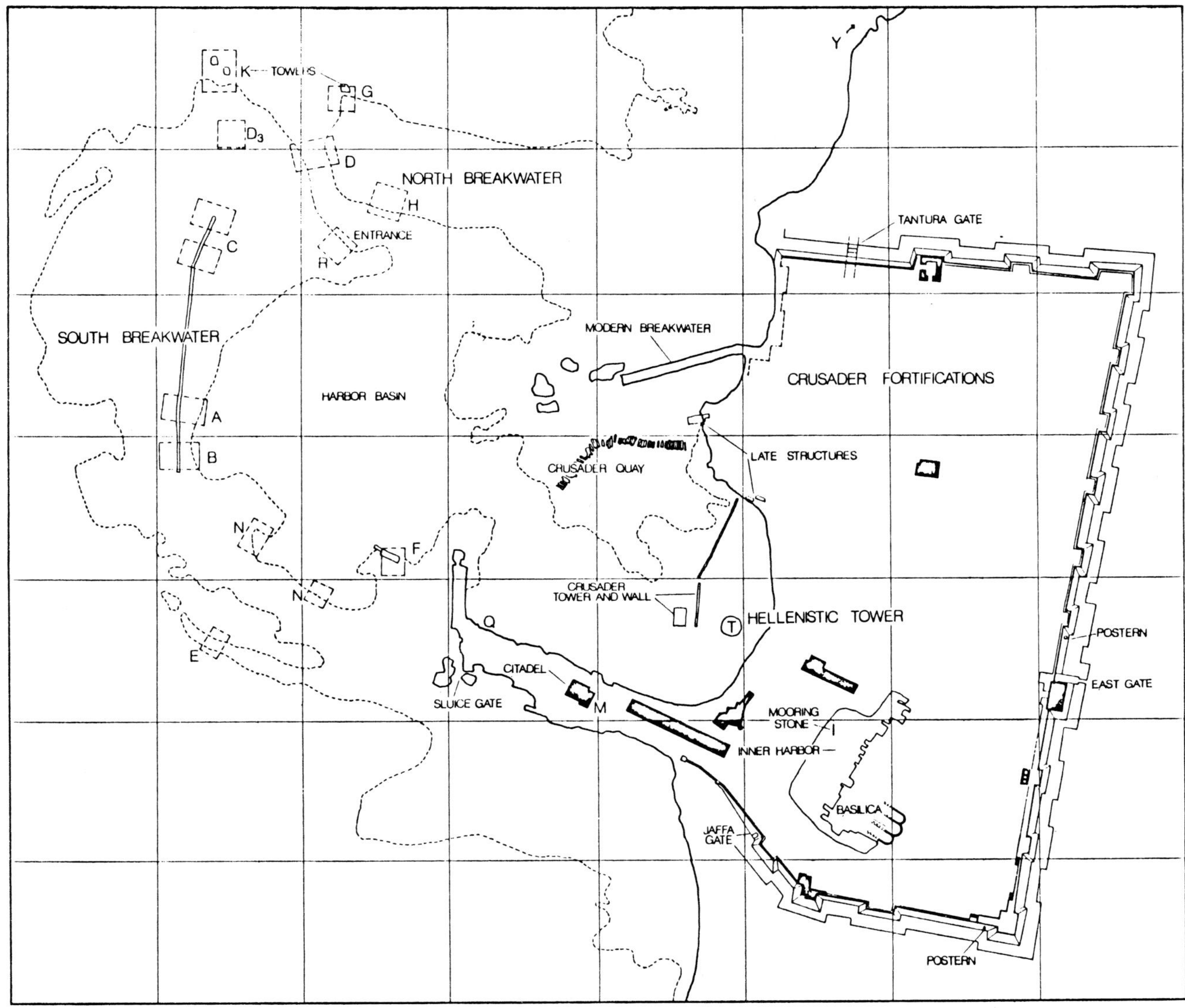

Figure 25.
CAHEP site map showing areas excavated since 1976. CAHEP has explored remains of harbor facilities on land as well as underwater.
CAHEP drawing.

the mooring stone was used. The fossils of marine organisms are still encrusted on the face of the wall, beginning above the abrasion notch and extending some distance below it. Anxious to date the quay wall, the excavators dug all the way to the bottom of it, which meant working in mud and water because the trench was below the fresh-water table. In the end their hard work was rewarded, for they discovered that the quay wall had been founded on bedrock, and indeed that the bedrock had been cut away to a considerable depth to provide sufficient water beneath the keels of ships tied up along the quay. Their discovery means that the quay and the entire

Figure 26.
Eastern quay wall of Hellenistic-Herodian inner harbor basin, looking eastward. Pierced mooring stone, abrasion notch cut by the sea, and encrusted marine fossils confirm the identity of this structure.
Mark Little photo.

Figure 27. Masonry inside southernmost vaulted building supporting Herodian temple platform, looking south. Here building stones with hewn margins have been laid alternately as headers and stretchers.
Aaron Levin photo.

harbor basin located on what is now dry land belonged to the Hellenistic period and to Strato's Tower. It was normal in that period for harbor engineers, following Phoenician practice, to excavate harbor basins inward from the coast, thus creating ports that were well protected from the prevailing winds and heavy coastal seas.

CAHEP has almost certainly located the northern and southern harbors of Strato's Tower, no mean feat in view of the fact that excavation necessarily occurred along or near the shore in areas heavily disturbed by wave action (fig. 25). Similar challenges accompanied the next step in the search for Strato's Tower, the identification of the city wall from that period. The team's attention was drawn first to a striking ruin located near the southern harbor and apparently aligned with it. Negev had also cleared the southernmost vaulted building of the series that supports the great Herodian temple platform (fig. 54). He found that this vaulted building, presumed to be from the time of Herod, had actually been constructed in two distinct styles of masonry that had originated in two distinct periods. Relatively small sandstone ashlars (rectangular blocks) formed the northern wall and vault of the Herodian structure, whereas the stones of the southern and eastern walls of the building were large and had margins on their exposed faces (fig. 27). The builders of the southern and eastern walls, but not those who constructed the vault and the north wall, had laid the stones in each course alternately as headers (with the small, squared end facing outward) and stretchers (with the rectangular length facing outward). Because the builders of the north wall and the vault had laid the stones of the vault itself on *top* of the southern and eastern walls, those two walls, with their different style of masonry, had to have *predated* the construction of the vault. Obviously, the builders of the vaulted building had incorporated earlier walls within its structure.

Proceeding from the assumption that the southern and eastern walls of the Herodian vaulted building belonged to Strato's Tower, CAHEP archaeologists employed a standard technique of stratigraphic archaeology in an attempt to secure a firm date for them. In the constricted space within the vaulted building, where Negev had worked earlier, there was no hope of digging a full-scale trench stratigraphically. Even so, CAHEP could locate and date the foundation trench of the building's south wall, the trench the builders of that wall had dug below ground level for the purpose of laying the wall's foundations. To accomplish this the archaeologists dug a sounding, a trial trench 1 by 2 meters in size, directly against the wall in question, continuing downward until they reached either bedrock or sterile soil.

The CAHEP trench penetrated two distinct layers: the upper layer is described in the field notes as a gray clayey layer and the lower one as buff-colored, sterile sand. The foundation trench penetrated the upper layer and part of the lower. At the bottom of their trench, the builders of the wall had first laid stone rubble to level the foundation and then the first course of wall stones. When they reached ground level, they filled in their foundation trench, forming a deposit still visible to CAHEP's excavators. For dating purposes the potsherds contained within that fill were crucial to the archaeologists because the sherds necessarily came from vessels that predated the construction of the wall. The foundation trench yielded no datable sherds from vessels made later than the late second or early first century B.C.E. Because the CAHEP team found no later pottery in the foundation trench, they were confident that the southern and eastern walls of the Herodian vault had belonged earlier to Strato's Tower.

What the function of those walls was is not clear from the context in which they survive, but they do resemble closely another set of walls known to archaeologists at Caesarea. In 1963 and 1964 the Italian Mission excavated a 120-meter section of a defensive city wall north of the Crusader fortifications, including two round towers that originally had a gate between them and a polygonal tower some distance farther to the east (fig. 28; cf. fig. 16). The Mission did not offer ceramic or other stratified evidence for dating the wall, but even a quick glance at one section of it reveals that its masonry is virtually identical with that of the walls within the Herodian vault (fig. 29; cf. fig. 27). In both, large blocks with margins drafted on their exterior face were laid in courses of alternating headers and stretchers. The similarity indicated to

CAHEP archaeologists that the walls were built at the same time, that the walls within the Herodian vault also functioned as defensive walls, and that all belonged to the same defensive system. CAHEP identified still another round tower, again nearly identical in construction with the two in the northern wall, that may have belonged to this system. It, however, is underwater, just offshore from the open space within the Crusader fortifications, where the enclosed harbor of Strato's Tower once existed (fig. 25).

Figure 28.
North wall and towers uncovered by Italian Mission 1963–64, south at top.
PICTORIAL ARCHIVE
(Near Eastern History) Est.

Figure 29.
Section of north wall between round and polygonal towers, looking north. Masonry is identical in style with that pictured in fig. 27.
Aaron Levin photo.

When all of these features are drawn on a site map, there emerges what CAHEP has proposed for a working version of the city plan of Strato's Tower (fig. 24; cf. fig. 11). It includes the suggested line for the defensive walls, incorporating the walls within the Herodian vault, the offshore tower, and the section of wall with towers that the Mission discovered. The suggested line also incorporates both the northern and southern harbors, the enclosed harbors typical of the Hellenistic period. The offshore tower would have stood guard over the entrance to the southern harbor, securing it from enemy attack.

If we extend the dating secured for the segments of wall within the great Herodian vault to the entire defensive system, we have a historical context for the transition of Strato's Tower from unfortified town to walled city. By the last quarter of the second century B.C.E., ancient Palestine and much of the Near East had fallen into anarchy. The mighty Seleucid monarchy, which had wrested control of the country from the Ptolemies of Egypt in 200 B.C.E., had been reduced to a shadow of itself, and the Romans were still more than half a century away from assuming responsibility for security in the region. The situation enabled a number of petty rulers, or "tyrants," to establish independent ministates. One of them, Zoilus, ruled Strato's Tower and also the city of Dor 12 kilometers to the north. It is more than a plausible hypothesis that Zoilus fortified Strato's Tower. The ceramic evidence that CAHEP found accords well with a date for the defensive walls in the last quarter of the second century B.C.E. Moreover, a petty tyrant like Zoilus would have needed fortifications, because a more powerful state had emerged nearby from the chaos of the Seleucid monarchy: the kingdom of Judaea ruled by the Jewish Hasmonaean dynasty, descendants of Judah the Maccabee. Zoilus maintained his independence against the expansionist Jewish kings until 103 B.C.E., when King Alexander Jannaeus overthrew him and incorporated both Dor and Strato's Tower into the Jewish state.

Despite CAHEP's plausible reconstruction, not all archaeologists, including those with JECM, accept its conclusions. In fact, they are debated, as will become clear in chapter 3. The Italian Mission, which excavated the important section of north wall, suggested a Herodian date, and JECM insists that its own careful stratigraphic work in area G.8 supports the Italians' conclusion. CAHEP's position is that the ceramic evidence on which JECM bases its case does not exclude the wall's having been built by Zoilus. Thus, the search for Strato's Tower continues. Because in archaeology mathematical precision is possible only for measurements, each team expects that only further excavation can produce the evidence that will tip the balance of their interpretations. For all archaeologists "the answers lie below."

CHAPTER 3

King Herod's City

Figure 30.
Tell Samaria, ruins of Herod's temple to Augustus, looking south. The temple stood on an artificial platform reached by the broad staircase in the foreground.
PICTORIAL ARCHIVE (Near Eastern History) Est.

"I would rather be Herod's pig," said Caesar Augustus, "than his son." The Roman emperor, for whom Caesarea was named, must have known Herod well. The king, although hardly a pious Jew, abstained from pork and publicly observed other Jewish dietary laws to avoid offending his subjects, with whom he was already unpopular. But he executed three of his own sons when he began to suspect that they were plotting against him. Behind the emperor's witticism lay unpleasant facts.

The life and character of Herod the Great (ca. 73–4 B.C.E.) are important to our understanding of Caesarea and ancient urbanism in general. Cities in antiquity did not spring up spontaneously, nourished by anonymous developers and impersonal economic forces. Herod willed Caesarea into being, for reasons of policy, to make a profit, and as a colossal act of self-expression. The city figured prominently in his career, a manifestation of his personality and his dreams.

Herod was from Idumaea, a land in the southern part of the Jewish kingdom, whose inhabitants had accepted Jewish rule and the Jewish religion at sword's point only two generations before he was born (fig. 31). Herod's mother was a Nabataean princess. The Nabataean Arabs ruled Petra, the "rose-red city" in what is now Jordan, and territories on the desert fringe to the south and east of Judaea. His father, Antipater, was a brilliant Idumaean general and politician who had been a chief minister and power behind the throne to one of the last of the Hasmonaean kings. When Antipater died in 43 B.C.E., murdered with Hasmonaean connivance, Herod resolved to succeed him, and to rule over Judaea not for the Hasmonaeans, but in his own right.

One formidable barrier stood in Herod's way. Herod was only an Idumaean "half-Jew." He did not belong to one of the Jewish priestly houses and therefore could not combine civil and military authority, as the Hasmonaeans had, with the powerful office of high priest. Most Jews would never accept him willingly because they wanted either no ruler at all or a ruler in the high priest's robes presiding in the Temple at Jerusalem over the cult of God. Herod had, however, inherited some potent advantages from his father. These included vast wealth that came principally from estates in Idumaea and throughout the kingdom of Judaea. Herod had also inherited the loyalty of Antipater's soldiers (along with the means to pay them) and his father's exceptional military and political capabilities. Above all, Herod learned from his father to befriend the Romans.

The general Pompey the Great had first brought Roman arms to the corner of the world occupied by the Jewish kingdom in 65 B.C.E. In Syria, where the Seleucid monarchy had finally expired, Pompey established a Roman province and, as part of the process, sent one of his generals with an army to bring a Roman peace to Jerusalem. From that point on, it would have been obvious to a clear-thinking man that the Romans would decide who would rule over the Jews.

Antipater, the Idumaean, was such a clear-thinking man, and so was his son. After his father's death, Herod remained the power behind the Hasmonaean throne, along with his brother Phasael, until 40 B.C.E., when their enemies managed a coup. Taken captive, Phasael cheated certain execution by committing suicide; Herod escaped, and, after harrowing adventures, reached Rome before the end of the year. The Roman senate issued a decree declaring Antipater's surviving son king of the Jews, and shortly thereafter Herod joined in a procession up Rome's Capitol Hill to sacrifice to the Roman deities Jupiter, Juno, and Minerva and to deposit the senate's decree in their temple. Leading the procession, to Herod's left and right, were the new king's chief benefactors, the general Mark Antony and a young politician named Octavian, who, thirteen years later, would take the name Caesar Augustus and reign as the first Roman emperor. The spectacle is instructive. After a century of Roman civil war, Octavian and Antony had jointly seized absolute authority over Rome and the Mediterranean world. The king of the Jews sacrificed to the pagan gods of imperial Rome, shoulder to shoulder with the most powerful Romans of the day.

Once king, Herod had to master his kingdom, a labor that extended over three long and difficult years. As the new king might have expected, the Romans gave him little concrete support. Not until the bitter end, during a five-month siege of Jerusalem in 37 B.C.E., did a Roman general arrive with an army. Then, although entrenched as a Roman client king, Herod faced other kinds of peril. In the decade before their final showdown in the battle of Actium (31 B.C.E.), Antony and Octavian divided the world between them, with the entire East going to Mark Antony. This partition made Antony Herod's patron, to whom he owed absolute obedience. Antony, however, had joined forces with Queen Cleopatra of Egypt, one of the last Ptolemaic rulers of that wealthy land, and Cleopatra coveted Herod's kingdom. Despite her insistence Antony refused to depose Herod, who had been useful to him on several occasions, and the queen had to content herself with the gift of the Mediterranean coast of ancient Palestine, which included the future site of Caesarea.

Herod's punctilious loyalty to Antony became a serious liability after the battle of Actium, where Octavian prevailed. Within a year Antony and Cleopatra took their own lives. As on other occasions, Herod demonstrated courage and resourcefulness. Not long after the decisive battle, he sailed to the Greek island of Rhodes to meet Octavian in person. It must have been a moment of high drama. Herod entered the victor's presence without his royal diadem, leaving it to Octavian to judge Herod's capabilities and trustworthiness and to decide whether to execute him or to retain him as king of Judaea. As Herod had calculated, Octavian restored the diadem. What might have been the king's final hour became the occasion for enhancing his power. Octavian actually enlarged Herod's kingdom (fig. 31). He restored to it the coastal territory that Antony had given Cleopatra and that included the site of Strato's Tower, by then ruinous and dilapidated. Despite occasional conflicts with his Jewish subjects, and increasing difficulties within his family, Herod reigned in relative peace and security until his death in 4 B.C.E.

This, in outline, is the story of Herod the Great, known to us principally from ancient literary sources, from Macrobius who wrote in about 400 C.E. and preserved Augustus's witticism, and from Flavius Josephus, whose works are by far the richest written sources for Herod's life. An aristocratic Jew, Josephus organized the defense of the Galilee (in the northern part of ancient Palestine) during the Jews' revolt against Rome in 66 C.E. When his mission failed, he became a turncoat, spent the rest of the war (66–70 C.E.) in the Roman camp, and then lived out his life in Rome under the protection of Titus, the general responsible for the destruction of Jerusalem and the Jewish Temple, and his father, the emperor Vespasian.

In his *Jewish Wars* and *Jewish Antiquities*, Josephus defends his own conduct and that of his people, the Jews. In doing so he discusses both Herod and Caesarea in detail. Because Josephus wrote his books roughly eighty years after Herod's death, scholars assume that he took his information from earlier accounts. These

Figure 31.
Herod's Kingdom at its greatest extent.
Robin Ziek drawing.

would have included the *History* of Herod's court historian, Nicolaus of Damascus, and the king's memoirs. Although his sources were obviously biased, Josephus's account of Herod preserves authentic information, enough to help historians to reconstruct a detailed and accurate portrait.

The portrait is of a man with a passion for power and gifted with the wealth, political and military genius, tenacity, and daring to achieve it. Herod understood the Romans and the Jews. He had to deal with the competing demands of being faithful to his Roman patrons and of placating Jewish religious sensitivities. He never managed to resolve the contradiction. Thus Herod feared for his crown and for his life, and paranoia eventually directed his suspicions and cruelty even toward members of his own family.

Herod the Master Builder

Not only is the literary portrait of Herod far from complete, but we lack a portrait bust even on Herod's coins. Jewish law did not permit human images, and wherever possible Herod avoided giving offense. What do exist in abundance, however, are the remains of Herod's buildings. As much as Josephus or any formal portrait, these mute stones reveal Herod's personality, fears, tastes, and ambitions.

Apparently Herod feared the Jews but was clever and ambitious enough to win them over, despite his questionable origins and his friendship with the hated Romans. To that end he rebuilt the Second Temple in Jerusalem, probably between 23/22 and 15 B.C.E., to give the Jews a new and more splendid setting in which to offer sacrifices to God through the agency of their priests. Herod's building replaced an earlier version of the Second Temple, which went back to the sixth century B.C.E., and had been expanded and embellished a number of times.

The Romans destroyed the Second Temple in 70 C.E. Archaeologists cannot search for its traces because the Muslim Dome of the Rock, itself a building of unsurpassed holiness and beauty, now occupies the site (fig. 32). But the visitor can gain some impression of the Temple's setting, and of the effort and expense that went into its construction, by examining the platform on which Herod placed it, the Temple Mount, now called the *Haram esh-Sherif* ("Noble Sanctuary") by its Muslim occupants. This spacious platform, which measures 485 meters on its west side—nearly one-third of a mile – and 285 meters on the south, is supported by massive retaining walls. Much of the original masonry survives, including what Jews call *ha-kotel ha-ma'aravi* ("the Western Wall"), Judaism's most sacred place

Figure 32. The Western Wall (Hebrew ha-kotel ha-ma'aravi*), sometimes called the "Wailing Wall," in Jerusalem. Above it, the Muslim Dome of the Rock occupying the approximate position of the ancient Jewish Temple, destroyed by the Romans in 70 C.E. View looking east. The Western Wall formed part of one retaining wall of the immense platform on which the Temple stood. Its Jerusalem limestone blocks date from the time of Herod the Great and present a good example of the monumental masonry of the Herodian age.*
Kenneth Holum photo.

Figure 33.
Model of Herod's Second Temple, view toward the west, part of the model of Herodian Jerusalem located in the garden of the Holyland Hotel, Jerusalem. Scale of the model 1:50.
Zev Radovan photo.

(fig. 32). Some of the limestone blocks, which are carefully dressed with margins at their exposed edges, reach 1.85 meters in height and 12 meters in length, and at least one weighs more than 100 tons. Even more impressive is the original height of the platform, much of which is hidden beneath the debris and soil that have accumulated over the centuries. Between 1867 and 1870, during archaeology's heroic age, an Englishman, Lieutenant Charles Warren, dug a vertical shaft at the southeastern corner of the Temple platform that reached bedrock and the foundations of the Herodian structure 24.4 meters below ground level. At that point, the original retaining wall must have towered at least 50 meters above the valley floor, the height of a fifteen-story building.

Atop the high retaining walls, columned porticoes, or porches, surrounded the paved outer Temple court on the north, east, and west. A great hall, called the Royal Portico, stood on the south. No trace of these exists, but the details are described in the works of Josephus and of the early rabbis. The same sources devote even more

Figure 34.
Aerial view of Masada looking southeast. Roman siege camp visible in foreground, and to the south of it the earthen ramp that the Romans built to gain access to the summit when they attacked the Jewish occupants in 74 C.E. The left (northern) profile of the mountain reveals the three terraces of Herod's Northern Palace.
PICTORIAL ARCHIVE (Near Eastern History) Est.

detail to the inner Temple courts, the Altar of Burnt Offerings, and the Temple itself. The literary sources describe a magnificent and holy building, sheathed in white marble, with a facade 50 meters high and 50 meters wide, that gleamed in the morning sun like a snowy mountain (fig. 33).

The Second Temple expressed not only Herod's need to placate the Jews, but also his taste for the beautiful and the grandiose and his ability to organize manpower on a large scale. We see this in all Herodian architecture, particularly in what the Israeli archaeologist Ehud Netzer has called the mountain palace-fortresses. Herod built or rebuilt royal residences set on top of easily defended mountains and fitted out with splendid living quarters for him and his household, including cisterns and magazines for the supplies he would need to withstand an extended siege. A line of them – Alexandrion, Doq, Cypros, and Masada – extended north–south along the western escarpment of the Jordan Valley and the Dead Sea, guarding the eastern approaches to Jerusalem, while Machaeros, where one of Herod's sons later beheaded John the Baptist, lay farther to the east, in what is now Jordan (fig. 31). Herodion and Hyrcania, positioned in the Judaean desert to the south and southeast of Jerusalem, protected the capital's southern flank and provided the king with his most accessible places of refuge. The palace-fortresses functioned also as administrative centers, strongpoints from which Herod's troops could control the surrounding countryside, and as prisons in which he confined members of his family whom he considered a threat. The palaces had lavish rooms with stunning views over the desert. Herod could receive guests in them while on vacation from the capital. They also provided him with a secure but appropriately royal retreat he would need if his enemies overthrew him. Two at least, Herodion and Masada, in the boldness and originality of their architectural conception, reveal a brilliant and daring esthete at work.

Masada towers mesa-like in the remote desert, its nearly flat top reaching more than 400 meters above the Dead Sea, a short distance to the east (fig. 34). The late Israeli archaeologist Yigael Yadin excavated Masada in 1963–65 with an army of volunteers and colleagues. The visitor who ascends the mountain today by foot or cable car can inspect the well-preserved double defensive wall, or casemate, a large block of storerooms, and capacious cisterns (holding 40,000 cubic meters of water) hewn out of solid rock. On the mountain's northern summit are the remains of a Roman-style bath, with the cold, tepid, and hot rooms typical of contemporary bathhouses in Italy.

Most impressive, however, are the palaces. In the western palace, Herod's

builders installed mosaic pavements decorated with colorful geometric patterns, similar to those in lavish Hellenistic houses but without the human or animal figures that would have offended the Jews. The northern palace descends the mountain's steep northern scarp in three terraces, the lowest one perched precipitously above the abyss and supported in part by a massive buttressing wall that required of its builders both consummate engineering skill and readiness to work in difficult and dangerous circumstances (fig. 34). On this lowest terrace stood a square peristyle building, consisting of ranges of half-columns set on low walls (fig. 35). Against the

Figure 35.
Masada, view toward south of the peristyle building on the Northern Palace's lowest terrace.
Aaron Levin photo.

back wall, sandstone Hellenistic-style Corinthian capitals topped stone half-columns with plaster vertical fluting (figs. 35–36). Between the columns, painted plaster imitated a multicolored, marble revetment – a style of decoration also popular in the Hellenistic East and reminiscent of the houses of the wealthy at Pompeii and elsewhere in Italy. In the southeastern corner of this lower terrace, Yadin and his teams uncovered another Roman-type bath. This building obviously served only the pleasure of the king and his guests, who could, from that lofty perspective, gaze over the Dead Sea and a vast expanse of savagely beautiful desert.

Figure 36. Masada, Northern Palace, lowest terrace. Engaged Herodian capital, Corinthian order, carved from sandstone.
Aaron Levin photo.

Figure 37.
Herodion, remains of Herod's Mountain Palace-Fortress, looking east. Judaean Desert and Dead Sea visible in the background.
PICTORIAL ARCHIVE
(Near Eastern History) Est.

Figure 38.
Herodion, Herod's Mountain Palace-Fortress, remains of peristyle court, looking south. Base of eastern tower at left and in the background a triclinium (dining room) later used as a synagogue.
Kenneth Holum photo.

At Herodion Herod did no less than reshape an entire mountain (fig. 37). Upon the summit of what is now called, in Arabic, the *Jebel Fureidis* ("Mountain of Herod") Herod built a circular structure 63 meters in diameter. Its outer and inner walls had corridors in multiple storys between them. Earth and stone fill were poured against the outer wall to create the mountain's artificial conical shape. A flight of steps, ascending from the northeast and partly covered by the fill, provided the only access to the cylinder's interior. The space within the circular walls contained a luxurious peristyle to the east, and to the west a formal dining room, living quarters, and still another Roman-type bath (fig. 38). The hot room of this bath was roofed with a dome – one of the earliest surviving examples of this characteristic Roman building technique. Above the circular space, at the cardinal points of the compass to the north, west, and south, semicircular towers rose, and to the east a full round tower that may have stood 45 meters high above the original mountaintop. The bases of the towers were solid masonry, but above them were rooms; there were probably royal apartments in the eastern tower, perhaps with a

small bath like the one in the northern palace at Masada. From the galleries on top of the eastern tower Herod would have had a spectacular view of the Judaean hills and could easily communicate by signal mirror or fire with similar towers in Jerusalem.

According to Josephus, Herod built this palace-fortress to be his tomb. Thus, architectural historians have traditionally identified the mausoleum of Caesar Augustus in Rome as the source of its design. There may be some truth to this theory, but clearly Herodion also reflects Herod's own esthetic principles. Its bold design combined defensive capability with luxurious dwelling accommodations, as at Masada, and it drew freely on Hellenistic and Roman building techniques and decoration.

Herod built other palaces, although not heavily fortified ones, in the valley below Doq and Cypros, where the Wadi Qelt egresses from the western escarpment of the Jordan Valley. The Hasmonaean kings had already constructed a winter palace there, not far from the oasis of Jericho, and Herod redeveloped the site to suit his taste. The latest Herodian palace on the site, excavated recently by Netzer, was built on both sides of the Wadi Qelt. On the north side of the wadi, the palace's northern wing was fronted by a long portico (fig. 39). We know from the remains that this wing consisted of a series of magnificently appointed rooms, the grandest of which was a huge reception room, 19 by 29 meters (left, fig. 39), where Herod could sit in state to receive distinguished guests, embassies, and petitioners. Roofed and surrounded on three sides by colonnades, it had a floor of deluxe *opus sectile*, a type of marble paving with geometric patterns in various colors. To the east of this reception room lay two open peristyle courts, a large dining room, and a complete Roman-type bath, parts of which were constructed with Roman concrete faced with *opus reticulatum*, small square stones laid in a fishnet pattern, rather than the mud brick native to the region (fig. 40). Across the wadi to the south, probably accessible by a bridge, were a monumental building – perhaps another bath – on a high mound, a large swimming pool, and a sunken garden luxuriant with exotic plantings that provided an engaging vista for those gazing across the wadi from the porticoes of the northern wing.

Herod's winter palace at Jericho reveals the same esthetic principles as the palace fortresses, and more besides. Individual building units – palace, pool, porticoes, bath, and garden – are arrayed in a singularly dramatic setting astride the wadi and in a relationship to one another that emphasizes their belonging to a single organic design. The same is true at Herodion, where Netzer recently turned his attention to the lower slopes of the mountain, facing north. There Herod's architects laid out a number of other buildings: a second palace overlooking what appears to be a

Figure 39.
Jericho, northern wing of Herod's palace, looking northeast with Wadi Qelt in the foreground.
PICTORIAL ARCHIVE (Near Eastern History) Est.

Figure 40. Jericho, northern wing of Herod's palace, opus reticulatum *in the* frigidarium *(cold room) of the Roman bath.*
Kenneth Holum photo.

racetrack, an unidentified monumental building, service buildings, and a large ornamental pool with a circular structure in its center. All of these buildings are oriented perpendicular to a line drawn through the north–south axis of the mountain palace-fortress. All seem to be part of the same building program and to have been purposely positioned in exact relationships with each other.

We have seen that in antiquity rulers devoted themselves to building cities. In addition to Caesarea, Herod founded two towns, or small cities, named for members of his family: Antipatris (biblical Aphek) in the Plain of Sharon northeast of Joppa and Phasaelis in the Jordan Valley. In 27 B.C.E. he refounded Samaria, the ancient capital of the northern kings of Israel, and named it Sebaste (Greek for

Figure 41.
Tell Samaria, where Herod founded Sebaste, sister city of Caesarea, likewise named for his patron, Caesar Augustus. The ruins of ancient Samaria and Sebaste lie on top of the hill. Aerial view, looking southeast.
PICTORIAL ARCHIVE (Near Eastern History) Est.

Augustus) in honor of his patron, Caesar Augustus. This city occupied a steep hill in the region of Samaria, about 38 kilometers southeast of Caesarea (fig. 41). Refounding it meant not only giving it a new name, but increasing its economic resources and population and constructing new buildings. For Sebaste, according to Josephus, Herod provided six thousand colonists, many of them non-Jewish veterans from his army, an increased amount of arable land, and new fortification walls more than 3.2 kilometers in circumference. On the summit of the hill Herod constructed a large platform, like the Jerusalem Temple platform, and had a temple to Augustus placed on it, with an altar in front and a spacious forecourt (fig. 30). Sebaste associated Herod with the ancient tradition that rulers founded cities, and like the palace-fortresses, strengthened his grip on the country. With its fortification wall and veteran colonists Sebaste served, in Josephus' words, as "a stronghold against the entire nation."

This brief catalog by no means exhausts Herod's building projects within his kingdom, not to mention equally important projects abroad, most of which benefited cities and urban life. To various cities he donated fortifications, temples, marketplaces, porticoes, aqueducts, baths, and fountains. From him the great city of Antioch in Syria received the gift of a paved street 3.2 kilometers long and flanked by roofed colonnades in the latest fashion. In 16 B.C.E. Herod even presided over the Olympic games in Greece, giving a permanent endowment to support the venerable contests and receiving in return the title of permanent president. These benefactions reinforce the view that Herod devoted his wealth and energy to building both to satisfy his longings for personal security and luxury, and because he wished to be remembered in the company of the great builders of the past.

Herod Founds Caesarea

Herod created Caesarea, Sebaste's sister city, within a relatively brief period, 22–10/9 B.C.E. Josephus, in the *Jewish War* (3.408–15), describes the enterprise:

> *Along the coast Herod discovered a city that was in decay named Strato's Tower, whose location was well-suited to receive his generosity. This he rebuilt entirely in marble and ornamented with a most splendid palace. In this project he displayed his genius for grand designs, because the entire seacoast from Dor to Joppa, between which the new city lay, had lacked a harbor, and as a result any vessel sailing from Phoenicia to Egypt had to remain at sea buffeted by the southwest wind. Here even a moderate breeze dashes the waves against the rocks with such force that the backflow churns up the sea far off the coast. Thus, by lavish expenditure, the king conquered nature herself, constructing a harbor larger than the Piraeus,* and providing deep anchorages in its innermost recesses.*

After a detailed account of the harbor, Josephus describes the city itself:

> *Adjacent to the harbor stood the buildings, they too fabricated in marble, and leading toward it were the streets of the city, laid out at equal*

*The harbors of Athens.

distances from one another. Directly opposite the harbor entrance, upon a high platform, rose the temple of Caesar, remarkable both for its beauty and for its great size. In it stood a colossal statue of Caesar, not inferior to the Zeus at Olympia, which was its model, and one of the goddess Roma, equal to the Argive statue of Hera. Herod dedicated the city to the province, the harbor to those who sailed along its coast, and the honor of the new foundation to Caesar. For he named the city Caesarea.*

*The other public buildings – the amphitheater, the theater, and the marketplaces – Herod constructed in a style worthy of the city's namesake. Then he established athletic contests, to be held every fifth year, likewise named for Caesar. Herod himself presided over the inaugural games in the one-hundred-and-ninety-second Olympiad,** offering highly valuable prizes.*

Certainly Josephus knew Caesarea well – the stiff onshore breeze and the crashing surf. Josephus also appears to have understood Herod well and to have assessed correctly his motives for founding Caesarea. Herod displayed "generosity" on a kingly scale. He had recognized the site's promise, and with his extraordinary intelligence and foresight, along with a fabulous outpouring of wealth, even conquered nature. Moreover, in founding Caesarea, Herod combined his desire to ingratiate himself with Caesar Augustus with an economic motive: the desperate need for adequate port facilities on that part of the Mediterranean coast. There were no doubt two further considerations that Josephus does not mention. If inhabited by a loyal populace, Caesarea would fortify Herod's grip on his kingdom. Like Sebaste farther inland, and like its predecessor Strato's Tower, the new seaport would provide ready access to world markets for agricultural products from the Plain of Sharon. By linking Sebastos with east–west trade routes, Herod could make his new city a major emporium and could expect a profit from harbor and market fees. The scale of Herod's harbor works has even suggested to some archaeologists that he wished it to compete with Alexandria in Egypt for first rank among seaports in the southeastern Mediterranean. If so, Herod would have rivaled in statesmanship and high policy the great Macedonian conqueror who founded Alexandria and gave it his name.

Josephus also illuminates the actual process of founding a city in the ancient world. In a passage of the *Jewish Antiquities* (15.331–41) that parallels closely the *Jewish War* description, he wrote about Herod's "design" providing for all of the city's needs on a lavish scale. It probably included a formal city plan, in which

*The Zeus at Olympia and the Hera of Argos, both in Greece, were created in the fifth century B.C.E. by Phidias and Polycleitus, respectively. They ranked as two of the most celebrated works of classical sculpture.

**In 10/9 B.C.E.

Herod's architects and planners laid out the harbor, streets, temples, and public buildings. But designing a city required more than placing buildings on a plan. In the ancient conception, as in the modern one, a city was to be a living organism that could thrive on its own, and therefore in designing one Herod had to provide the necessary constituent elements.

The conception of necessary constituents varied. The Greek author Pausanias, who wrote the second-century C.E. equivalent of a Baedecker or *Blue Guide* for tourists from abroad, denied the title "city" to a hamlet in his country because it had "no government offices or gymnasium, no theater or marketplace or water flowing from a fountain." Thus, some kind of municipal administration and recreation facilities, along with running water, were required constituents, as were the temples and streets Josephus mentions. Obviously, to be ranked as a city, a community would also need a substantial population, including a landholding aristocracy, craftsmen, and slaves, and a viable economy. No doubt the plan for Caesarea was that much of its wealth would come from its harbor, but it would also need fields. The assumption in antiquity was that a city's economy would be based on its arable land; this "territory" (*territorium* in Latin and *chora* in Greek) was land under the city's authority. The aristocrats owned much of it but preferred to live in town, either leasing their property to peasant farmers or exploiting it directly with slaves and slave overseers. Other lands in the city's territory belonged to the city itself. Because municipal taxes were virtually unknown, the income from this land was the principal source of a city's revenues. Finally, a proper city had to have a fortification wall, separating the built-up area within – with its temples, marketplaces, and other facilities – from the territory outside. Even in peacetime the city wall provided symbolic confirmation of the city's independence and of its ability to defend itself. Hence, Caesarea's city goddess, the Tyche, or divine embodiment of the city, wore a crown that represented the city wall (see pp. 13, 15).

When Herod and his architects designed Caesarea, their plans provided for all of the necessities. Because Strato's Tower had been practically deserted, they had, as well, to populate the new city. Several distinct ethnic and social groups made up the population, but we do not know the proportion of each. Many of those who arrived were Greek-speaking pagans who frequented the temple to Roma and Augustus that Herod had built, but Jews also flocked to claim the economic advantages that Caesarea offered. Not long before the outbreak of the Jewish War in 66 C.E., the Jews of Caesarea argued that the city should belong to them because its founder, Herod, had been a Jew. The pagans responded that Herod would not have put temples and statues in Caesarea if he had intended it to be Jewish.

Among the landholders, the city's aristocracy, were veteran soldiers who had served in Herod's army and had been rewarded with farms on their retirement. Many of the tenant farmers who actually tilled the soil were neither Jews nor pagans but Samaritans – worshipers of the God of Israel for whom the sacred mount was not Zion but Mount Gerizim near modern Nablus. Although the ancients were notoriously indifferent to statistics, Josephus does report that, at the outbreak of the Jewish War, Caesarea's pagans massacred the city's entire Jewish community of twenty thousand, except for a few whom the Roman governor seized and sent in chains to labor in the city's dockyards. If this figure is anywhere near accurate, the total population in 66 C.E. must have numbered at least fifty thousand, which would have ranked Caesarea among the twenty or so largest cities in the Mediterranean world.

Little is known of Caesarea's municipal institutions in Herod's day. He gave his new city a tripartite constitution that resembled those of other Greek and Roman cities: an assembly of the entire citizen body (a "town meeting") that had little actual power, a town council of the leading citizens to supervise day-to-day government, and magistrates who presided over lawcourts and allocated the city's revenues appropriately. As in other ancient cities, a small group of wealthy men actually ran Caesarea, subject, of course, to Herod himself. The king stationed one of his officers in the city with the title general (*strategos*), and placed a body of royal troops under his command.

Of the cities on ancient Palestine's coastal plain, Caesarea possessed the largest territory, donated to it by its founder (fig. 42). It extended about 35 kilometers north to south, from the Chorseos River (modern Nahal Daliyya) in the north to the Bdellopotamos (Nahal Poleg, south of Netanya). To the east Caesarea's territory extended in a few places 27 kilometers or more inland from the coast. The total area of Caesarea's territory therefore amounted to over 100,000 hectares. To the northeast and east, rocky hills occupied part of this area, but much of it was the rich farmland of the northern Plain of Sharon (fig. 43). Prosperous farms, country villas, and small towns were arrayed across the landscape, all of them subject to Caesarea and its rulers. Herod had seen to it that the new city's economy would have a solid agricultural base.

In recent years our knowledge of Caesarea's territory has expanded enormously. Apart from indications of its extent in ancient texts, the Archaeological Survey of Israel, a research effort supported by the government of Israel, has sent experienced archaeologists out to walk the countryside to locate all the ancient remains visible at ground level and to prepare survey maps. They note the varieties of

Figure 42.
Caesarea's city territory, the lands given to it by Herod. The city's frontiers are known only approximately. Territories of other cities, some of them founded later, bordered Caesarea's. By the end of the second century C.E., an excellent system of paved highways radiated from Caesarea, connecting it with several of these cities. Also included on this plan is the city's aqueduct system to the north of the city, developed between the time of Herod and the fifth century C.E.
Robin Ziek drawing.

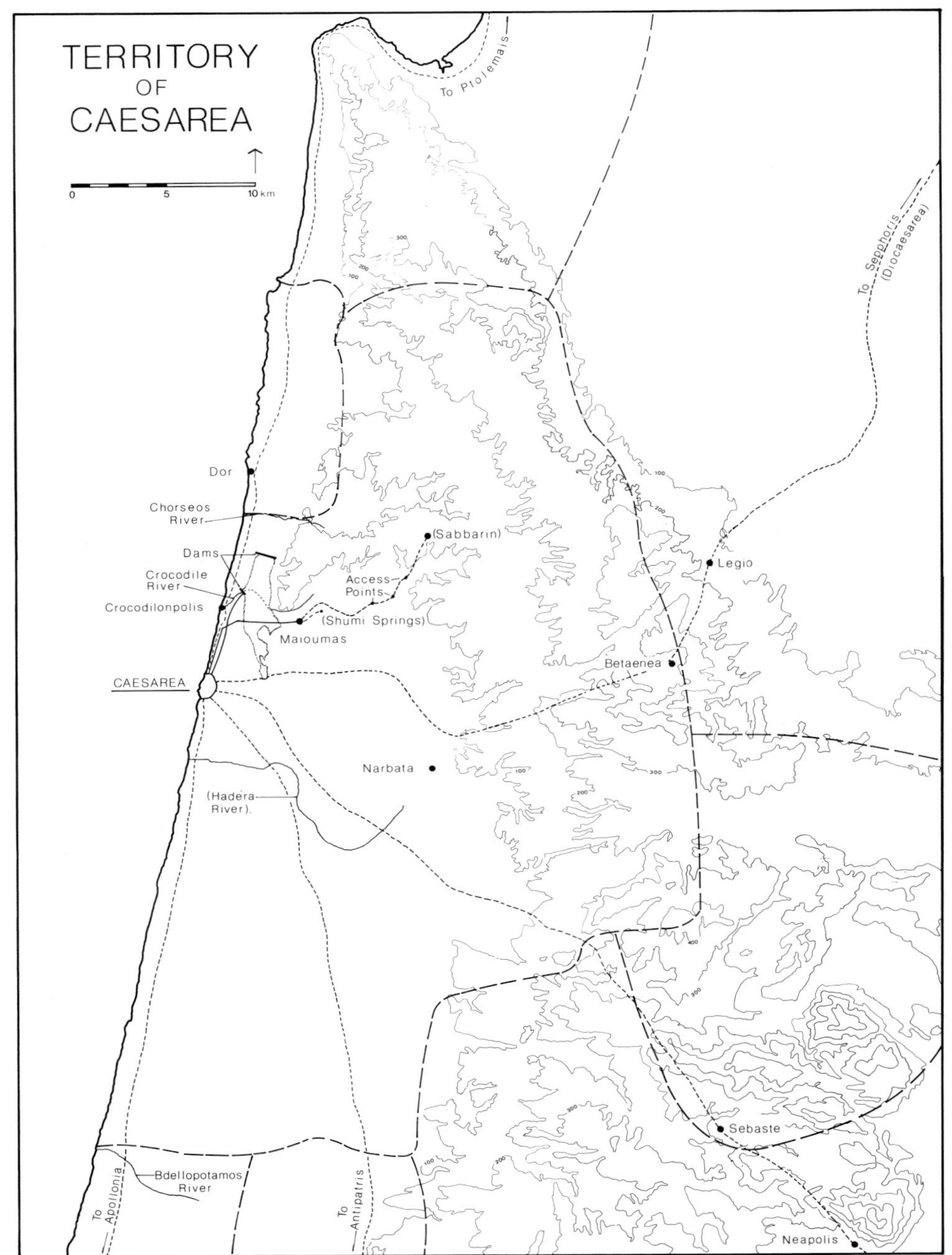

Figure 43. Rich farmland in Caesarea's territory, about five km northeast of the ancient city, looking southwest toward Caesarea. In the distance, below the slopes of the Carmel range, a Turkish khan (caravan rest house) built over the ruins of an ancient theater marks the site of Maioumas, one of the city's subject towns. Aaron Levin photo.

sherds they find and photograph and draw significant artifacts. These kinds of information enable archaeologists to estimate land use and population density for all historical periods.

Archaeologists also have much to say about the city's architecture and its harbor – the necessary constituents that Herod provided when he founded Caesarea. They have, for example, excavated and studied Caesarea's aqueduct system, which supplied water for the city's needs from sources to the north and northeast. The high-level aqueduct is well known (fig. 44). Less well-known is the fact it is actually two separate water channels; the eastern one was built first, but there are no reliable clues for dating it. Latin inscriptions on the aqueduct prove that the Emperor Hadrian ordered construction of the western, and later, channel in the second century C.E. (see p. 127). Because a water supply was an essential constituent of an ancient city – as Pausanias indicated in the passage quoted here – many archaeologists believe that Herod constructed the eastern channel when he founded Caesarea.

How archaeologists recognize Herod's work – the aqueduct and other building enterprises – and date it reliably is tied to the possibilities of stratigraphic archaeology, which one day will be applied to the eastern aqueduct channel. Excavations must proceed layer by layer, and the material-culture remains – the sherds and other refuse of human occupation – that appear in each layer are cataloged and compared with dated material from other sites. Especially useful for dating Herodian buildings is the ancient pottery classified generally as *terra sigillata*, a term derived from the fact that some pots of this type bear a stamp, *sigillum*, that is their potters' name or trademark (figs. 45–46). Archaeologists know that some forms of *terra sigillata* were made about the time that Herod founded Caesarea; those forms are therefore diagnostic for Herodian construction. Levels that contain such sherds – and none known to be later – most likely date to Herod's time. Also diagnostic for the period are sherds of certain forms of ceramic cook pot (fig. 47) and of *millefiori* glass vessels (fig. 48), and of course coins of Herod the Great. The so-called Herodian lamps, on the other hand, prove to be less useful for dating (fig. 49). An early form may date to the time of Herod or a bit later, but because variants were produced until the end of the first century C.E. and beyond, they cannot help the archaeologist recognize Herodian strata.

Using stratigraphic archaeology, literary sources, and a certain amount of educated guesswork, archaeologists have been able to draw an urban plan of Herod's Caesarea (fig. 50). These drawings leave many questions unanswered, questions that only further excavation will clarify.

In his description of the city's founding, Josephus fails to mention Caesarea's city wall. CAHEP archaeologists interpret this silence not unreasonably to mean that Herod did not build one. In their view the northern wall and towers excavated by the Italian Mission in 1959 dated from the late second century B.C.E. and remained in use after Herod's time only to protect the part of Caesarea that had earlier been Strato's Tower. JECM, on the other hand, points out that Herod built Caesarea, like Sebaste, in part as a military strongpoint, to be "a fortress for the entire country," as Josephus puts it in his *Jewish Antiquities* (15.293). In JECM's view he would hardly have left so much of the city unfortified, a point substantiated by the fact that, in general, Hellenistic city builders considered a wall to be one of a city's essential constituents. Furthermore, JECM archaeologists believe that the north wall and towers discovered by the Mission date to the late first century B.C.E., and are therefore most likely Herodian and are only part of the fortification wall

Figure 44. Caesarea's twin high-level aqueducts, where they parallel the coast just north of the city (cf. figs. 42, 83), looking north. Here masonry arcades carry the water channels across sand dunes. The western (nearer) aqueduct was built by the emperor Hadrian (second century C.E.) against the western face of the eastern (earlier) aqueduct, probably from the time of Herod. The dividing line is clearly visible within the arches.
Aaron Levin photo.

Figure 45.
Ceramic Terra sigillata *tableware – bowls and plates – from Caesarea (restored). Diameters 12.0–27.0 cm, dates from the later first century B.C.E. to the second century C.E. In this group, an Arretine bowl from Italy (lower left) and a plate of eastern manufacture (upper right) date approximately to the time of Herod the Great. IDAM collection, at the Center for Maritime Studies, Haifa.*
Danny Friedman photo.

Figure 46.
*Footprint (*planta pedis*) stamp from the Arretine bowl in fig. 45. It reads P.CLO.PR and identifies the potter as P. Clodius Proculus, known to have been from Arezzo in Italy. Such stamps (*sigilla*) characterize* terra sigillata.
Danny Friedman photo.

Figure 47.
Ceramic cook pot from CAHEP area J1 (restored). Height 20.5 cm, date first century B.C.E.-first century C.E. IDAM collection, at the Center for Maritime Studies, Haifa.
Danny Friedman photo.

Figure 48.
Glass vessels used in the time of Herod. To the left a ribbed drinking bowl, 12.1 cm in diameter, and to the right a millefiori *cup, 9.4 cm in diameter. Provenances unknown, but sherds of such vessels occur at Caesarea. Courtesy of IDAM.*
David Harris photo, Israel Museum.

Figure 49.
Group of "Herodian" oil lamps manufactured in ancient Palestine from late in the first century B.C.E. to early in the second century C.E. Lengths (including spout) 8.6–10.5 cm. Some archaeologists consider the form at the upper right to be diagnostic of the time of Herod the Great. Provenances unknown, but sherds occur at Caesarea. DIAR collection.
Aaron Levin photo.

Figure 50.
Urban plan of Herod's Caesarea in 10/9 B.C.E. based on archaeology and literary sources, mainly Josephus.
Robin Ziek drawing.

Herod provided for all of Caesarea. It would have followed roughly the line indicated in fig. 50.

To test this hypothesis JECM excavated along the north wall. Chapter 2 presented CAHEP's case for a Hellenistic dating of this disputed wall, and here JECM's arguments, based, like CAHEP's, on stratigraphic excavations, attempt to show that the wall was built late in the first century B.C.E., almost certainly by Herod. This is no mere archaeologist's quibble, for a Hellenistic dating would mean that Herod had incorporated the wall of Strato's Tower into his own city, reducing the originality of its urban plan.

JECM's case rests on their stratigraphic excavation of field G, area 8, the square we used to illustrate stratigraphic technique in chapter 2. The layers that JECM discovered in G.8 are reproduced in one of the south balks (fig. 14). As the excavators proceeded down outside the wall (locus 8001, fig. 14), they went through a succession of soil loci – layers distinguished from one another by soil color, compaction, particle size, and other variables. The soil in locus G.8018 contained sherds of many ceramic vessels and lamps that could be dated between the early first century B.C.E. and the early first century C.E. Loci G.8119, G.8123, G.8124 produced, respectively, sherds from the late second and early first century B.C.E., the late second century B.C.E., and the second century B.C.E. Locus G.8122 contained only virgin sand. Cutting through loci 8119, 8123, and 8124 was locus G.8125, the foundation trench for wall G.8001.* This contained numerous sherds from the second and early first centuries B.C.E., including a fragment of a cook pot that belonged to the first century B.C.E. or the first century C.E.

JECM's interpretation of this evidence is straightforward. The layers represented by G.8119, 8123, and 8124 predated the wall but do suggest late Hellenistic habitation, Strato's Tower. When Herod's builders arrived on the scene in 22 B.C.E., they dug a trench for the foundations of the city wall, laid the foundations in it, and filled up the remainder of the trench with soil from the vicinity. That soil, locus G.8125, contained both fragments of the pots used by the inhabitants of Strato's Tower and sherds from the first century B.C.E., following the decline of Strato's Tower. Both the trench and the wall date, therefore, to the time of Herod. Locus G.8018 represents the early years of Caesarea, preserving as it does fragments of pots used by the first inhabitants of Herod's city.

Outside the line of the Herodian walls, archaeologists have identified two major public buildings that date from Herod's time – the theater to the south and the amphitheater to the northeast (fig. 50). Because the contests with which Herod inaugurated the city in 10/9 B.C.E. included chariot races, a hippodrome or circus

*In fig. 14 the foundation trench, G.8125, is shown penetrating only G.8119 and part of G.8123. The reason for this apparent anomaly is that only this portion of the foundation trench could be distinguished clearly from surrounding loci and excavated separately. All of the pottery used to date G.8125 came from the portion of the foundation trench indicated in fig. 14 as G.8125.

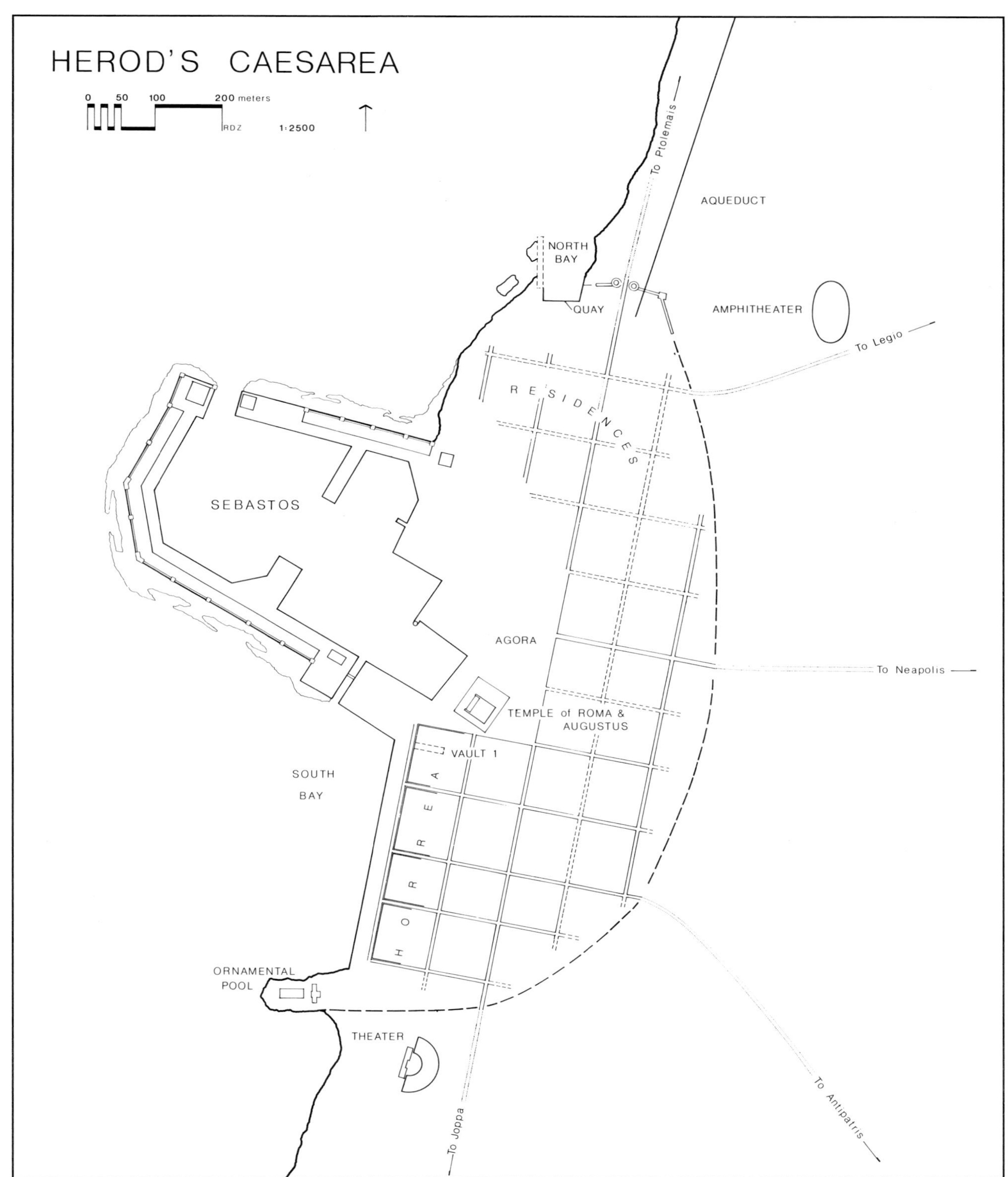
HEROD'S CAESAREA
0 50 100 200 meters
RDZ
1:2500
To Ptolemais
AQUEDUCT
NORTH BAY
QUAY
AMPHITHEATER
To Legio
RESIDENCES
SEBASTOS
AGORA
To Neapolis
TEMPLE of ROMA & AUGUSTUS
VAULT 1
SOUTH BAY
HORREA
ORNAMENTAL POOL
THEATER
To Joppa
To Antipatris

probably also belonged to the original plan. It would have been a wooden structure located in the same place the Romans later built a similar structure in stone. Herod and his advisers apparently placed these facilities outside the fortification walls for a reason: following the ribald and sometimes obscene mimes and other performances in the theater, the races in the hippodrome, and especially the beast fights and gladiatorial combats in the amphitheater, crowd control may have been easier in the open than in the narrow city streets.

Figure 51.
The Caesarea theater, constructed by Herod the Great and remodeled several times between the first and the fourth centuries C.E. In the sixth century C.E., no longer in service, it was incorporated into a fortress that included the wall and towers visible in the foreground. Excavated by the Italian team in the early 1960s, the building has been restored and brought back into use for concerts and dance. View toward southeast.
PICTORIAL ARCHIVE (Near Eastern History) Est.

Figure 52.
Site of the Caesarea amphitheater, heavily robbed – exploited as a quarry – between its abandonment in the fourth century C.E. and modern times. Beyond the amphitheater, the line of Caesarea's Byzantine fortification wall is visible. View to the northeast.
PICTORIAL ARCHIVE (Near Eastern History) Est.

The Italian Mission excavated the theater (fig. 51) between 1959 and 1963. After distinguishing the original Herodian design from later phases, they estimated that the theater's original *cavea*, the concave structure with stone bench seats rising in semicircular rows, had accommodated about 3,500 spectators. In Herod's time, a floor colorfully painted with geometric designs decorated the *orchestra*, the semicircular space in front of the *cavea*, and the *proscaenium* (the stage) had a facade behind it ornamented in the Hellenistic manner with a rectangular central niche flanked by two semicircular ones.

That Herod incorporated an amphitheater into the original urban plan of Caesarea attests his devotion to Roman culture. The stone-built amphitheater as an architectural form had originated in Italy, and the combats exhibited there represented Roman taste in public entertainment. Little remains of Caesarea's amphitheater beyond an oval depression in the terrain, first discovered in aerial photographs (fig. 52). Recent survey work has located a small portion of the stone retaining wall that separated the *arena* – the sand-covered floor where gladiators and beasts fought

Figure 53.
Caesarea, the rocky promontory seaward from the theater. Netzer proposes this as the location of Herod's royal palace, what he calls the Promontory Palace, identifying the rectangular pool visible here as a fresh water swimming pool that was part of the palace's facilities. Others interpret the pool as a commercial fish pool (piscina).
Aaron Levin photo.

one another – from the spectators' seating. Surveyors reckon the arena's dimensions at about 60 meters on its east–west axis and 95 meters north–south; it was therefore larger than the arena of the Colosseum in Rome, the amphitheater the emperor Vespasian and his sons constructed in the Eternal City a century later.

In his description of Herod's building program at Caesarea, Josephus emphasizes the magnificent palace Herod had built there. Although this palace has not been located for certain, Netzer proposes identifying it with what he calls the Promontory Palace, located on the rocky promontory that extends into the sea near the theater, roughly where the Herodian fortification walls must have reached the coast (fig. 53). The large pool (18 by 35 meters) cut into the rock, suggests to some investigators the kind of salt-water tank used in Roman times for commercially breeding and storing fish. Netzer, however, has noted small cuttings in the rock, which may have belonged to a peristyle surrounding three sides of the pool, and channels, which indicate that originally fresh water, not sea water, had filled it. Thus the pool might have been a luxurious swimming pool, like the one at Herod's palace at Jericho. The stunning setting at Caesarea, some distance out to sea, recalls the equally dramatic siting of Herod's palaces at Masada and Herodion. The excavation of associated structures to the east of the pool has not yet provided evidence for its date, but further work there may confirm that this was indeed one of Herod's royal dwellings.

Inside the fortification walls, the city's streets were arranged, according to Josephus, "at equal distances from one another." This means that at Caesarea Herod embraced the Greek tradition of orthogonal (or "rectangular") city planning that is associated with the fifth-century B.C.E. urban designer Hippodamus of Miletus. In a Hippodamian urban plan, the streets delimit regular city blocks, which archaeologists call *insulae* ("islands"). Josephus reports in another passage (*Jewish Antiquities* 15.340) that Herod devoted equal effort to constructing sewer passages that ran below the streets, also "at equal distances from one another," from the landward side into the harbor and the sea. Although so far no remains either of streets or sewers that can be dated stratigraphically to the time of Herod have turned up, JECM has been able to deduce a large part of the Herodian street plan (fig. 50). Numerous Roman- and especially Byzantine-period street pavements and sewers have been excavated (pp. 133–34 and 175–76). Because they align exactly with features of the Herodian city plan – the twin gate towers in the northern portion of the city wall, for example – JECM assumes that the layout of the streets must follow the original Herodian plan. These streets do lie "at equal distances from one another." By JECM's measurement the standard *insula* of Herodian Caesarea measured about 80 meters east–west and 120 meters north–south.

To their dismay archaeologists have not yet located one of the key elements in the Herodian city plan that Josephus mentions, Caesarea's *agora*, or marketplace. It must have been rectangular in plan, surrounded by colonnades, and the length of one or two city blocks. It was probably positioned equidistant from the harbor and the city's gates. The marketplace in fig. 50 corresponds roughly in size to the one that Herod's builders had laid out at Sebaste only a few years before.

Some of the evidence that the street plan of Roman and Byzantine Caesarea was Herodian comes from JECM excavations in field C, to the south of the Crusader

fortifications. There, fronting the Mediterranean shore, JECM found a large number of vaulted buildings that had been built as warehouses (*horrea*) for storing grain, wine, and other goods that passed in and out of Caesarea's harbors. There is stratigraphic evidence that the vaults were part of Herod's original design, and they do align with the projected layout of Herodian streets.

The discovery of these vaults was the result of some detective work by JECM. When they began excavating in 1971, they observed a series of five stationary sand dunes lined up along the coast to the south of the Crusader fortifications. Condor and Kitchener had called attention to these dunes when they surveyed the site in 1873 (fig. 7), and they intrigued the JECM team in their initial site survey. The fact that the dunes had not moved suggested that there might be massive ruins within them, a hypothesis the team investigated. One result was the discovery of vault 1, one of the richest archaeological finds made thus far at Caesarea (figs. 50, 105). Following two seasons of excavation in 1973 and 1974, the vault was revealed to be a rectangular structure 31.30 meters long east–west, 4.95 meters wide, and 4.94 meters high. It could be dated by ceramic evidence (which will be discussed subsequently, pp. 134–36) to the time of Herod. The king's builders had laid the foundations directly on bedrock and used rectangular ashlars for the walls and wedge-shaped vaulting stones, voussoirs, carefully cut from local sandstone and fitted neatly together. Vault 1 opened onto a paved street to the west and proved to be only one of at least fourteen similar vaults arranged in a block beneath the northernmost dune. If similar blocks lie concealed beneath the dunes to the south, Caesarea must have boasted at least fifty vaulted buildings in its southwestern quarter. They would have presented an imposing sight to mariners approaching the harbor and are a striking illustration of how Herod equipped Caesarea to be a major port city.

Figure 54. Caesarea, Herodian temple platform, view toward the east. King Herod built his temple to Roma and Augustus on a platform composed of at least seven vaults, of which five are visible here. In the southern vault (right in the photo) CAHEP identified remains of the city wall of Strato's Tower. In the foreground, remains of buildings from later periods.
Aaron Levin photo.

There is a second series of at least seven vaulted chambers located inside the Crusader city, just to the east of what had been the southern harbor of Strato's Tower (fig. 54). Although larger in size, this second series of vaults, like the first, no doubt functioned as *horrea* associated with the adjacent harbor. They also served another purpose, however: together they formed the "lofty platform" that Josephus speaks of, on which Herod had built his magnificent temple to Roma and Augustus. There are no certain traces of this temple. As Josephus describes it, the temple housed colossal statues of Herod's patron Augustus and of the goddess Roma, who embodied the Eternal City exactly as Caesarea's Tyche embodied Caesarea. On the altar that stood before this temple, the inhabitants of Caesarea sacrificed to the goddess who was the genius of Rome and at the same time to the immortal genius of Augustus. The temple's size, elaborate decoration, and position in Caesarea's urban landscape, on the lofty platform that dominated the city and the harbor, made it the city's most sacred place (figs. 50, 62). According to Josephus, sailors approaching Caesarea could see it from far out at sea. Herod made visible the ties that bound him to Augustus and Rome.

A careful look at the city plan (fig. 50) reveals that the vaults that formed the temple platform did not align with the vaults to the south of the Crusader fortifications or with the streets of the city. Although it dominated the city, the temple to Roma and Augustus took its orientation from the harbor, which incorporated the inner harbor of Strato's Tower and preserved the orientation of the old city. Thus, in the urban plan of Caesarea, the temple linked the city with its harbor.

The Search for Herod's Harbor

In both the *Jewish War* and the later *Jewish Antiquities*, Josephus provides virtually identical descriptions of the harbor that Herod built at Caesarea:

> *Having calculated the relative size of the harbor, . . . he let down stone blocks into the sea to a depth of 20 fathoms [approx. 37 meters]. Most of them measured 50 feet long, 9 high, and 10 wide [15.25 by 2.7 by 3.05 meters], some even larger. When Herod had finished the submarine foundation, he laid out the part of the breakwater above sea level, 200 feet across [61.0 meters]. Of this, a 100-foot portion was built out to break the force of the waves, and consequently was called the outer barrier. The rest supported the stone wall that encircled the harbor. At intervals in this wall great towers rose, the tallest and most magnificent of which was named Drusion, after the stepson of Caesar.*
>
> *There were numerous vaulted chambers for the reception of those entering the harbor, and the whole curving structure in front of them offered a wide promenade for those who disembarked. The entrance channel faced north, for in this region the north wind always brings the clearest skies. At the harbor entrance stood colossal statues, three on either side, set up on columns. A massively built tower supported the columns on the port side of boats entering harbor, those on the starboard side, two upright blocks of stone yoked together, higher than the tower on the other side (*Jewish War *1.411–13).*

When Herod completed the harbor, he gave it the name Sebastos. Like the city itself, the harbor would honor the king's principal Roman patron, for "Sebastos" is simply Augustus in Greek. The harbor also glorified members of the emperor's family. The colossal statues flanking the harbor entrance to left and right represented six of his relatives. The harbor's loftiest tower took its name from Drusus, who was the son of Augustus's wife and a successful general and highly popular family member. At the time the tower was being constructed, Drusus had a good chance of succeeding Augustus as emperor of Rome.*

*This tower's name confirms that Herod completed building the city and the harbor by 10/9 B.C.E. Drusus died accidentally in 9 B.C.E. Thereafter, because the Romans used buildings to glorify the living and tombs to memorialize the dead, Herod would probably have chosen another name for the tower.

Josephus's description of Herod's harbor works at Caesarea once seemed fantastic. Archaeologists first established that there were underwater remains that resembled his description in 1960, when an American, Edwin A. Link, explored the site from his boat the *Sea Diver*, using divers with scuba equipment. Even so, the feats Josephus implies – in particular the transporting of huge rocks to construct the breakwaters – still seemed beyond the technological expertise of Herod's engineers. Could a completely artificial harbor of such magnitude have been built out into the sea along an unstable, sandy coast, and in a brief twelve years? Once created, could such facilities be maintained in spite of winter storms and the strong south-to-north longshore current, laden with sand, that still silts up Israel's harbors? Would a man even of Herod's temperament dare to extend a city's buildings out over the open water? Was Josephus guilty of the accusation of "grandiloquent hyperbole," made by the cleric W. M. Thomson in 1861, or had he reported accurately an engineering accomplishment as sophisticated and innovative as any the ancient world had ever seen? The answers to these questions were to come from the sea, from the submerged ruins of the ancient harbor itself. CAHEP set out to find them.

When the sea is relatively calm and the sun is bright, the harbor ruins show up clearly in aerial photographs (fig. 55). To the south (right, fig. 55), submerged harbor installations extend from the shore for about 800 meters to the west and north of the small modern fishing jetty and anchorage. These installations form what CAHEP calls the southern breakwater. In places they seem almost in working order, but elsewhere bottom sand, storms, and currents have disfigured them. To the northwest (left, fig. 55), a small breach with a sandy bottom marks the ancient entrance channel and separates the southern breakwater from another enclosing arm. This installation, which CAHEP calls the northern breakwater, extends almost due west from the shore for about 280 meters. It too now lies slumped beneath the sea.

Archaeologists who work underwater face some special problems. Although they seek the same results and ideally use the same techniques as their colleagues on land, stratigraphic excavation in a marine environment is always difficult and sometimes impossible. The sea simply does not respect the integrity of an archaeological trench. Often an excavator working down through layers that are apparently stratified and contain successive material from the Byzantine, Roman, and Herodian periods arrives at the bottom of the trench and finds modern roof tiles or a tennis shoe. If a tennis shoe could work its way down into the sand several meters below the sea floor, so can potsherds, coins, and other artifacts. An experience like this erodes archaeologists' confidence in stratigraphic archaeology under water.

Still, undisturbed strata do appear occasionally, and they are so much the more precious for being infrequent. In area D, for example, located across the ancient harbor entrance (fig. 25), CAHEP hoped to learn which historical periods had witnessed the most ship traffic in the great harbor basin that is enclosed by the

Figure 55.
Caesarea, aerial view of the submerged remains of Sebastos, Herod's harbor, looking east. Easily visible are the southern breakwater, curving from right to left, the shorter northern breakwater, and the entrance channel between them.
Bill Curtzinger photo, © National Geographic Society.

northern and southern breakwaters. The team suspected that the current flowing out of the entrance had deposited, in successive layers, miscellaneous datable artifacts dropped from ships or from the quays inside the harbor. In fact, in area D the team did discover a continuous layer of viscous mud or clay, about 0.25-meter thick, protected beneath a layer of rubble that had washed off the southern breakwater and that rested in turn directly on sterile sand. This clay layer probably represented the original bottom of the ancient harbor, formed in part by dredging and dumping within the harbor basin and from the residue of organic pollutants introduced during the harbor's earliest period of use. To CAHEP's satisfaction the clay layer contained a large quantity of pottery and lamps datable to the end of the first century B.C.E. through the mid-first century C.E. Also among the debris in the clay layer were a sheave block from an ancient merchant ship (fig. 56) and a beautiful bronze oil jug (fig. 57) of types consistent with a date early in the first century C.E. The discovery of this layer was reasonable proof that the harbor enclosed by the northern and southern breakwaters – the installations visible in the aerial photographs – did date from Herod's time and was the one that Josephus describes.

Figure 56.
Sheave block, made of boxwood, probably used in the running rigging of a Roman ship of the first century B.C.E. or the first century C.E. Height 13 cm. Found in CAHEP area D7. IDAM collection, at the Center for Maritime Studies, Haifa.
Robert Hohlfelder photo.

Figure 57.
Bronze aryballos (oil jug), height 8.1 cm, found in CAHEP area D2. Perhaps manufactured in Italy, this object would have been used in the baths. IDAM collection, at the Center for Maritime Studies, Haifa.
Robert Hohlfelder photo.

Figure 58. CAHEP dive raft, positioned over the entrance to Herod's harbor. From this platform, compressed air is distributed to divers at work in underwater trenches. Tied up to the dive raft is one of CAHEP's Zodiac boats, used to transport divers to and from work sites. Robert Hohlfelder photo.

Pursuing the same goals as their colleagues on shore, underwater archaeologists employ equipment suitable to the marine environment. While their terrestrial equivalents walk to work or ride in a van, the divers don their wetsuits and breathing apparatus and catch a lift to the work area in a Zodiac boat, an inflatable dinghy powered by an outboard motor. Often their first stop is the dive raft, a collection of oil drums lashed together, which is anchored above the entrance to the ancient harbor (fig. 58). This ungainly craft is the mother ship for underwater operations; from it, pressurized air, brought in a main air line from a diesel compressor on shore, is distributed to the divers and their equipment. To increase mobility and the time they can spend underwater, CAHEP divers sometimes disconnect their air tanks at the excavation site and use the so-called hookah breathing apparatus, which employs a subsidiary air line that is attached to the main system at the dive raft.

Once at work CAHEP archaeologists use a number of devices developed especially for undersea exploration. An air probe is used to locate parts of the ancient harbor buried beneath the sea floor and to determine their shape, or profile (fig. 59).

Figure 59.
CAHEP divers use the air probe to trace the profile of structures concealed beneath the sea floor. A jet of air introduced into an iron pipe quickly burrows into the sand until it encounters an obstacle. Depth beneath the sea floor is then read from a metric scale on the iron pipe.
Harry Wadsworth photo.

Figure 60.
CAHEP divers working an air lift, the principal apparatus for excavating on the sea floor. In a large-diameter flexible tube, a jet of air introduced from the compressor sets up a flow of water that removes sand like an underwater vacuum cleaner.
Mark Little photo.

A jet of air fed from scuba tanks through an iron pipe burrows its way through bottom sand until it encounters a solid object. The operator then reads the depth of sand above the object from a metric scale marked on the pipe. A series of such measurements taken along a steel cable fixed at both ends produces a profile. If the decision is made to excavate, the archaeologist uses not a trowel but an air lift (fig. 60), a large-diameter, flexible hose that works much like a vacuum cleaner. Compressed air sets up a flow of water that removes sand, mud, gravel, small stones, and other bottom debris – and that will suck up potsherds, coins, and other artifacts as well if the operator does not use it cautiously. One advantage of excavating underwater is the absence of muscle wear and tear in transporting heavy objects out of a trench. The diver uses an air bag, filled from the breathing apparatus, which lifts objects to the surface with ease (fig. 61).

CAHEP archaeologists, like their land-based counterparts, began work on the harbor by surveying and mapping its bottom features. For control purposes the

Figure 61.
CAHEP divers use an air bag to lift heavy objects from the sea floor. The air bag is filled with air from the diver's regulator.
Harry Wadsworth photo.

Figure 62. Sebastos, the harbor that Herod the Great built at Caesarea, perspective view looking southeast (cf. fig. 50). Visible to the left is the northern breakwater, in the foreground colossal statues of the Roman imperial family mounted on columns, the harbormaster's house to the left of the harbor entrance, and the lighthouse named Drusion to its right. Curving south and eastward from the lighthouse is the southern breakwater with vaulted buildings for receiving and storing goods.

J. Robert Teringo painting, © National Geographic Society.

team identified excavation areas, designated with letters of the alphabet (fig. 25). Supervisors take elaborate notes, using plastic notepads and pencils that write underwater. As on land, a photographer keeps a continuous record of excavations, and the dig architects prepare top plans and section drawings. Because of the action of the sea, which obliterates trench walls, the excavators cannot rely on balks to control stratigraphy in a trench. Indeed, heavy seas have often brought a day's work to a premature end.

Employing these techniques, CAHEP archaeologists have not only located the harbor that Josephus describes and confirmed its date, but have proved that, by and large, his description is not "grandiloquent hyperbole" but a reliable record. Josephus reports that the width of the southern breakwater was 200 Roman feet. Its ruins, visible here in the aerial photograph (fig. 55), actually vary from 80 to 220 meters in width. CAHEP's survey work and excavation indicate an original width in the neighborhood of 70 meters, just about the 200 feet Josephus reports. The disparity in these measurements was the work of heavy seas, which caused rubble to spill from the buildings on top of the breakwater, widening it. CAHEP's investigations also confirmed that Herod's engineers purposely left undeveloped what Josephus calls the outer barrier – the outer half of the breakwaters – and that a stone sea wall with towers did encircle the harbor, separating the inner and outer halves of the breakwater. Neither the wall nor the towers survive intact, but concentrations of rubble, including worked blocks of stone, do appear at regular intervals along the southern breakwater, presumably the remains of the towers. The mass of rubble that has spilled to the east testifies to the existence of the vaulted chambers on the breakwaters that Josephus mentions and to the "wide promenade for those who disembarked." Indeed, the correspondence between Josephus's text and the results of archaeological investigation is so exact that CAHEP has been able to reconstruct the original design of Sebastos in surprising detail (figs. 50, 62).

Josephus does not mention a lighthouse specifically. In antiquity lighthouses, like the one at Alexandria in Egypt, were high towers capped with a platform for beacon fires. Herod's harbor must have had one to guide mariners to the harbor entrance whether they were sailing at night or during the day. Presumably the edifice named Drusion served that function, for it was, Josephus says, the "tallest and most magnificent" tower in the harbor complex. The CAHEP team believes that it has located the remains of the Drusion tower in a zone of massive stones adjacent to the western side of the channel entrance. The position is just right, and the volume and size of these stones suggest a building of exceptional dimensions, appropriate for a lighthouse 80 to 90 meters tall (fig. 62). Perhaps Herod and his architects called the

structure Drusion with special symbolism in mind: they might have thought it fitting to name a lighthouse with a beacon for Augustus's likely successor.

Like the Link expedition before it, CAHEP searched for the six colossal statues Josephus mentions as having been set up on columns, three on each side of the harbor entrance. The team succeeded in finding the two blocks that supported the statues to the right of the entrance and the massive foundation for those that stood on the left (fig. 62), but there is no trace of the statues or their columns.

In addition to confirming the accuracy of Josephus's description, CAHEP has acquired a wealth of information from survey and excavation to embellish the historical record with significant details. For example, it is now clear that Herod's architects incorporated the southern harbor of Strato's Tower into Sebastos as an inner harbor basin, just in front of the platform that supported the temple to Roma and Augustus. This inner harbor may be one of the "innermost recesses" that Josephus mentions in the passage quoted earlier (p. 72). In the main harbor basin, one or more projecting platforms may also have increased the harbor's docking capacity. Furthermore, roughly 20 meters to the south of the main southern breakwater, the team examined what may have been a subsidiary barrier (visible in the aerial photograph, fig. 55), designed to impede the crashing of the heaviest seas against the main breakwater. In that main southern breakwater, not far out from the shore, CAHEP discovered a channel, or sluice. It may be one of several that admitted water from the heavy seas into the harbor basin. The sluice's opening would have created an outflowing current to carry away the silt that is a perennial problem there. Finally, by excavating at a number of points on the sea floor, the team has exposed foundations on which Herod's massive harbor works were built: a layer of pebbles and stone rubble that supported the immense blocks of the superstructure. This type of foundation, which is still used in harbor construction, held the sand in place and prevented undercutting by the heavy seas.

One of Josephus's remarks does appear exaggerated at first: he claims that in size Herod's harbor at Caesarea surpassed Piraeus, the harbor of ancient Athens. The northern and southern breakwaters of Sebastos enclose an area of roughly 200,000 square meters (20 hectares). Even if the inner basin is included in the figure, Herod's new constructions at Caesarea did not approach the capacity of the three harbor basins and other anchorages available at Piraeus. If, however, additional anchorages at Caesarea are brought into the calculation, even this report may turn out to be accurate. CAHEP has discovered that Herod rehabilitated the northern harbor of Strato's Tower and that in fair weather ships that called at Caesarea could also use the south bay as an anchorage, off-loading their cargoes onto small boats.

Josephus definitely was mistaken in one instance. He claims that when they constructed the harbor Herod's builders "let down stone blocks into the sea to a depth of 20 fathoms [approx. 37 meters]," and that those stones were as large 50 by 10 by 9 feet. Entirely apart from the extreme depth,* it is hard to understand how Herod's engineers could have handled blocks of that size, or even smaller ones, from boats maneuvering offshore. CAHEP has discovered a surprising solution to this puzzle. Herod's engineers did use stone blocks in the harbor, although of more

*We should not take these figures seriously. The medieval scribes often garbled figures when they copied ancient texts. The clay level found in area D, and identified by CAHEP as the ancient harbor bottom, now lies about 10.5 meters below sea level; however, the sea bottom offshore has slumped about 5.0 meters below its ancient elevation (see p. 141), so the depth of the harbor in antiquity could not have been more than 5.5 meters.

manageable dimensions than Josephus reports. However, when they needed extremely large blocks they did not use stone, they used hydraulic concrete.

The Romans had already invented concrete construction, *opus caementicium*, by the beginning of the second century B.C.E. Roman concrete should not be confused with modern concrete or cement. It consisted of a mass of aggregate, or stone rubble (*caementa*), bonded together by means of a special mortar made of lime and *pozzolana*, a volcanic ash from central Italy. For ordinary construction purposes, builders normally laid the concrete mass into a form of hewn stones or brick, but it was the concrete that had the necessary strength and structural integrity. Early on, builders in Italy also discovered that mortar made with *pozzolana* hardened when it came into contact with water, and they therefore made use of it for bridges and harbor jetties.

Herod the Great imported Roman concrete into his kingdom and employed it extensively in building the harbor at Caesarea. CAHEP has found numerous large concrete blocks in the harbor breakwaters. Josephus's "massively built tower" and "blocks of stone" that supported colossal statues flanking the harbor entrance turned out on investigation to be made of concrete. The best example, however, is the giant concrete block that forms the western end, or pierhead, of the northern breakwater, which CAHEP explored in its area G (fig. 25). The excavation revealed that the block is 11.5 by 15.0 meters long and wide, and 2.4 meters high from its bottom, which rests on sand, to its eroded upper surface. Its dimensions far surpass those of the blocks that, according to Josephus, Herod "let down into the sea." When the team exposed the vertical faces of this block, they also discovered parts of the wooden forms into which the builders had poured the concrete (figs. 63 and 64). The formwork had been constructed from large wooden base beams with uprights and horizontal planking inside and out. The elaborate carpentry included lap joints and mortising. To prevent collapse during pouring, the builders had passed tie beams through the volume to be filled with concrete.

The materials CAHEP excavated from this construction were sent to analytical laboratories, where carbon 14 analysis of wood samples produced a dating of 1,970 years B.P. ("before the present"), plus or minus seventy years, which is about right for Herod's reign. Botanists report that species of spruce, pine, fir, and poplar are represented among the wood samples, and all are of European origin. The stone rubble, or aggregate, in the concrete came from local sources, but the mortar may contain *pozzolana* from Italy. It is reasonable to suspect that the materials and technology used at Caesarea came with Roman engineers Augustus sent to assist Herod's architects with the harbor project.

Figure 63. CAHEP area G. Diver inspects large wooden beams uncovered at the bottom of the underwater trench, part of the formwork into which Herod's builders poured concrete, making the large concrete block visible above the diver. Bill Curtzinger photo, © National Geographic Society.

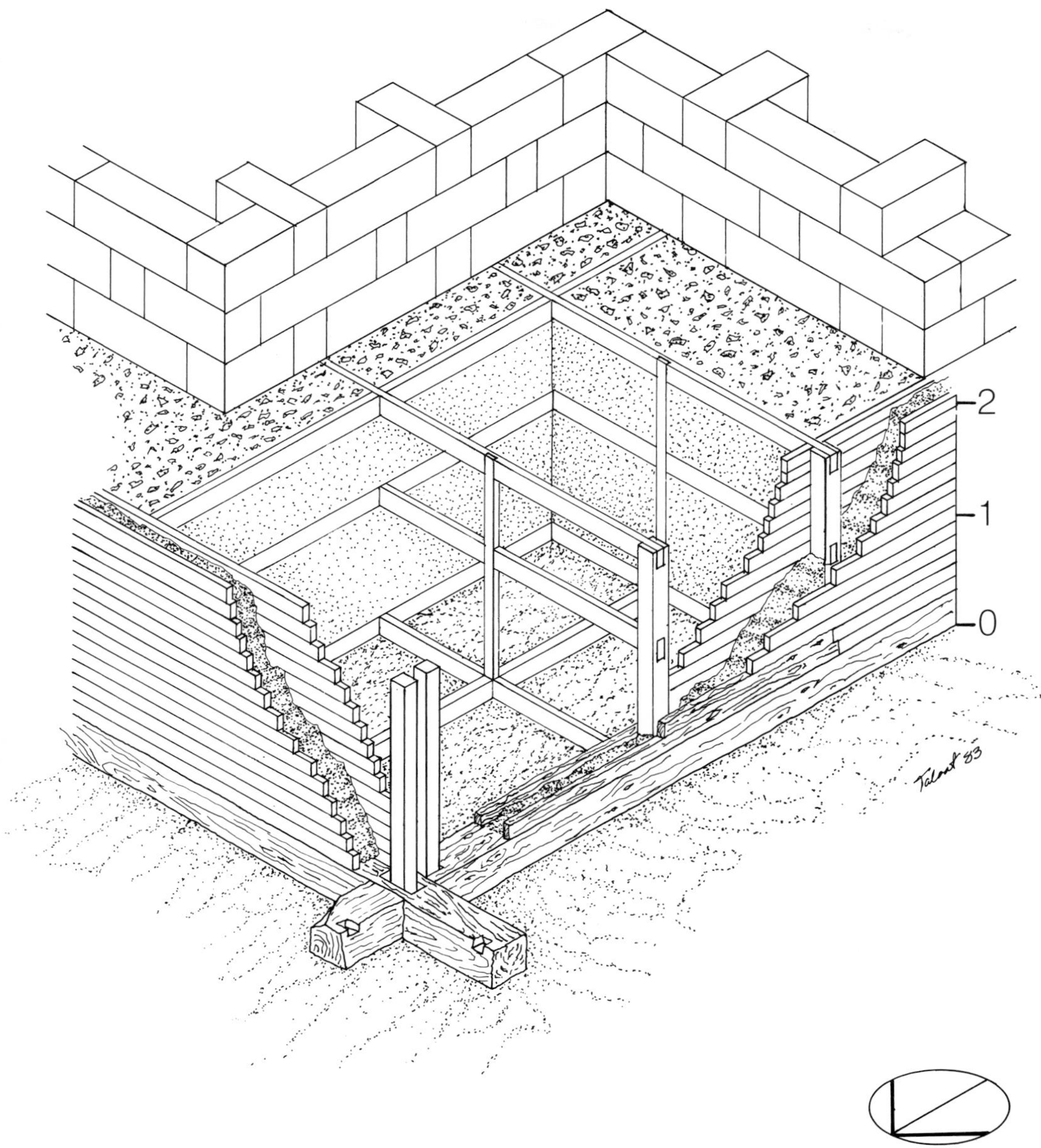

Figure 64.
Reconstruction of the wooden formwork found in CAHEP's area G. The builders made these forms of wooden base beams, uprights, horizontal planking, and tie beams for strengthening.
CAHEP drawing.

The remains that the CAHEP team found in its excavations suggest a scenario for the construction (fig. 65). Thousands of workmen, both slaves and conscripts, would have labored at a furious pace to bring the project to completion in twelve years or less. In places they used stone blocks quarried in the vicinity in sizes they could easily manage from boats. Workmen put together the forms for the concrete work on or near shore and then sledged and towed them into position. Professional divers (called *urinatores* by the Romans because of their predictable physiological response to spending long periods under water) had already prepared the sea floor to receive the formwork. Workers inserted mortar into the cavity between the inner and outer planking of the forms, causing the forms to sink into place. Others lowered the stone rubble (*caementa*) and mortar, probably in leather buckets, into place beneath the sea's surface. As each huge concrete block was completed, stonemasons laid down a pavement of limestone blocks above it, fragments of which CAHEP found. Still other laborers dropped stones along the block's outer edge to create a sloping barrier, or *berm*, to protect the base of each block from undercutting. The berm protected the wooden formwork as well. Fragments of it have enabled modern archaeologists to reconstruct the ancient engineering.

Thus the king built a city. Herod must have devoted much of his time to Caesarea during the twelve years of its construction. Although no portraits of Herod of any kind have survived, in our mind's eye we can if we try picture him walking around what had been Strato's Tower, engaged in animated discussion with his architects, poring over plans, barking orders. It must have been that way, because this project reflects so much and so faithfully the man's personality as we understand it from his splendid construction projects elsewhere. Filled with enthusiasm for all things Roman, Herod brought Roman entertainment, Roman gods, and even Roman concrete into his kingdom. At Caesarea, as at Masada, Herodion, and on the Temple Mount in Jerusalem, he conceived designs of unsurpassed scale and boldness. Above all, Herod meant to have his name among those of the great builders of the past, with Alexander and the Seleucids, with the fabulous kings who had devoted themselves since time began to founding and nurturing cities. Like them he wanted a monument to ensure his fame, a great city that would flourish far into the future. That essentially was King Herod's dream.

Figure 65.
The construction of Sebastos, Herod's harbor at Caesarea. In the foreground divers help position formwork for the large concrete block that CAHEP discovered in area G. Beyond and to the left other laborers lower cement and stone rubble in leather buckets into a form already in place.
J. Robert Teringo painting, © National Geographic Society.

CHAPTER 4

The Daughter of Edom: Caesarea in the Roman Period

The Talmud, the compilation of Jewish legal and moral teaching, preserves a cryptic and provocative comment by Rabbi Isaac Napaha of Caesarea. In it the rabbi, who lived about 300 C.E., cryptically refers to Caesarea as the "daughter of Edom." What he meant was "daughter of Rome." More than a thousand years earlier, in the time of the Israelite kingdom, the nation's implacable foe had been neighboring Edom. In Rabbi Isaac's time Rome was the new Edom and Caesarea, her daughter, symbolized the very antithesis of Jewish values. As Rabbi Isaac put it, again somewhat cryptically:

> *Caesarea and Jerusalem [are rivals]. If someone should say to you, "both have been destroyed," do not believe it. [If someone should say,] "both are prospering," do not believe it. [But if someone says,] "Caesarea is destroyed and Jerusalem prospering," or "Jerusalem is destroyed and Caesarea prospering," then you may believe it.*

The rabbi was not predicting the physical extinction of either Jerusalem or Caesarea. The Romans had long since established their renowned peace among the cities of the Mediterranean world. The issue Rabbi Isaac had in mind was whether the Jewish people could preserve their unique culture and religion in the face of Roman ways.

It is significant that Isaac considered Caesarea, a city, to be a threat to the Jews. The ancient rabbi would perhaps have agreed with Mumford that "buildings, and monuments and public ways . . . leave an imprint on our minds," that cities are

Figure 66. Sebaste, remains of colonnaded street probably constructed in about 200 C.E. The ancient pavement followed the line of the modern paved road. The columns supported a roof that shaded sidewalks flanking the street, and shops opened onto the sidewalk. Although evidence is sparse, Caesarea's patrons probably financed construction of similar streets in the same period. For the structure of a similar street from the Byzantine period, see fig. 128.
Aaron Levin photo.

transmitters of culture. Isaac knew that Caesarea's splendid monuments turned Jewish heads and that Jews who lived there tended to be more Roman than Jewish.

The Romans wanted Jews and other national minorities within the empire to assimilate. Having embraced the mission to "subject the world to the rule of law," as the poet Virgil expressed it, they realized instinctively that they could not rule effectively without the acquiescence of those they had conquered. To secure that acquiescence the Romans did what some other imperial peoples, both ancient and modern, have refused to do – they opened their own citizenship, along with full protection of the laws and the right to hold office, to those they had subjected, provided that they would adopt Roman culture. The result was the phenomenon called Romanization, the spread of Roman culture across the Mediterranean world and beyond its frontiers. Generally, Romanization was voluntary. To hasten it, the Romans adopted a policy of building cities and of encouraging cities that already existed to become more Roman. So far as possible, cities were to emulate Rome in social and political order, in religion, in private life and morality, and in appearance. The Romans agreed with Mumford and with Rabbi Isaac Napaha of Caesarea that cities transmitted culture. Thus, at the culmination of a process that lasted more than three centuries, Caesarea became the daughter of Edom.

The Process of Romanization

Of course Herod had already made Caesarea Roman. To a Hippodamian city plan of Hellenistic type Herod had added specifically Roman features, the amphitheater and the temple to Roma and Augustus. He had imported construction materials and probably craftsmen from Italy to build the harbor, and he may have employed them also in the royal palace that Josephus mentions. But King Herod's city also had a Jewish face. Apparently Jews made up nearly half of the population. In the 50s and 60s C.E., half a century after Herod's death, the city's Jews demanded that they receive the same citizenship rights as the pagan community because the city's founder had been a Jew.

Upon Herod's death in 4 B.C.E., the Romans installed Archelaus, one of his surviving sons, as his principal successor, though with the title ethnarch ("ruler of a people") instead of king. Archelaus proved incompetent, so in 6 C.E. the Romans packed him off to what is now southern France for permanent retirement. Henceforth Rome ruled its province directly. Because Jews formed a large part of its population, the new province received the name Judaea.

For Caesarea the change in government meant increased Romanization. Its loyalty to Rome and its excellent communications, by land and sea, made Caesarea a natural choice for the provincial capital. That choice was enough of a reason for the Jews to think of the city as the "daughter of Edom," for she then represented Roman political and military authority in Judaea.

Moreover, in 6 C.E. a Roman officer had arrived to take office as the first governor. Initially, the governor was of low rank and under the supervision of the governor of Syria. Although he was expected to spend part of his time in Jerusalem, Caesarea was to be his main duty station, and he probably moved at once into what had been King Herod's palace. One of the governor's principal duties was to preside over trials, most of which were to be held in Caesarea, and he supervised the apparatus that the Romans established for collecting taxes from the provincials. In 6 C.E., when the Romans made Herod's kingdom into a province and Caesarea its capital, they conducted a census in the country, directed from Caesarea, to determine individual tax liability. This was the census that took place "when Quirinius was governor of Syria," according to Luke 2:2. Also according to Luke, it brought Joseph and his wife Mary to Bethlehem, where their child Jesus was born.*

The governor also commanded the body of troops responsible for keeping order in that turbulent country. They were second-line troops, what the Romans called auxiliaries, instead of legionnaires, but they spoke Latin, at least when on duty, and fought in the Roman fashion. Some of the soldiers came from more Romanized provinces and even from Italy, like the Italian Cohort mentioned in the New Testament book, Acts of the Apostles. Together with the staff of clerks, accountants, and orderlies that the governor brought with him to help carry out his duties, this personnel increased the Latin-speaking, Romanized element in Caesarea's population.

One of the most sensational archaeological discoveries at Caesarea was made in 1961 by the Italian Mission. They were excavating the theater, which had been extensively remodeled in the fourth century C.E., when they found a stone in reuse in a small stairway. A brief Latin inscription on the stone (fig. 67) identified a small temple that had stood on the site centuries earlier and named the temple's builder. The text of the inscription, with appropriate restorations, reads:

[———]S Tiberiéum
[. Po]ntius Pilatus
[praef]ectus Iud[ae]e
*[dedit dédicavit]***

The New Testament records that Pontius Pilate was the officer who presided over the trial of Christ. The inscription confirms that a man named Pilate once served as

*According to Matthew 2:1 Jesus was born "during the reign of Herod," i.e., before 4 B.C.E. Scholars believe that Luke confused the census of Quirinius with an earlier one conducted by C. Sentius Saturninus, who was governor of Syria from 9–6 B.C.E.

**Conventionally, square brackets are used to indicate that letters have disappeared from the stone and round brackets to fill out the abbreviations that appear so frequently in Latin inscriptions.

Figure 67. Latin inscription mentioning Pontius Pilate, found by the Italian Mission in 1961 reused as part of a stairway in Caesarea's theater. Height 82 cm, width 69 cm. The inscription records that Pilate dedicated a temple ca. 26–36 C.E. to the Emperor Tiberius. IDAM collection, on display in the Israel Museum.
Israel Museum photo.

governor of Judaea and could indeed have presided over the trial, as the New Testament declares.

Only three lines of the inscription survive, along with a mark called an *apex* over one of the letters in what would have been the fourth. The fourth-century reuse destroyed the left side of the inscription, so that only about half of the letters remain. Nevertheless, much of the original sense can be restored. Reading and restoring inscriptions belongs to one of the subspecialties of archaeology, *epigraphy*.

Despite their having examined many comparable inscriptions from the period, epigraphers have been unable to find a satisfactory restoration for the first word of the inscription, which ends with an "S." The next word, *Tiberiéum*, is a temple dedicated to the divine genius of the Emperor Tiberius, who succeeded Augustus on the latter's death in 14 C.E. The name in line two, Pontius Pilate, is familiar. Line three was also easily restorable; it gives Pilate's title, "prefect of Judaea." Line four probably contained a familiar formulaic expression meaning "gave and dedicated." Except for one missing word, the restored inscription would thus read: "Pontius Pilate, the prefect of Judaea, gave and dedicated a temple of Tiberius." The epigraphers also know the date, because Pilate's tenure of office, during which he must have dedicated the temple, extended from about 26 to 36 C.E.

The inscription also makes available to us a detail of Roman administration: the precise title, prefect of Judaea, that Pilate and other governors held. In addition, the Pilate stone records a previously unknown episode of Romanization, namely that in Caesarea Pontius Pilate dedicated a new temple at which citizens could declare their allegiance to the Roman order by offering sacrifice to the emperor's genius. The language is itself interesting. In that part of the Mediterranean world, most natives spoke a Semitic tongue – and probably Greek as well, which was a lingua franca in the region by the end of the Hellenistic Age. But Pontius Pilate ordered this stone inscribed in Latin. If he did not order the inhabitants of Caesarea to learn the imperial language, public inscriptions like this one emphasized that it was in their interest to know it.

The case of Saint Paul, recorded in the New Testament book, Acts of the Apostles (21–25), shows the Roman governor at work in Caesarea and illustrates the advantages of being Roman. In 58 C.E. the Roman officer in charge of Jerusalem arrested the Christian Apostle Paul, whom the Jews were accusing of having caused a riot. Because the officer had discovered that Paul was a Roman citizen, he did not flog the prisoner, the normal procedure for learning the truth, but instead sent him with a large escort of soldiers to Caesarea. There the governor, Antonius Felix, kept Paul in custody "at his headquarters in Herod's palace." A few days later, Felix conducted a trial. The high priest and other Jewish leaders came to Caesarea to testify against the prisoner. Paul delivered a speech in his own defense, but the governor did not reach a verdict. Paul remained in Caesarea under open arrest for almost two years, until a new governor named Porcius Festus arrived. Festus held a second trial, at which Paul uttered the famous words, "I appeal to Caesar," and Festus responded, "You have appealed to Caesar, to Caesar you shall go!" Paul had exercised his right as a Roman citizen to escape the jurisdiction of a provincial magistrate like the governor of Caesarea and to have his case heard at the emperor's court in Rome. From Caesarea's harbor Paul traveled by ship to Rome, where, a few years later, he was executed.

The revolt that became the Jewish War of 66–70 C.E. broke out in part because Caesarea's pagans slaughtered twenty thousand Jews, nearly the entire Jewish community. During that war, the Roman commander, Vespasian, made Caesarea his base of operations, and his son Titus continued the practice when the troops had declared Vespasian emperor. During the winters of 67 and 68 C.E. Vespasian quartered two of his legions there, more than ten thousand soldiers, thinking that the riches the city offered would be good for morale. Following the Roman victory, Titus celebrated his brother's birthday at Caesarea with a display of beast fights and

Figure 68.
Bronze coin of Nero struck at Caesarea. Diameter 2.1 cm. The reverse of the coin features Caesarea's Tyche, in this case without the small god Sebastos at her lower left. The Greek legend reads "Caesarea by the harbor Sebastos." The Greek numeral 14 appears to the left of the figure, giving the year during Nero's reign, 67/68 C.E., when the coin was minted. Museum of Ancient Art, Haifa.
Aaron Levin photo.

man-to-man combats in the amphitheater. Forced to fight as gladiators, twenty-five hundred Jewish prisoners-of-war met their deaths. The Caesareans no doubt enjoyed the spectacle and the profits reaped from catering to Roman troops. The war that ended with the destruction of the Jewish Temple in Jerusalem brought Caesarea even greater prosperity and made it even more Roman.

Armies have always run on money. Vespasian required large quantities of gold and silver coins to pay his troops, and the troops in turn needed smaller bronze denominations so they could patronize Caesarea's petty shopkeepers, inns, and brothels. The imperial mints in Rome issued the gold and silver. To supply bronze coins the city fathers of Caesarea set up a mint that, like other city mints in the provinces, continued to manufacture bronze coins for use as small change until the middle of the third century C.E.* Hardly an elaborate affair, a mint consisted of a few skilled workmen who engraved obverse and reverse dies and then made a coin by striking a blank piece of metal between them. Still, possessing a mint was both profitable and prestigious. The emperors conceded to municipal mints the right to select the designs on their coins' reverses, so these were a way of advertising a city's local traditions, its gods and goddesses, and even some of its important buildings.

The first coins from the new mint of Caesarea appeared in 67/68 C.E., during the first winter Vespasian's troops spent in the city. The coin in fig. 68 (reverse) is typical of those with which the archaeologist and numismatist normally work – that is, it is badly worn from long periods of circulation and, before cleaning, was corroded from lying for centuries in the soil. The obverse of this coin features a bust of Nero, the reigning emperor; and the reverse has the now familiar figure of the Caesarea Tyche. On this coin the obverse and reverse legends are in Greek, the language commonly used on coins issued in eastern provincial cities of the time. The obverse legend identifies the emperor, "Nero Caesar Augustus." The reverse gives, in Greek numerals, the date, year fourteen of the emperor Nero, or 67–68 C.E., and the name of the city in a curious form: "Caesarea by the Harbor Sebastos." This legend suggests that for the ancient inhabitants of Caesarea the city and the harbor Sebastos were in some way separate entities. This information leads us to consider that, while the streets and other buildings in Caesarea were aligned on the Herodian town plan, the temple to Roma and Augustus, the vaults that formed its platform, and the entire harbor may have preserved the earlier orientation of Strato's Tower.

Numismatists contribute to stratigraphic archaeology by dating coins, which, in turn, are useful in dating archaeological strata. But each coin is also a minute historical document. As such, the Nero coin is instructive about the process of Romanization. It is the earliest type of coin on which Caesarea's Tyche appears, and

*Some numismatists believe that both Herod the Great and the prefects had struck coins at Caesarea earlier.

Figure 69. Bronze coin of Trajan minted 115–17 C.E. The reverse (pictured here) shows the emperor in a toga sacrificing over an altar. In his left hand he holds the cornucopia, the horn of plenty. The Latin legend reads COL(onia) PRI(ma) FL(avia) AVG(usta) CAESARIENSIS, which was Caesarea's full name after Vespasian had refounded the city as a Roman colony. Diameter 2.3 cm. Minted at Caesarea, now in the Museum of Ancient Art, Haifa.
Aaron Levin photo.

Figure 70. Bronze coin of Trebonianus Gallus minted at Caesarea 251–53 C.E. The reverse (pictured here) features Caesarea's Tyche with Sebastos holding an anchor. The legend gives Caesarea's ultimate numismatic signature, COL(onia) P(rima) F(lavia) AVG(usta) F(elix) C(oncordia) CAES(area) METR(opolis) P(rovinciae) S(yriae) PAL(aestinae). By this time, Caesarea had received the honorific title of metropolis of the province of Syria Palestine. After issuing these coins, the mint of Caesarea closed forever. Now in the Caesarea Museum.
Bill Curtzinger photo, © National Geographic Society.

indeed it represents the earliest evidence of any kind for the city's goddess. It is significant that the coin type bearing the Tyche's image came from the Caesarea mint precisely when thousands of Roman troops were lodged in the city, for the image chosen for the Caesarea Tyche resembles in many ways the goddess Roma. Roma also stood with her foot on the prow of a ship, held the bust of the emperor in her right hand and a spear in her left, and wore the short sword, the *parazonium* (cf. figs. 3, 4, 6). Like the goddess Roma, Caesarea's Tyche normally wore a short cloak that left one breast bare, in the manner of an Amazon. It is therefore probable that the designers at the Caesarea mint modeled the Caesarea Tyche on the coins after the goddess Roma, using the statue in Herod's temple to Roma and Augustus as a prototype. Presumably the city fathers directed them to do so to express both their solidarity with the Roman troops and the degree of their own assimilation to Roman ways.

Vespasian and Titus had reason to be pleased with the reception Caesarea's citizens gave them and with the expressions of loyalty and assimilation reflected in the Tyche coins. The emperor and his son rewarded the city by promoting it to the status of Roman colony. Like individuals, cities in the empire had rank, and colonies were the elite. In theory a colony came into being when a body of Roman citizens left Italy to establish a miniature copy of Rome in a distant land. In the case of Caesarea, however, agents of Vespasian and Titus simply screened the city's existing citizen body, excluded any who knew no Latin or otherwise did not meet the qualifications, and made the rest colonists in the new Caesarea, which brought with it automatic Roman citizenship. At the same time Vespasian and his son settled veterans in the new colony, fulfilling their obligations to the soldiers who had fought with them in Judaea. The same agents who had screened the existing population assigned land to the veterans in the territory of Caesarea – in some cases, no doubt

Figure 71. Marble cylinder with Latin inscription honoring Marcus Flavius Agrippa, found at Maioumas near Caesarea in 1889, now in the Rockefeller Museum, Jerusalem. Height 80 cm, diameter 58 cm. Cuttings in the upper surface show that this stone was the base for Agrippa's statue. The inscription on the stone, dated sometime in the period 70-ca. 200 C.E., demonstrates that Caesarea had a Roman-style constitution.
Kenneth Holum photo.

farms that had belonged to the Jews massacred before the outbreak of the war. These and their descendants became the new citizen body. Although a few un-Romanized Jews and many other natives still lived in Caesarea and its countryside, contributing to the city's economy as craftsmen, laborers, and tenant farmers, they were a faceless underclass with few rights and no role in governing the community.

Caesarea's mint proudly advertised its new rank on the coins it issued – an effective medium of propaganda, because ordinary people in Caesarea and throughout the East used these coins as small change. On a coin of the Emperor Trajan (98–117 C.E.), Caesarea's impressive official name appears in full: *Colonia Prima Flavia Augusta Caesariensis* (fig. 69). The language of the coin legend, once Greek, became Latin, appropriate for a Roman colony. The city adopted the titles *Flavia* and *Augusta* from its founder, Vespasian Augustus, whose family name had been Flavius. The word *Prima* in the title meant that Caesarea was the first colony

Figure 72.
Squeeze of the Marcus Flavius Agrippa inscription (fig. 71) made of filter paper. This medium provides an exact mirror image of the original. The upper right part of the squeeze reflects damage to the stone since it was found in 1889.
Aaron Levin photo.

Vespasian founded. By the middle of the third century C.E., on a coin of the emperor Trebonianus Gallus (251–53 C.E.), the name had become even more ponderous: *Colonia Prima Flavia Augusta Felix Concordia Caesarea Metropolis Provinciae Syriae Palaestinae* (fig. 70). The length of the name testifies to the pride that the citizens of Caesarea had in their city, by now "metropolis of the Province of Syria Palestine." This version turned out to be Caesarea's ultimate numismatic signature, because after the reign of Trebonianus Gallus changes in the economy and imperial policy closed the mint forever.

Another document that speaks of profound Romanization, a marble cylinder now housed in Jerusalem's Rockefeller Museum, first came to light nearly a century ago in Caesarea's territory, at the place called Maioumas (figs. 42 and 43). Late in the first or in the second century C.E., the Caesareans ordered a statue of one of their leading citizens erected, for which this cylinder was the base (fig. 71). The statue has long since disappeared, but cuttings on the upper surface of the marble indicate where it had been placed. On the rounded face of the stone, a brief text was inscribed, in Latin, that identifies the notable and his services to the city.

A squeeze was made of the Maioumas inscription so that epigraphers could study it (fig. 72). A squeeze is an impression of a text. It is especially useful when a text, like this one, which is rounded, cannot be easily photographed. To make a squeeze the epigrapher commonly uses an industrial-grade filter paper that is dampened and beaten into the letters of the inscription with a stiff brush. Five to eight layers of paper is the thickness usually required. When dry, the squeeze is not

Figure 73.
Bust of an unknown woman, reportedly from Caesarea, now in the Museum of Ancient Art, Haifa. Marble, 28.6 cm high. The style recalls the Greek sculptor Praxiteles (fourth century B.C.E.), so the bust probably is a Roman-period copy of a Greek or Hellenistic original.
Aaron Levin photo.

Figure 75.
Marble funerary relief, 60.5 cm high and 37.0 cm wide, found at Caesarea east of the hippodrome, now in the Caesarea Museum. The deceased, a young man, appears as an athlete, with a victory palm and a prize vase, as in Graeco-Roman funerary art. Probably carved at Caesarea in the third or fourth century C.E.
Aaron Levin photo.

Figure 76.
Ceramic oil lamp, 10.3 cm long, from the later first or early second century C.E. Said to be from Caesarea, it is now in the Museum of Ancient Art, Haifa. This is a typical Roman-style lamp, common at Caesarea. Volutes flank the nozzle, and on the discus, the lamp's circular upper body, two men play a board game.
Aaron Levin photo.

Figure 74.
Group of ceramic loom weights, 2.0–2.5 cm in diameter, found by JECM in area A.1, courtesy of IDAM. Roman or Byzantine in date. When vertical threads, the warp, had been attached to a loom, such weights were attached to the threads' lower end to keep them in place during the weaving process. Weaving was women's work, done normally in the home or a small shop.
Aaron Levin photo.

Figure 77.
Group of glass vessels, either found at Caesarea or typical of the glass that occurs there in Roman layers. Left in the photo: unguentarium *(cosmetic bottle) of the tear bottle type, with a bronze cosmetic stick, height of the bottle 10.9 cm, courtesy of IDAM. Top center: another* unguentarium *of the candlestick type, height 11.0 cm. The sheen was caused by weathering. Courtesy of IDAM. Lower center: date bottle, 7.6 cm long, probably also used for cosmetics, in the Israel Museum (gift of Emma Mazur in memory of Norbert Mazur). Lower right: bowl with collared rim, 7.5 cm in diameter, courtesy of IDAM. Upper right: jug with strap handle, height 14.7 cm, probably used as a decanter for wine or water, in the Israel Museum (Dobkin collection).*

only accurate but flexible, portable, and reasonably permanent. The squeeze of the Maioumas inscription contains the following text:

> *[M(arcum) Fl(avium) A]grippam pontif(icem)*
> *II viral(em)*
> *col(oniae) I Fl(aviae) Aug(ustae) Caesareae ora-*
> *torem ex dec(reto) dec(urionum) pec(unia) publ(ica)**

In free translation, the text means that the senate (*decuriones*) of Caesarea ordered a statue erected, with funds from the city's treasury (*pecunia publica*). The man depicted, Marcus Flavius Agrippa, had filled the municipal office of *duumvir*, one of the "two men" who headed the municipal government. He also held the distinction of priest (*pontifex*) in the cult of one of the pagan gods and had served as the city's ambassador (*orator*), perhaps as part of a delegation to the emperor. The exact date of the statue and the inscription is unknown. The municipal senate could have erected the statue at any time between circa 70 C.E., when Vespasian founded the new colony, and the third century, when city constitutions like the one revealed in this document disappeared.

Nearly every word of this inscription bears on Romanization. The man's three names, typical of the Roman naming system, prove that he, like Saint Paul, held Roman citizenship. In fact, the family name Flavius means that Marcus, or one of his forebears, had received citizenship from Vespasian or Titus and, like the colony as a whole, in appreciation had adopted the emperor's name. It is a good guess that the family of Marcus Flavius Agrippa numbered among the Romanized Jewish or Greek families that had made the grade when Vespasian and Titus first founded the Roman colony of Caesarea. Now Marcus had become one of Caesarea's proudest sons. The descendant of eastern Greeks or Jews, he had embraced a life of service to his native city, like one of the famous Romans of the past. As one of the "two men," he had held the magisterial office that corresponded, on the municipal level, with that of the two consuls of Rome, the officials for whom the year was named and who, in republican times, had headed the Roman state. The *decuriones* who honored Marcus formed the local equivalent of the august senate of Rome. With such citizens and Roman-style institutions, cleansed of its un-Romanized elements, infused with Roman blood and, to judge from the coins and inscriptions, having adopted Latin as its official language, Caesarea had truly become a small version of Rome. The rabbis may rightly have suspected her of being the "daughter of Edom."

*A large piece of the stone cylinder, with the first four letters of the inscription, is missing. The letters could be restored because the stone's original discoverer, K. Zangemeister, published a complete text in 1890.

A good way of understanding what the rabbis meant is to look at Caesarea's material culture, at the artifacts that CAHEP and JECM archaeologists have found in their trenches and at objects from Caesarea in museum collections. Local and regional styles did not lose their influence, but ceramic pots, cups, plates, and lamps, objects of fine art like mosaic pavements and sculpture, and even the paraphernalia of everyday life – what the archaeologists call *instrumenta domestica* – reflect more and more classical Greek and Roman tastes and a common Mediterranean lifestyle (figs. 45, 73–79).

Figure 78.
Mask of Tragedy, part of a mosaic pavement, mounted on a panel 52.8×47.7 cm, probably from a villa near Caesarea, now in the Museum of Ancient Art, Haifa. The mask, a king or hero, is a stylized version of the masks worn by actors on the Greek stage. Similar images occur in Italy, at Pompeii, and at Antioch in Syria. Probably from the third or fourth century C.E.
Aaron Levin photo.

Figure 79.
Mask of Comedy, part of the same mosaic pavement as fig. 78, mounted on a panel 55.5 × 53.4 cm, also in the Museum of Ancient Art, Haifa. This mask represents one of the slaves who were characters in Greek New Comedy. Again, parallels are known from Pompeii and Antioch.
Aaron Levin photo.

Figure 80.
Bronze cuirassed statue of the Emperor Hadrian, height of the head 34 cm, of the cuirass 52.5 cm, now in the Israel Museum. The head, cuirass (breastplate), part of the arms, and other fragments of a standing statue were discovered near Beth Shean, Israel, in 1975. The emperor wears the military cloak (paludamentum) *and a muscle cuirass, on which three pairs of nude warriors are depicted fighting. Hadrian, who reigned 117–38 C.E., was one of Caesarea's principal imperial patrons.*
Pierre-Alain Ferrazzini photo, Israel Museum.

The Patronage of the Emperor

Romanization was expensive. The municipal senate had paid for the statue of Marcus from the city treasury, out of the profits from agriculture on city-owned estates in Caesarea's territory. Like their modern counterparts, however, ancient cities chronically overspent their resources and consequently depended on their leading citizens to finance public construction projects and even essential services, like providing fuel to heat the city's baths. The Maioumas inscription does not speak explicitly of Marcus's generosity with money, but honors like priesthoods, ambassadorships, and the office of the "two men" went to rich citizens who had made financial contributions. The rewards for such patronage also included statues and inscriptions in public places, visible proof that a man had achieved what every Roman wanted most, a measure of *gloria* ("renown") in the eyes of his fellow citizens.

When a city's needs surpassed the resources even of its richest citizen, the emperor was inclined to step in. The emperor, of course, had more wealth than anyone else, derived from estates in all parts of the empire, and he employed his vast resources to further Romanization. A city that had demonstrated its enthusiasm for Roman ways could expect results from an embassy pleading for improvements in its water supply, sewage system, or entertainment facilities. Moreover, the Roman emperors had embraced the Hellenistic notion that building cities was a sign of statesmanship and a claim to power, and they set out to establish themselves as the leading urban patrons in all parts of the empire.

The Flavian emperors Vespasian and Titus had already patronized Caesarea by establishing a colony named for themselves and granting Roman citizenship to many of its inhabitants. The next emperor whose generosity toward the city has been recorded was Publius Aelius Hadrianus, known as Hadrian, who reigned from 117–38 C.E. Hadrian had a penchant toward lavish building projects and refined living – as visitors to the sprawling ruins of his villa at Tivoli outside of Rome discover, with its baths, audience halls, gardens, and ornamental pools. He adored Greek culture – in a safely Romanized form – and identified his own genius with the Greek god Zeus of Olympus. Devoted to urbanism and the well-being of his subjects, Hadrian traveled tirelessly through Rome's provinces, founding new cities and colonies and spending money freely to beautify existing ones. According to one ancient source, he "built something in almost every city."

Roman Judaea and its capital, Caesarea, ranked high among Hadrian's concerns. To embody his imperial presence in the land, an unknown donor erected a

Figure 81.
Bronze coin of Hadrian, minted 117–38 C.E., diameter 3.0 cm. The reverse (pictured here) shows the emperor plowing the ritual furrow that marked the founding of a colony. He drives a yoked bull and cow, while above the goddess Nike (Victory) extends a crown to place on his head. The legend above and below the figures gives the city's official name: COL(onia) I(Prima) FL(avia) AVG(usta) CAESAR(i)EN(sis). Minted at Caesarea, now in the Museum of Ancient Art, Haifa.
Aaron Levin photo.

bronze statue of him that was found recently near Beth Shean (ancient Scythopolis), about 55 kilometers east of Caesarea (fig. 80). It surely ranks as one of the most imposing emperor portraits that have survived from antiquity. Hadrian also toured the east. In 129–30 he wintered at Gerasa, now Jerash in northern Jordan, and then spent a good part of the spring and summer in Judaea. During the visit he initiated many projects to encourage urbanism, probably more than we know from written sources and the archaeological record: at Gerasa itself a new city quarter, perhaps including a hippodrome; trunk roads connecting Judaea with major cities beyond her frontiers; at Tiberias, on the Sea of Galilee, a temple to Hadrian, probably equating him with Zeus; and at Neapolis (modern Nablus) a temple to Zeus. Hadrian refounded Sepphoris in the Galilee, naming it Diocaesarea after himself. (*Dio-* is a form of "Zeus," so the name meant "the city of Zeus-Caesar," i.e., of Hadrian.) Similarly, he announced that he would rebuild Jerusalem, which had lain mostly in ruins since the Jewish War of 66–70. Jerusalem was to become a Roman colony named Aelia Capitolina, also after Hadrian himself (Aelius Hadrianus) and Jupiter Capitolinus, the equivalent of Zeus and chief god of the Roman pantheon.

As its crowning monument, Aelia Capitolina would boast a splendid temple to Jupiter Capitolinus that would overshadow the site of the destroyed Jewish Temple. Although Hadrian had intended his project only to benefit the local population and encourage them to become more Roman, he obviously underrated Jewish devotion to Jerusalem and the Jews' hatred of Roman rule. Hadrian's intentions so infuriated the Jews that they revolted, under a leader called Bar Kokhba, whom some considered the messiah, and engaged Rome in a second bloody Jewish War (132–35). After a hard-won victory, Hadrian built Aelia as planned, unleashed a savage but ineffective persecution to put an end to Judaism, and, hoping further to consign the Jews to oblivion, changed the name of the province from Judaea to Palestine. Henceforth Caesarea would be known as the capital city of Syria Palaestina.

Hadrian also went to Caesarea. No written source mentions his visit, but he would not have omitted paying honor to a loyal city that was the seat of the provincial governor. For the occasion the city mint of Caesarea issued a special coin (fig. 81) with the bust of Hadrian on its obverse and on its reverse, the emperor ceremonially founding the city, driving a yoked team (a bull and a cow) that is plowing a ritual furrow around the settlement's perimeter. The coin legend uses the city's existing name, *Colonia Prima Flavia Augusta Caesar(i)ensis*, so we can assume that Hadrian did not refound Caesarea. The coin expresses symbolically Caesarea's warm welcome to Hadrian, thanking him for his patronage, for benefactions that justified designating him the colony's founder.

Figure 82.
Porphyry statue of an emperor, 2.45 m high, uncovered in 1951 in the so-called Byzantine esplanade east of the Crusader fortifications (cf. figs. 112, 136 for the setting). This statue, from the second century C.E., probably represented Hadrian and may well have been the cult statue in his temple, the Hadrianeum.
Aaron Levin photo.

Among Hadrian's benefactions for Caesarea was a *Hadrianeum*, a temple to himself like the one at Tiberias. This temple has not survived, but in 1951 the Israeli archaeologist Shmuel Yeivin may have uncovered one of its components. Among later ruins, he found the colossal figure of a Roman emperor, datable to the second century C.E., carved in porphyry, an extremely hard, reddish-purple stone imported from Egypt that was generally reserved for divine or imperial statues (fig.

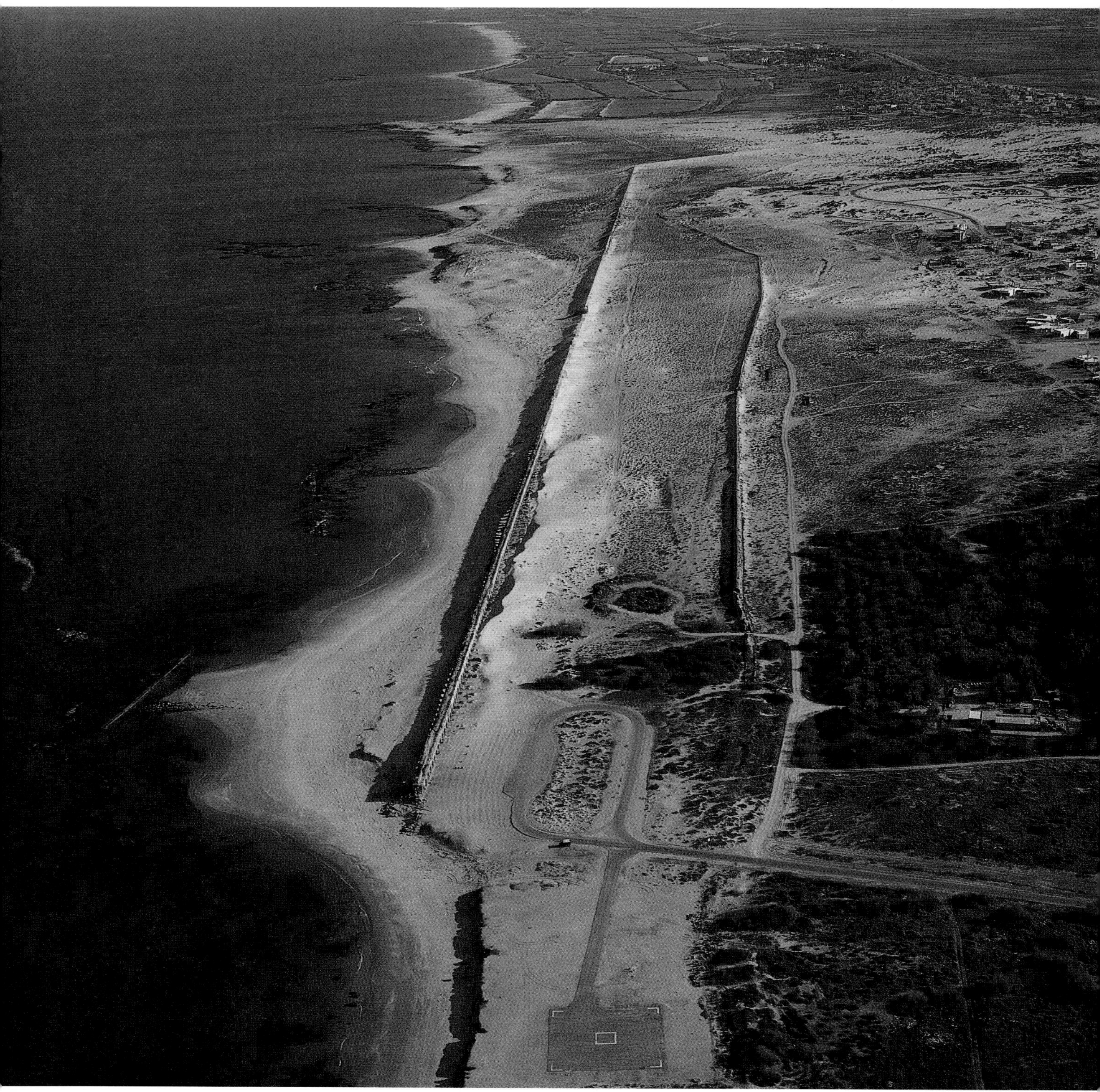

82). The head, hands, and feet of the figure had been fashioned separately in another material, presumably marble, but are not preserved. The figure wears the emperor's civil costume, a Roman-style tunic and toga. The late archaeologist and art historian Michael Avi-Yonah concluded that the statue copied a throned Hadrian, holding the scepter in his left hand and the globe in his right, that had stood near the forum in Rome. If so, the Caesarea porphyry statue very likely was the cult statue, the principal object of worship, in Caesarea's *Hadrianeum*. Nearly three meters high, it still impresses visitors as one of Caesarea's most splendid monuments.

Hadrian also ordered the refurbishing and expansion of Caesarea's aqueducts, in part, no doubt, because increasing Romanization meant more public fountains and bathing establishments (both common features of Romanized cities), which would have strained existing facilities. No baths are preserved from the period, but the aqueduct system that would have fed them is in remarkably good condition and deserves careful study. The stone-built aqueduct that approaches the city from the north (figs. 42, 44, 83) actually is two channels supported on masonry arcades, one aqueduct to the east and a second, later one constructed against it. Archaeologists believe that Herod built the eastern aqueduct when he founded Caesarea (pp. 78–79). It brought water from the Shumi springs near ancient Maioumas (fig. 43), a distance of about 6 kilometers to the northeast of Caesarea's harbor. The aqueduct does not follow a direct route, however (fig. 42). From the base of the Mount Carmel range, it first heads nearly due west 2.5 kilometers across the plain, tunnels for 400 meters beneath a modern Arab village and through the sandstone ridge that parallels the coast, and then continues southwest for nearly 1 kilometer before turning for the final 2.6-kilometer leg to Caesarea.

The earlier aqueduct remained in service through the Roman period. To increase the water supply, Hadrian's engineers located springs farther to the east along the Wadi Sindaya (Nahal Tanninim), the most distant of them about 14.5 kilometers to the northeast of Caesarea near the Arab village of Sabbarin. From that point the hydraulic engineers constructed a second aqueduct along the northern slopes of the wadi – much of it carried in tunnels cut into the rock – that followed a circuitous route until it joined with the earlier line near Maioumas (fig. 42). At several points along the route, shafts cut into the rock at an angle and fitted with steps permitted access to the tunnel during its construction and facilitated cleaning and ventilation once it was in service (fig. 84). In places the tunnel reaches about 45 meters below ground level and is 1.10 meters high and 0.80 meter wide. Small niches at intervals in the rock once held oil lamps to illuminate the tunnel head as workmen dug their way through the solid rock. The workmen used simple leveling

Figure 83.
Aerial view of the coast north of Caesarea, looking north. In the distance, the twin high-level aqueduct emerges from the sandstone ridge and turns southward to approach the city. Farther inland the low-level aqueduct, from the Byzantine period, is also visible.
PICTORIAL ARCHIVE (Near Eastern History) Est.

Figure 84.
One of the shafts cut into the rock that gave access to the subterranean portion of the Hadrianic aqueduct line.
Bill Curtzinger photo, © National Geographic Society.

devices to ensure that water would flow through the tunnel once it was completed. Aqueducts of this type were a triumph of Roman organization and engineering. Their cost and difficulty required resources on a grand scale such as only an emperor could provide.

There is no doubt that Hadrian ordered construction of the second, longer aqueduct line. At intervals along its exposed outer face, the builders inserted inscribed blocks into the masonry that record who was responsible for the work (fig. 85). Nine of those inscriptions have been found thus far, of which one example reads:

> *Imp(erator) Caes(ar)*
> *Tra(ianus) Hadr(ianus) Aug(ustus)*
> *per vexil(lationem)*
> *leg(ionis) VI Fe[r(ratae)]*

Figure 85.
The western aqueduct line north of the city. An inscription set into the masonry identifies Hadrian as the builder and his troops as the workmen. This portion of the aqueduct was built on sand, so buttressing, visible in the photograph, was needed to keep the water channels in service until the sixth century C.E.
Aaron Levin photo.

This text says that the Emperor Hadrian had constructed the aqueduct through a "detachment" (*vexillatio*) of the Sixth Legion, nicknamed "Old Ironsides." The other eight inscriptions also mention Hadrian and two other legions, the Tenth and the Second. Because it is otherwise known that these three legions served together in Judaea in the years immediately before the Bar Kokhba revolt (132–35), it is reasonable to connect the new aqueduct with Hadrian's visit to Caesarea in 130. The nine inscriptions together also demonstrate how Hadrian assembled the manpower he needed for such a huge project. Like other emperors Hadrian used the army to build aqueducts, highways, and similar urban projects, both to maintain the discipline of his fighting units during peacetime and to further his goal of enhancing city life.

It is likely that Hadrian (if not another second-century emperor) used his troops during peacetime to carry out another giant building project at Caesarea: the city's circus, or hippodrome, the facility for chariot racing. The remains of the

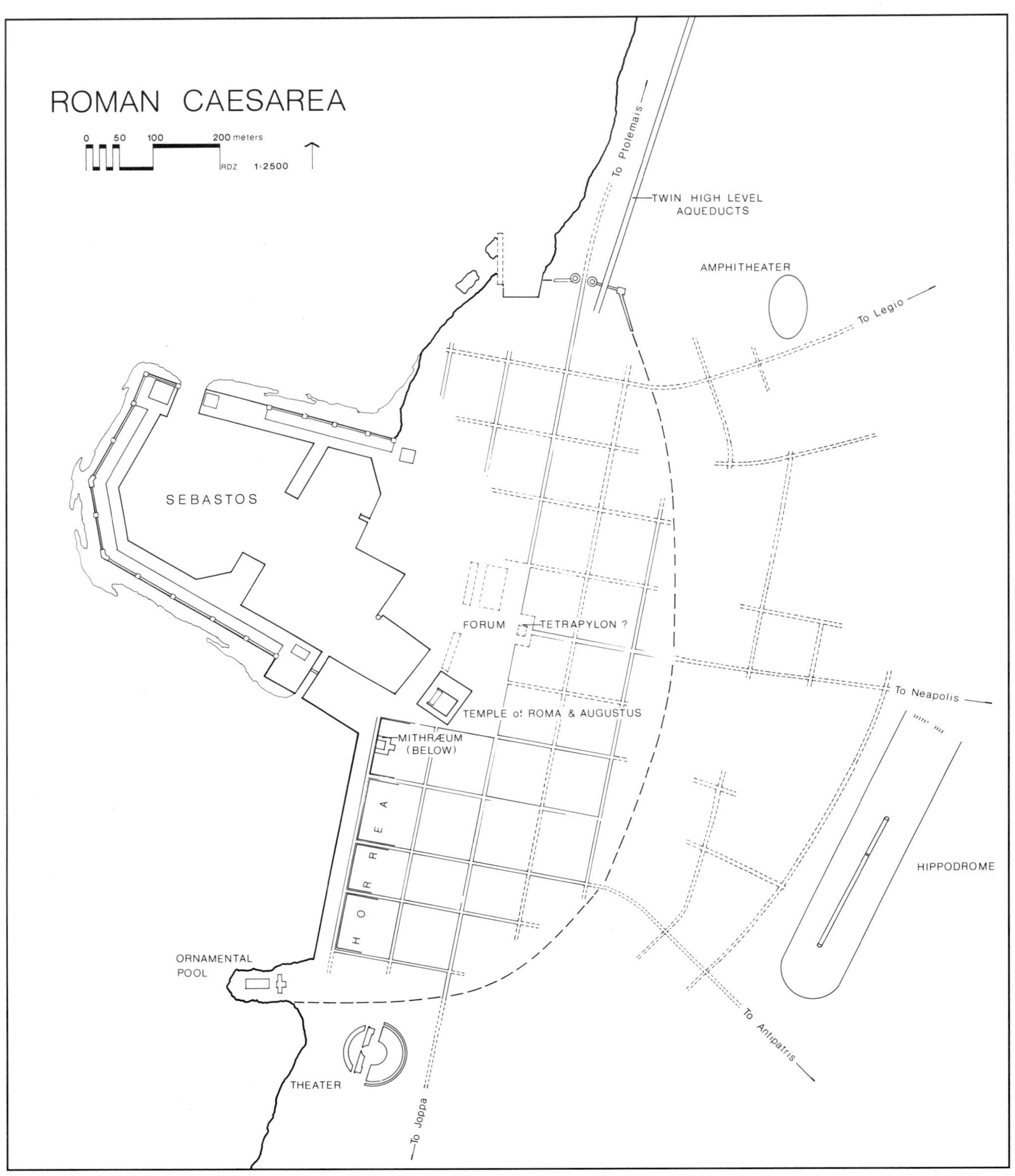
ROMAN CAESAREA
0
50
100
200 meters
RDZ
1:2500
To Ptolemais
TWIN HIGH LEVEL
AQUEDUCTS
AMPHITHEATER
To Legio
SEBASTOS
FORUM
TETRAPYLON ?
To Neapolis
TEMPLE of ROMA & AUGUSTUS
MITHRÆUM
(BELOW)
HORREA
HIPPODROME
ORNAMENTAL
POOL
To Antipatris
THEATER
To Joppa

circus are at the site's southeastern quarter, some distance outside the line of the Herodian fortification walls (fig. 86). Although farmers have converted the open area of the circus to agricultural use, most recently to raising bananas, the contours of the ancient structure still exist (fig. 1).

Figure 86.
Urban plan of Roman Caesarea about 200 C.E. By this time the city had expanded beyond the projected line of the Herodian city wall, but new fortifications had not yet been provided. The most visible additions to the city's topography were a new aqueduct line and the circus, or hippodrome.
Robin Ziek drawing.

To excavate the entire circus stratigraphically, at the deliberate pace of proper scientific work, would take decades, so JECM turned to surveying and sampling. John Humphrey, an authority on circuses, led a survey for JECM in 1973 that studied surface contours and remains, and in 1974 he excavated select portions of the circus. The work proved to be fruitful. The archaeologists discovered, for example, that ancient or medieval builders had robbed the stones from the superstructure of the *cavea*. However, the foundations of at least twenty rows of seats remained. This suggests an overall seating capacity in excess of thirty thousand – which, although not many if compared to the 260,000 or so that the Circus Maximus in Rome could accommodate, is still an impressive figure for a provincial city.

The running track, called an *arena*, like the surface of the amphitheater, formed a large oval, whose maximum dimensions were about 450 meters north–south and 90 meters east–west. The *cavea*, formed of stone seating that rose in rows supported by arches or vaults, much like the seating of both the theater and the amphitheater, surrounded the arena to the east, south, and west. Across the northern end, in a broad semicircle, lay the *carceres*, the stalls with gates that opened in unison to signal the start of the race. Up to twelve teams of two, four, or even more horses each, pulling racing chariots (fig. 87), bolted on signal from the *carceres* for a grueling seven-lap race run counterclockwise around the circus's raised central divider, or *spina*. To accommodate the wide turns necessary at high speeds, the designers of the circus oriented the *spina* about five degrees clockwise from the north–south axis, leaving a bottleneck as the teams approached the first turn, the *meta prima*, near the southern end of the circus. Jockeying for position there frequently caused fatal crashes, adding to the spectators' thrills. After making the second turn, the *meta secunda*, of the seventh lap, about two-thirds of the distance down the western leg of the running track, the horses crossed the finish line in front of a special section that provided seating for the judges.

Figure 87.
Ceramic oil lamp, 10.2 cm long, from the later first century C.E. On the discus a charioteer drives a biga, *a chariot drawn by two horses, to the right. Said to be from Caesarea, now in the Museum of Ancient Art, Haifa.*
Aaron Levin photo.

JECM also examined the three cones cut from hard Aswan granite, imported from upper Egypt, that had formed the *meta secunda* at the northern end of the *spina* and the remains of a gigantic obelisk that once rose near its center – a spectacular single block of the Aswan stone perhaps 27 meters high when complete and capped by a shining pyramid of polished stone. Within the last few decades, agricultural workers moved the three granite cones (minus their upper portions, recently discov-

Figure 88.
Large fragment of the obelisk, made of granite from upper Egypt, that once ornamented Caesarea's hippodrome. It lies across the ancient spina, *where it fell during the Crusader period. Behind it portions of the* meta *cones are visible.*
JECM photo.

ered in the harbor) alongside the obelisk (fig. 88). The work in 1974 also demonstrated that long pools, roughly 7.4 meters wide, had decorated the *spina*. From the example of other sites, we can assume that at several points along the *spina* there were groups of statues.

The 1974 season provided a reliable date, based on stratigraphy, for the construction of this monumental stone circus. In area H.4 the team excavated a trench across the *cavea* foundations along the west side of the track, where they found three successive plaster surfaces that had been laid down just to the east of the inner *cavea* wall, where the *arena* surface came up against it. Beneath the lowest (earliest) plaster surface were three datable coins, all from the first century C.E., and a substantial number of datable potsherds, the *latest* of which belong in the first half of the second century C.E. Because the team associated the earliest plaster surface at this point with the earliest *arena* floor, it is likely that the monumental stone hippodrome – as opposed to an earlier temporary structure already in use in King Herod's time – was

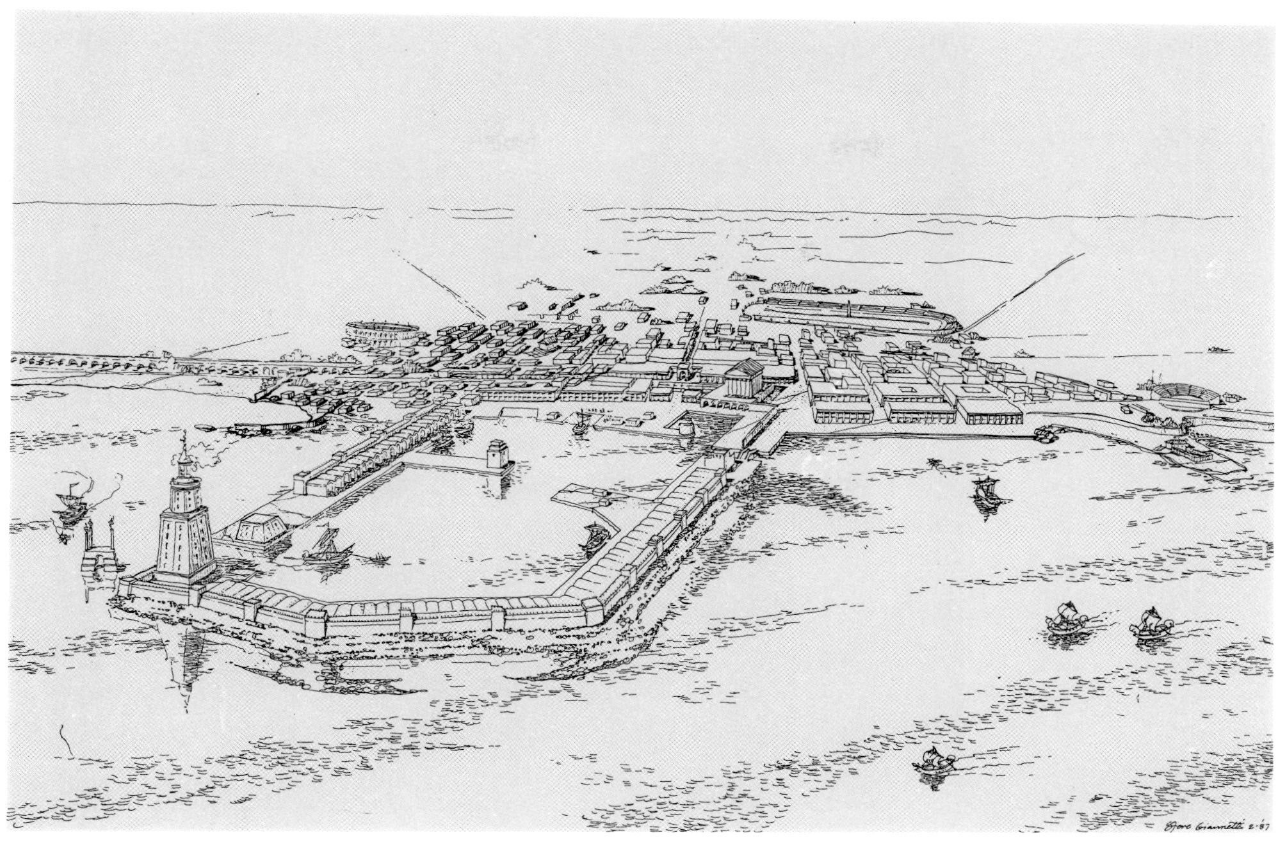

Figure 89.
Roman Caesarea about 200 C.E. Hypothetical perspective view looking east.
Stephen Giannetti drawing.

constructed in the first half of the second century C.E., and perhaps by Hadrian, who is known to have benefited Caesarea in the same period.

Although the Greeks had a long history of devotion to horses and chariot racing, already evident in the culture depicted in Homer's *Iliad*, the revived taste for such contests in the first and second centuries C.E. was principally Roman, and hence represents Romanization. Besides the circus, other major construction projects in the second century C.E. made Caesarea more and more the "daughter of Edom." For example, late in the century the emperors sponsored the building of monumental streets flanked by colonnades, sidewalks, and shops, much like the ones explored at Caesarea's sister city, Sebaste, in the 1930s (fig. 66). Some of Caesarea's street colonnades may date from Herod's time, but most of the column capitals that have turned up at the site come from the late second century or early third. Most likely the emperors Septimius Severus (reigned 193–211) and his son Caracalla (reigned 211–17), both of whom honored Caesarea with imperial visits,

Figure 90.
*Group of transport amphora sherds found by JECM in vault 1, now at DIAR. Largest example (handles at lower right) 31.5 cm high. These sherds represent vessels made in Italy, Yugoslavia, the Aegean basin, and Spain and used for wine, olive oil, fish sauce (*garum*), and grape syrup (*defrutum*). The vessels represented dated from the late first century B.C.E. to the third quarter of the first century C.E.*
Aaron Levin photo.

also beautified her by funding large-scale reconstruction of her major streets. The project may have continued under the last emperor of the dynasty, Severus Alexander (222–35 C.E.), who exalted Caesarea among the cities of Palestine by promoting her to the rank of metropolis.

From the modern perspective patronage on an imperial scale could best contribute to Caesarea's well-being if devoted to keeping her economy vibrant. The Roman emperors did use their resources to develop a first-class system of paved roads in Palestine, as elsewhere in the empire, employing the army for this purpose. Caesarea occupied a key position in this system, with excellent links to other urban centers and to caravan routes beyond the empire's frontiers (fig. 42). Heavy commercial traffic moved to and fro along those routes, by pack train and wagon. Combined with the agricultural production of the Plain of Sharon, this traffic kept Sebastos and those who labored there busy and prosperous.

JECM's work on vault 1, located just south of the Crusader fortifications, demonstrated lively activity at Caesarea's port in the first century C.E., when Sebastos welcomed trading vessels from the farthest reaches of the known world. It was specifically ceramic analysis of the pottery found in vault 1 that demonstrated

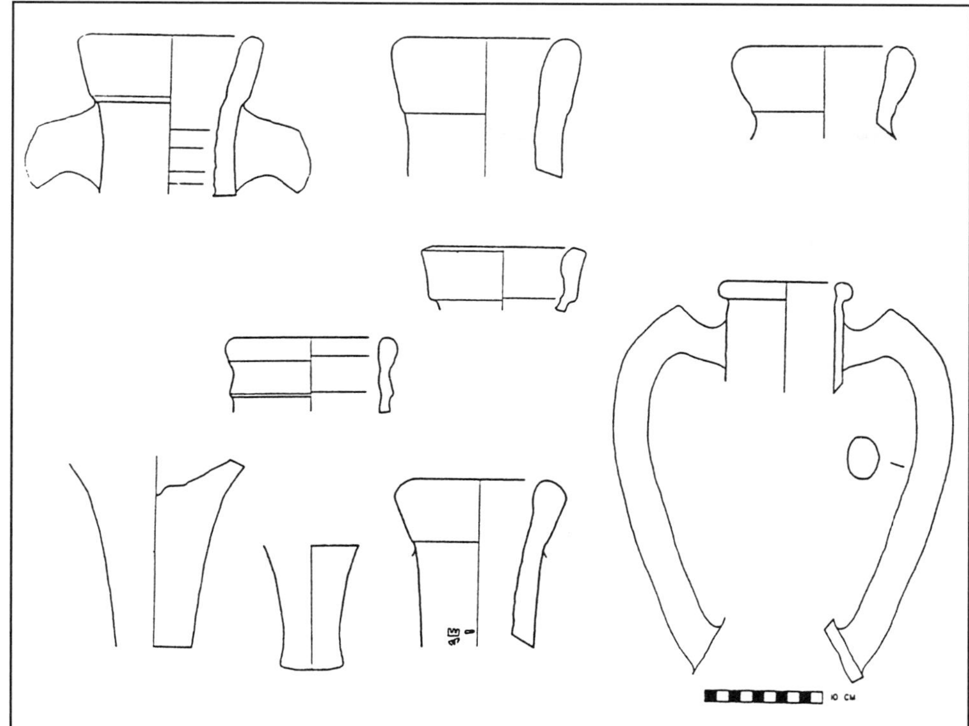

Figure 91. Computer-generated profiles of the sherds in fig. 90. Ceramicists use profiles of this type to communicate the results of their research in published reports. Profiles courtesy of Archeological Assessments Incorporated, Nashville, Arkansas, and Jeffrey Blakely.

this. Herod, it will be remembered, had ordered the vaults built as part of the original conception of Sebastos, to serve as warehouses, *horrea*. When the team excavated within vault 1, they penetrated thirteen distinct occupation layers. Layers 1 and 2 – situated at the lowest level, immediately above the bedrock on which the vault's foundations were laid – contained numerous sherds. Although they are just broken pieces of pottery, in the hands of an experienced ceramicist the sherds had a story to tell (fig. 90). Of the forty-one sherds saved from layers 1 and 2, thirty came from vessels known as transport amphoras. From these miscellaneous diagnostic sherds – rims, handles, and bases – the specialist recognized amphoras made in Spain (six examples), Italy (three), Yugoslavia (four), the Aegean basin (nine), and perhaps North Africa (one). The vessels typically contained wine (twelve examples), olive oil (six), *garum* – a popular sauce made of putrid fish and used with food as a condiment – (three), and *defrutum* – a syrup of grape sugar used as a sweetener, a preservative, and a beverage – (one).

The sherds have the power to evoke for us the bustling activity that once took place at vault 1 and in the harbor Sebastos, or *Portus Augusti*, as it was known in Latin. From the ships that arrived at Caesarea's quays, longshoremen unloaded

Figure 92.
Transport amphora used for shipping wine. Although later in date – third century C.E. – this complete specimen belongs to the category of vessel in figs. 90–91. Height 82.5 cm. Examples of this form have turned up in the Athenian agora, in Iraq, at Jerash in Jordan, in Jerusalem, and at Caesarea. Found in Israel in a tomb, now in the Museum of Ancient Art, Haifa.
Aaron Levin photo.

cargoes of popular commodities – gourmet items, some of them shipped at great expense from far away. The laborers brought the amphoras that contained these goods to the warehouses for temporary storage and then consignment or resale to the merchants or middlemen who would put them on the market in the city, the countryside, and in the broader region Sebastos served. From this business many of the humble citizens of Caesarea made a decent living. On the macroeconomic level the sherds from vault 1 tie Caesarea into an international trade network within the ancient Mediterranean world and beyond. The extent of this trade is testified to by sherds similar to those from vault 1 that archaeologists have found at other sites (fig. 93). These sherds show that distant markets received the same goods as Caesarea.

The pottery from vault 1 is also a paradigm of the methods ceramicists use to make sense of potsherds. The insights discussed here depended, first of all, on ceramicists classifying the sherds found: the exact shape, or profile, of each sherd; the particle size of the clay from which it was made; the color of its fabric after firing; and whether the surface of the sherd was painted or otherwise decorated. To do this ceramicists searched through published reports of pottery from other sites, looking for parallels – examples of the same classes of vessel. For most of the sherds numerous parallels existed: scholars had already published examples of whole vessels like the ones from which the sherds came; they had discovered, from inscriptions or remains inside the vessels, what the vessels typically contained; they had located the clay beds in distant countries where the potters had extracted the clay to make the pots; and they had found enough examples in layers dated by stratigraphy to estimate the period during which the pots were manufactured and used.

Significantly the sherds from vault 1 all belonged to vessels first manufactured late in the first century B.C.E., and none were dated later than the middle or third quarter of the first century C.E. The sherds confirmed, therefore, that the vault dated to King Herod's reign, and that the heyday of its use as a warehouse extended over the following hundred years.

The ceramicists' task did not end with classifying and comparing the sherds or with the insights these procedures provided; they next had to publish their research to make it accessible to their colleagues. Where once an artist would have had to draw each profile by hand, today profiles are created and stored by computer. In the examples in fig. 91, a vertical line divides each profile in half. To the left of the line is the sherd's external profile, to the right its internal one. Each indicates the pot's shape and decoration. Besides using drawings ceramicists describe each sherd verbally, using their own jargon: "The ware [fabric of the vessel] is sandy and contains volcanic inclusions [bits of volcanic material mixed with the clay]." They give the

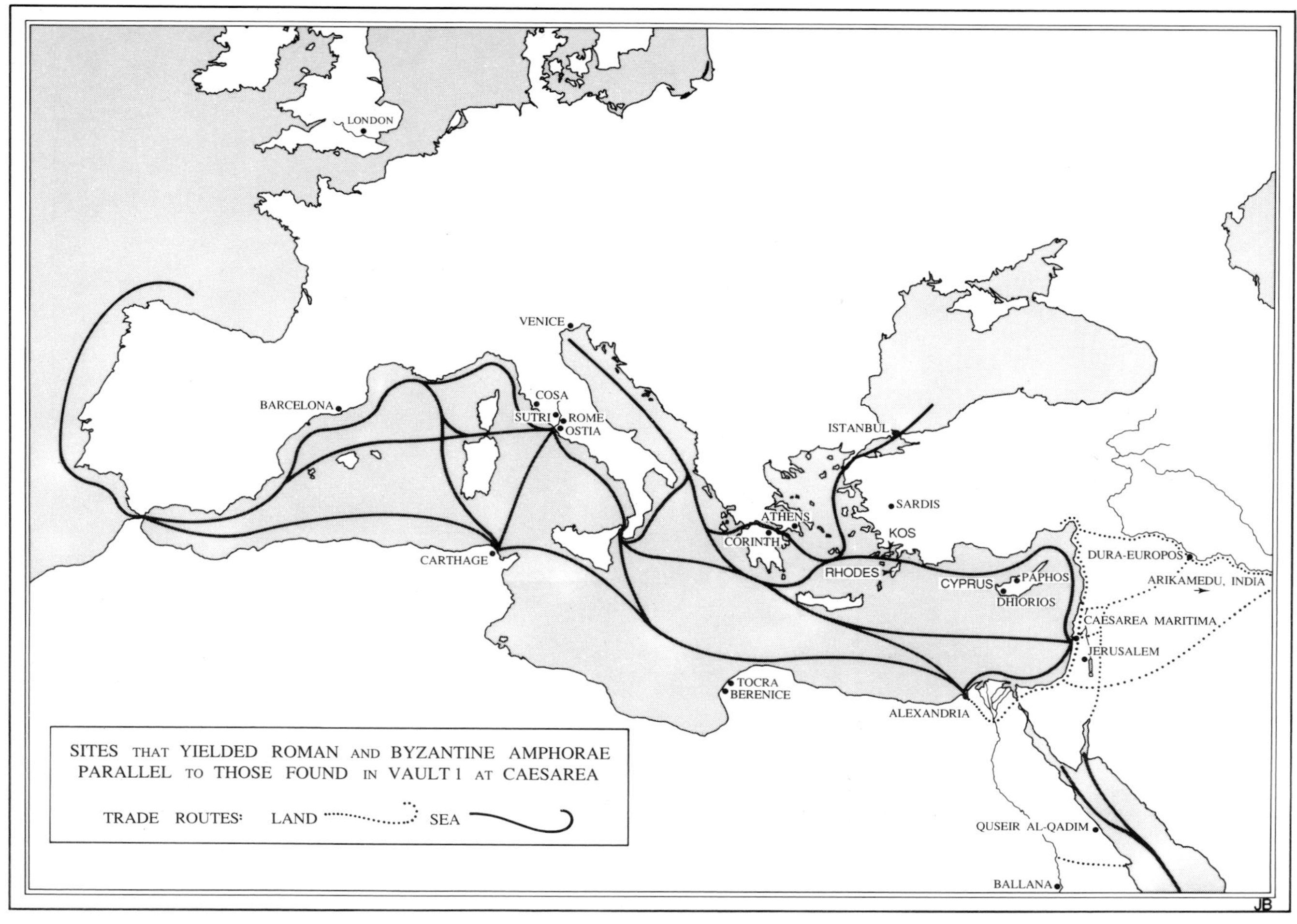

color of the sherd in the codes in the standard *Munsell Soil Color Charts*. The code 2.5Y8/2, for example, means a specific shade of light yellow. Ceramic reports do not make easy reading, but they do communicate the archaeologist's findings precisely, and specialists depend on them.

Another kind of evidence adds to our picture of the bustling Caesarea harbor. Because of powerful winds and currents, some ships did not reach the harbor entrance, but ran aground on the breakwaters or on shore and were lost with their cargoes. Hence, evidence of shipwrecks litters the sea bottom and the ruins of the harbor breakwaters. Most of those wrecks survive only as concentrations of pottery from cargoes, but in one case much of the ship's hull survives. In 1983, 1984, and 1986 CAHEP examined the remains of that wreck, which lies in the bay north of the

Figure 93.
Map showing trade routes that connected Caesarea and its harbor Sebastos with the Mediterranean world and more distant lands. Also indicated are sites where sherds like those in vault 1 have been found in archaeological trenches.
JoAnn Boscarino drawing.

Figure 94.
CAHEP divers uncover remains of a merchant ship in the bay just north of Caesarea, area Y, in only 2 m of water. The ship proved to be a merchant vessel of the first century C.E.
Bill Curtzinger photo, © National Geographic Society.

Hellenistic-Herodian wall, just off the beach, in only 2 meters of water (fig. 94). Using the special techniques of shipwreck archaeology, the CAHEP team removed the overburden of sand and fixed a grid of 25-centimeter squares in place to help their architects prepare drawings with accurate measurements (figs. 95 and 96). Divers also searched the sea floor in the vicinity for remains of the ceramic vessels

Figure 95.
To facilitate accurate drawing of the shipwreck in area Y, CAHEP's underwater architects fixed a grid of 25×25 cm squares over it. Murky water is a frequent problem.
Mark Little photo.

Figure 96.
The area-Y shipwreck, plan of preserved planking. The remains indicate a vessel about 40 m long with a beam of about 12 m.
Lauren Goldberg drawing.

Figure 97.
Fragment of a wooden frame, with dowel holes, from the area-Y shipwreck. Beneath the sea floor, the wood survived in remarkable condition. Height 11 cm. IDAM collection, at the Center for Maritime Studies, Haifa.
Robert Hohlfelder photo.

that had held the ship's cargo and, using a magnetometer, for metal objects concealed beneath the sand. The heavy surf, especially strong in shallow water, quickly reburied the remains of the hull, so that CAHEP will need to reexcavate it in future seasons.

For the present CAHEP can confirm that the wreck in the north bay was a merchant ship from the late first century B.C.E. or early first century C.E., when Herod's harbor first attracted international commerce. For its period the ship had a large capacity. Its hull measured about 40 meters long and 12 meters in beam. The ship's stout planking, more than 8 centimeters thick and sheathed with lead, was nailed through dowels to closely set frames, the ship's ribs (figs. 96 and 97). In a general way it would have resembled the ship depicted sailing into Portus Augusti, Rome's harbor, on a marble relief (fig. 98). The cargo remains found in the northern bay included fragments of large storage jars that had been manufactured in the western Mediterranean and typically were used on shipboard as containers for both liquid and dry commodities. It appears, therefore, that the ship plied long-distance trade routes and had sailed to these waters from Italy or elsewhere in the West, Caesarea ranking high among ports of call in the eastern Mediterranean.

The north-bay ship, the amphoras from vault 1, and other finds evoke an image of lively activity in Sebastos and the adjacent anchorages during the century or so after Herod. For the rest of the Roman period the picture is less clear. Some archaeologists believe that artifacts from the clay layer found in the harbor entrance prove that the Herodian basin went virtually unused after the third quarter of the first century C.E. We saw in chapter 3 that this layer, the floor of the Herodian harbor, contained no remains datable to later than the first century C.E. The archaeologists who make this point argue that to keep the facilities of Sebastos in operation required constant attention. Despite its antisilting capabilities, the enclosed basin would tend to clog if it were not dredged. Heavy seas, especially when driven by winter storms, had the capacity to destroy stone and concrete installations over a period of decades. There was another factor operating, moreover, that neither Herod nor the Romans could have predicted. At least one active geological fault extends along Israel's coast just offshore, and seismic action along it caused the harbor breakwaters to tilt downward from their elevations in antiquity. In addition, the weight of the massive breakwaters and other structures caused them to settle into the sandy bottom. Hence their ruins now lie 5 to 8 meters below sea level. No one knows when these processes began or how quickly they proceeded, but it is certain that Sebastos required not only dredging if it were to remain in service, but also the frequent restoration and enlargement of the breakwaters themselves.

*Figure 98. The Torlonia harbor relief, marble, 0.75-m high and 1.22 m wide, dated late second century C.E., from Portus, Rome's seaport, where the emperors Claudius and Trajan built artificial harbors in the first and second century C.E. The relief shows bustling harbor activity. One ship, to the right, has tied up to a quay, by the same type of mooring stone that CAHEP found at Caesarea (fig. 26) and a longshoreman is unloading its cargo, wine shipped in amphoras. A second ship, to the left, in general appearance much like the north bay ship from Caesarea, has just entered the harbor and has already furled its headsail (*artemon*). Between the two ships stands Neptune, the sea god, with his trident. Behind the second ship, the harbor's lighthouse is visible with a beacon on top. The statuary in the background, to right and left of the lighthouse, probably represents actual sculpture that ornamented the entrance to Ostia's harbor, like the statues of Augustus's family at Caesarea (fig. 62).*
Photo from the Fototeca Unione at the American Academy in Rome.

Josephus says that Herod, in constructing the great basin of Sebastos, "conquered nature herself." Further human intervention – further organization and the expenditure of immense sums of money – was needed to keep the harbor in operation, as it was for Caesarea as a whole. The entire city was an artificial creation that could not flourish unless the Roman emperors, with their reserves of wealth and manpower, devoted themselves to its well-being. Perhaps in the end the emperors found it easiest to support urban beautification projects, like colonnaded streets, circuses, and aqueducts, which contributed to the immediate gratification of its citizens or made a city more Roman. Such projects had immediate rewards, for they increased an emperor's popularity and encouraged the loyalty of his subjects. It was the economic infrastructure of an ancient city that was apt to suffer from neglect, as it is in some modern cities. Only further archaeological exploration will determine whether this was the case with the port Sebastos, a piece of Herod's dream that may early on have gone to ruin.

The City's Gods and Goddesses

In the ancient conception a city was first of all a religious community, composed of worshippers of the same gods and goddesses. In the first century B.C.E., the Roman orator Cicero had declared: "Let every community have its own cults." Inscriptions from everywhere in the Roman Empire, but especially from cities in the eastern provinces, herald the "gods and goddesses of our fathers" that "stand before" the city, keeping it safe from harm and seeing to its prosperity. Temples to these deities occupied the most conspicuous places in the city's landscape, and there were small shrines in every neighborhood. Anyone could offer private sacrifice for his personal benefit, but more often people came to the temples for the public festivals that crowded the city's calendar, welcome respites from work and the tedium of daily life. Arrayed in splendid costumes, priests and priestesses officiated over parades of citizens decked out in their finery, over the singing of hymns, over ritual slaughter, and over the kindling of altar fires. The distribution of sacrificial meat gave every member of the community the chance to enjoy the god's generosity. Many festivals featured performances in the theater, the amphitheater, and the circus; conversely, no public function – from senate meetings to chariot races, the opening of the sailing season, or welcoming the emperor – began without a sacrifice to the city's gods.

Herod the Great had given Caesarea her original "ancestral" gods, Roma and Augustus, whose temple occupied the artificial platform above the harbor. The cult of the city's Tyche probably also originated at Caesarea's founding, although the

Figure 99.
Ceramic oil lamp from the late first century B.C.E. or the first century C.E. Length 15.0 cm. On the discus, Zeus wields a scepter, and in the foreground an eagle, Zeus' bird, clutches a thunderbolt in his talons. This is a high quality Roman lamp, said to be from Caesarea, now in the Museum of Ancient Art, Haifa.
Aaron Levin photo.

Figure 100.
Bronze coin of Caracalla minted 211–217 C.E. The reverse (pictured here) depicts Caesarea's Tyche standing in a tetrastyle (four-columned) temple, with figures of other gods or emperors in the intercolumniations to left and right. This coin confirms that the city goddess had a temple, where the people of the city brought sacrifices to her. The legend reads COL(onia) PR(ima) F(lavia) A(ugusta) F(elix) C(oncordia) with CAESAREA below the temple. Struck at Caesarea, now in the Museum of Ancient Art, Haifa.
Aaron Levin photo.

earliest evidence for it is dated 67/68 C.E., the time of the emperor Nero (fig. 68). In the third century C.E., coins of Caracalla, who was emperor from 211–17, depicted Tyche in her temple (fig. 100). In the fourth century C.E. Caesarea's citizens still gathered there to celebrate her birthday. To preside over these cults, the city established public priesthoods, filled by men like Marcus Flavius Agrippa, the Romanized Caesarean aristocrat whose honorific inscription records that he had served as priest (see pp. 115, 118). We know from surviving inscriptions that in the first and second centuries temples and priesthoods were dedicated to the emperors Tiberius and Hadrian. Thus, it is clear from the available evidence that the gods and goddesses who "stood before" Caesarea, protecting her and guaranteeing her prosperity, were distinctly Roman. The imperial cult assumed unusual importance, and the city's Tyche resembled the goddess Roma, who embodied the imperial city.

Of course people also had personal gods and goddesses at home and where they worked. Deities appeared everywhere in the home: individual divine images and mythological scenes decorated oil lamps, ivory and bone boxes, and bronze pitchers and jugs (fig. 99). An exquisite marble head of Dionysus excavated by JECM in area

Figure 101. Head of Dionysus, marble, 16.3 cm high. A wreath of nine heart-shaped ivy leaves identifies this work as the wine god, as does the softly rounded, effeminate face. Roman copy of a late classical or Hellenistic original. Found in JECM's area B.3, IDAM collection. Aaron Levin photo.

B.3 may once have graced the urban mansion of a wealthy citizen (fig. 101). CAHEP archaeologists found a bronze statuette of Jupiter in area G2 that is just over 8 centimeters high (fig. 102). In art Jupiter often holds an eagle in one hand and a spear in the other. This Jupiter's spear is missing. Although individuals sometimes offered incense or other forms of sacrifice to such images, these were not objects of worship. They generally were kept to beautify a home and to remind their owners of the divine powers that inhabited the universe. Of interest to us is that the religious culture they reflect of Caesarea conforms to that in the rest of the Graeco-Roman East. Clearly the populace had embraced the Roman order even in the intimacy of their private lives.

Outside of their households and workplaces, the inhabitants of Caesarea turned to public cults, increasingly to those of gods and goddesses popular in the rest of the Roman Empire. There was a temple to the goddess Isis at Caesarea, for

Figure 102.
Statuette of Jupiter, bronze, height 8.1 cm. The eagle in his right hand identifies this nude male figure as Jupiter. In his right hand he probably held a spear. Similar figures come from the European parts of the Roman Empire in the second and third centuries C.E. Found by CAHEP in area G2. IDAM collection, at the Center for Maritime Studies, Haifa.
Aaron Levin photo.

example. Of Egyptian origin, she had been thoroughly Romanized and had a special regard for sailors, who considered her their main protector. Her festival occurred in the spring, at the beginning of the sailing season, when her priests and devotees brought her in a procession down to the shore so she could bless the seamen. Serapis, another Romanized Egyptian deity, and the Greek goddess Demeter appear frequently enough on coins from Caesarea's mint to suggest that they too had temples in the city. An inscription attests to the local worship of Jupiter Dolichenus, a god from Syria popular with the Roman army. The Greek god Apollo was honored early in the third century C.E. by the emperor Septimius Severus, who established local Pythian games at Caesarea, athletic and theatrical contests that became famous throughout the eastern empire. The Ephesian Artemis also found a home at Caesarea. She may have arrived with settlers from her original cult center, the city of Ephesus in Asia Minor, where Saint Paul, on one of his missionary journeys, ran

Figure 103.
Artemis of Ephesus, height 1.65 m, carved in white marble, probably from the second quarter of the second century C.E. Found by the Italian Mission in 1961 near Caesarea's theater, this figure represents the ancient fertility goddess of Ephesus, in modern Turkey. The goddess's upper torso has the polymastia, *the "many breasts" that evoked her ability to nourish human and animal life. The bees, flowers, and goats on the front panel attached to her dress symbolize fertility and the goddess's role as "mistress of animals." IDAM collection, displayed in the Israel Museum.*
Nāchum Slopak photo, Israel Museum.

Figure 104. The Caesarea Artemis of Ephesus (fig. 103), reconstruction based on other images of the same goddesses. Although numerous variants exist, most images show the goddess with arms extended and to her right and left a pair of stags. From her arms descend strands of wool, tied off at intervals with threads. The elaborate headdress restored here, topped with an image of the goddess's temple, is based on a statue found in Ephesus.
Ellen Talaat drawing.

afoul of her worshippers (Acts 19:23–41). In the ruins of Caesarea's theater, the Italian Mission discovered a statue of this exotic, many-breasted Artemis that may have been the cult image in her temple (figs. 103 and 104).

What is striking about this enumeration of Caesarea's gods and goddesses is that it contains no surprises. Caesarea worshipped almost the same deities – or at least the same kinds of deities – as cities in Roman Britain, Spain, North Africa, Greece, Asia Minor, and Rome itself. As people moved about from one part of the empire to another, they brought their favorite cults with them. In time the cults found acceptance in cities far from their places of origin, in the meantime having undergone a process of syncretism that made them more like other Roman cults. It was in the city, where its adherents could build a temple and display their awe-inspiring rituals, that a cult could attract an audience and win converts.

Figure 105. The Caesarea Mithraeum in field C, vault 1, looking east. Low benches, suitable for reclining to eat and drink, flank the walls to left and right. A beam of light from an aperture in the vault illuminates the altar area.
Paul Saivetz photo.

Through archaeology it has also been demonstrated that Mithras was among Caesarea's gods. The cult of Mithras is perhaps the best example of the process of religious syncretism. Mithras hailed originally from ancient Persia, where devotees of Zoroastrianism, the national religion of the Persians, knew him as the champion of Ahuramazda, the god of light and goodness, and the implacable enemy of Ahriman, the spirit of evil and darkness. In the first century B.C.E., a new cult arose on the soil of the Roman Empire that had Mithras as its central figure. Thoroughly Roman in character, this religion spread widely among merchants, the army, and the administration. Numerous Mithraic cult centers, or *Mithraea*, have turned up in Italy, on the Danube frontier, and in other parts of the Western Roman Empire.

Despite the cult's probable eastern origins, it has been found more commonly in the West. For that reason JECM's discovery of a well-preserved Mithraeum with some typical accoutrements was a cause for excitement. It appears that toward the

Figure 106. The Caesarea Mithraeum in field C, vault 1, reconstruction. Wooden shafts set in rectangular holes that JECM discovered in the vault's intrados *formed a splay that evoked the sun's rays and separated off the eastern 4.50 m of the Mithraeum, forming a kind of "holy of holies."*
JECM drawing.

end of the first century C.E., unknown devotees of Mithras converted vault 1 (south of the Crusader fortifications) into a Mithraeum (figs. 105 and 106). They separated the eastern 13.5 meters of the vault from the western part with a partition, of which only the foundations survive. To the east of the partition they built low benches 1.60 meters wide and 0.40-meter high along the northern and southern walls, and a similar bench, only 1.10 meters wide, against the eastern wall. A stone partition 0.32-meter high divided the eastern bench in two along the central line of the vault. In line with this partition, and 0.25-meter in front of the eastern bench, JECM found the remains of an altar 0.60-meter by 0.60-meter and 0.22-meter high. To judge from surviving fragments, plaster covered the benches, the front and side walls, and the vault itself. The converted warehouse resembled Mithraea known elsewhere. Typically, they occupied basements or windowless lower stories to support the fiction that each Mithraeum had in fact been the very grotto where the god Mithras had slaughtered a bull – the crowning event in the adventures of this god, equivalent to the Crucifixion in the Christian Gospels. Vault 1 had no windows, and although not actually subterranean, at least during its reuse as a Mithraeum it functioned as a basement. Another building was constructed above it, giving it the feeling of a grotto. Altars were normal Mithraeum furniture, as were the benches on which the cultists reclined for ritual meals.

The builders of the Mithraeum also opened two rectangular apertures in its ceiling to admit light. The western one is 0.30-meter wide and 0.80-meter long. Located 14.6 meters from the eastern wall, on the vault's center, it illuminated the entrance to the Mithraeum. The builders set the eastern aperture, 0.45-meter by 0.45-meter square, in a position 0.33-meter to the south of the vault's center line and 3.50 meters from its eastern end. This position appears to have been calculated: the excavators discovered, by observing the shaft of light created by this aperture, that in mid June, as the sun completes its progression southward in the sky toward the summer solstice, the shaft comes closer to the altar, until, at high noon on the day of the solstice, it illuminates it. At that time each year the worshippers may have performed a special sacrifice on the altar, and at the prescribed moment in the ceremony opened the aperture to admit a dazzling shaft of sunlight into the dark chamber. Ancient texts reveal, after all, that for worshippers of Mithras, the sun that fell on the altar was none other than "Mithras, the unconquered sun": *Sol invictus Mithras*.

A second theatrical device may also have brought the sun into the Caesarea Mithraeum. The team found a series of nineteen rectangular holes, 4.0 by 7.0 by 3.0 centimeters deep, cut equidistant from each other into the *intrados*, or inner surface, of the vault, 4.50 meters from its eastern wall, on a line perpendicular to its axis. The holes must have received the butt ends of wooden shafts. In one of the nineteen holes, the shape of the wooden shaft survives in the surface plaster that surrounded it. If the shafts corresponded in length to the radius of the vault (2.5 meters), they would have met at its geometric center to form a splay resembling the rays of the sun, positioned just half a meter west of the aperture that admitted sunlight (fig. 106). Apart from the symbolism, this construction served to separate the eastern third of the Mithraeum from the rest in a manner familiar from other sanctuaries of this type. It was in the eastern portion – the "holy of holies," as it were – that the cult's leaders performed its most sacred and esoteric rites.

The location of the cult center in an easily concealed artificial grotto and facilities to achieve theatrical effects with light and darkness remind us that Mithraism was among the so-called oriental mystery religions that swept through the

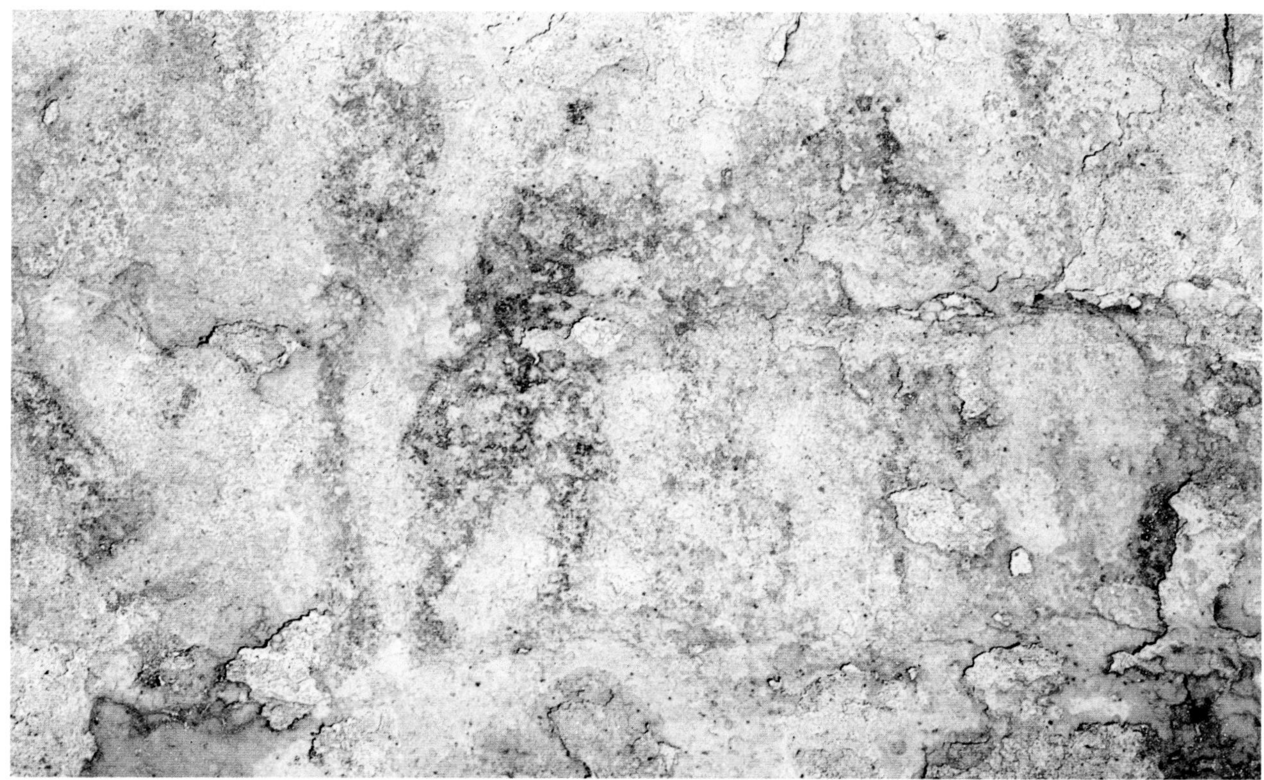

Roman Empire in the first three centuries C.E. Typically the cults kept their doctrines secret, sharing them only with those who had passed through a period of indoctrination and an initiation ritual that bore some resemblance to Christian catechism and baptism. In sharp contrast with the Christian communities, Mithraists and the adherents to other mystery religions kept no sacred books recording their beliefs. Like the Christians, however, they did express themselves in art. The walls of Mithraea were covered with paintings and relief sculpture expressing the most cherished doctrines of the faith.

Figure 107.
Fresco, badly preserved, on the south wall near the eastern end of the Mithraeum. Between two stylized trees that serve as panel dividers, two human figures, each 43 cm high, face each other above a rectangular object that is probably an altar. The figure on the left may be Mithras himself shaking hands with the figure on the right, perhaps Sol (the sun). JECM photo.

This was also the case at Caesarea. The fragments of blue plaster JECM found on the *intrados* of the vault indicate that it was painted to represent the vault of heaven. It may have had stars also, as in other Mithraea. The "unconquered sun" would break in through a darkened sky. Toward the front, on the walls of the holy of holies, there were paintings representing episodes in the career of Mithras and stages in the Mithraic life, including converts passing through the initiation ritual. Only three scenes survive, badly preserved, on the south wall of the Mithraeum near its eastern end (fig. 107). Before they could photograph, the team had to use a mist of

Figure 108.
The Caesarea Mithraic medallion, found in the Mithraeum in 1973, between the bench along the eastern wall and the altar. It is a marble disk, 7.5 cm in diameter and 1 cm thick. Its reverse side was left roughly dressed, while on its face Mithraic scenes are carved: in the upper register, Mithras slaying the bull (the tauroctone*), and in the lower (l-r) Sol kneeling before Mithras, Mithras and Sol banqueting, and Mithras riding the bull. This medallion may originally have been installed on the western face of the low masronry wall that divided the eastern bench (cf. fig. 106). IDAM collection, displayed in the Israel Museum.*
JECM photo.

alcohol and water to dissolve the layer of crystalized salt that was partly obscuring the paint. A painting of Mithras *tauroctone*, "slaying the bull," that, to judge from parallel examples, once occupied the eastern wall, has disappeared completely.

An object from the Caesarea Mithraeum preserves the iconography of the lost eastern-wall painting. During an excavation between the divider of the eastern bench and the altar, the team found a Mithraic medallion, carved in white marble and only 7.5 centimeters in diameter and 1.0 centimeter thick. Despite its small size, the object repeats some of the scenes that once decorated the Mithraeum walls (fig. 108). Mithras *tauroctone*, with his cape flying behind him, dominates the scene, like the cross or crucifix over the altar in a Christian church. By drawing back the bull's muzzle, thrusting his left knee into its flank, and pinning with his right foot the shank of its right rear leg, the god immobilizes the powerful creature and in the same movement thrusts a dagger into its heart. A snake rises to the wound to lick the bull's blood, and a scorpion – the rounded object beneath the point where the belly meets the flank – attacks its testicles. Above this scene to the left and right are the usual busts of Sol, the sun, and Luna, the moon. To the right and left of the *tauroctone* stand the traditional figures of Cautes and Cautopates, with their torches elevated and lowered, respectively.

In the lower register, separated by a ground line from the bull-slaying scene, are images of three episodes from the career of Mithras (from left to right): Sol kneeling before Mithras, Sol and Mithras banqueting together, and Mithras, with his cape extended behind him, riding the bull toward a recumbent figure, perhaps to be identified with Saturn or Ocean, two mythical beings of unknown significance in Mithraism. The carving here is especially crude, leaving the figures indistinct; to have had any meaning to the ancient viewer, they must have been painted. How worshippers could have seen an object so small in a setting as large and dark as the Mithraeum is perplexing. The medallion may have been used in the ritual. What is obvious is that the Mithraeum is keeping some of its secrets.

At some time during the second century C.E., a large building went up above vault 1 and the vaults that neighbored it to the south. The building was U-shaped, with two wings extending westward toward the sea. The northern wing lay just above vault 1 and the Mithraeum. Only parts of the building's foundations and traces of its deluxe marble flooring remain, but enough so that its former elegance is apparent. This and its large scale – its outside dimensions were 20.9 meters north–south and at least 19.0 meters east–west – indicate that it was a public building. Furthermore, within its ruins, or nearby, five Latin inscriptions from the second and third centuries were found that honor either Roman emperors or their officials. These discoveries led the JECM archaeologists to identify the U-shaped building as an honorific portico, an open public building in which portraits and inscriptions were displayed to honor officials.

It is not surprising that at Caesarea a Mithraeum and an honorific portico occupied the same neighborhood. The cult of Mithras, despite its secrecy, became an establishment religion, one of Caesarea's accepted cults, early in the city's history. Some of the Roman officials honored in the inscriptions above vault 1 no doubt ranked honorably among the Mithraic cultists who worshipped below. Because Mithraism appealed to such men, it worked its way easily into the fabric of urban society throughout the Roman Empire. The Persian god, made a citizen of Caesarea and of Rome, blazed a trail that Christ would soon follow.

We have seen that the people of Caesarea adopted traditional Graeco-Roman cults, like those of Artemis, Apollo, and Demeter, and also accepted the Romanized "oriental" ones of Jupiter Dolichenus, Isis, Serapis, and Mithras. In doing so Caesarea added a religious dimension to the process of Romanization that had begun when Herod founded the city. Her cults, like the ones in any Romanized city, exhibited a variety of potent, exotic, and colorful gods and goddesses that were worshipped with theatrical rituals and engaging entertainment in the theater, amphitheater, and circus. Caesarea's gaudy, richly bedecked religious face had the power to entice elements in the population that were insufficiently Romanized, and to transmit to them the majority religious culture. That is why Caesarea so offended and frightened the rabbis, and why they thought of her as "the daughter of Edom."

CHAPTER 5

The Advent of Christianity: Caesarea in the Byzantine Period

A man's dreams can get away from him. King Herod had founded a Greek- or Roman-style city, with protecting gods and goddesses of the traditional pagan type. He could not have foreseen that his city would reach the pinnacle of its prosperity and fame centuries later, in the fourth, fifth, and sixth centuries C.E., under the aegis of a new religion whose founder was born "in the days of Herod the King" (Matthew 2:1).

Figure 109. The Byzantine bath complex in Caesarea's northeastern suburbs, view toward the northwest of the frigidarium, *with the building housing the* caldaria *and* tepidarium *behind it. In the distance, the high-level aqueduct is visible, from which a ceramic pipe brought water to the bath.* JECM photo.

Jesus came from Nazareth, a small agricultural town, and his ministry hardly extended beyond the rural villages that fringed the Sea of Galilee. The new religion might have remained one of the minor sects within Judaism, had not the Apostle Paul redirected its mission toward non-Jews and made its message universal. Paul worked in the urban centers of the Eastern Roman Empire, and it was in the cities that the new religion first began to attract large numbers of converts. There was a good reason for this. In places like Antioch and the cities of Asia Minor that Paul visited, Gentiles seeking a compelling religious experience had already come into contact with vibrant Jewish communities. Attracted by the Jewish sense of community and the lofty theology and moral principles of Judaism, but unwilling to take on Judaism's dietary laws, circumcision, and other rigorous customs, these Gentiles flocked in large numbers to the fledgling church. It was the cities that transmitted the religious culture of Christianity.

For Paul's message, Caesarea was just the right place – a Gentile city with many Jews. Its proximity to Jerusalem, home of the first Christian church, meant that Caesarea learned of Jesus sooner than other cities, even before Paul began his work.

Indeed, the appearance of Christianity there dates back to the decade after the Crucifixion, which occurred in about 30 C.E.

The First Three Centuries

Despite years of investigation, archaeologists have not discovered any Christian artifacts or other physical traces of primitive Christianity at Caesarea. The situation is the same at other Christian sites. The reason is that the material culture of the earliest Christians did not differ from that of other inhabitants of Herodian and early Roman cities in ancient Palestine. For information about Caesarea's first Christians, researchers have to rely on precious literary evidence found in the New Testament book, Acts of the Apostles.

The Acts of the Apostles tells of Philip the Evangelist, a deacon in the Jerusalem church, who preached the Christian message in Samaria, north of Jerusalem, and in the towns near the Mediterranean coast, until he finally reached Caesarea (Acts 8:4–40). Philip must have recognized the opportunities that the city offered, for he stayed there and became the leader of the Christian community. About twenty years later, in 58 C.E., Saint Paul lodged with Philip at Caesarea; by that time Philip had fathered four daughters, each gifted with prophecy. When Paul resumed his journey to Jerusalem, members of the Caesarea community accompanied him, including a man named Mnason of Cyprus who had a house in Jerusalem where the apostle would stay (Acts 21:8–16).

The first recorded Christians of Caesarea – Philip, his daughters, Mnason of Cyprus, and the rest – were Jews, but Acts also relates how the city's Gentiles adopted the new faith. It describes the conversion of Cornelius, a man who typified many in Caesarea's growing first-century population: people who were not natives but had arrived from abroad to work in the bustling seaport Sebastos or with the imperial administration. Cornelius was an army man. His rank was centurion, a noncommissioned officer in the Roman forces. He served with the Italian cohort, one of the units stationed in Caesarea under the governor's command. Cornelius most likely received his posting to Caesarea before Pontius Pilate left Judaea in 36, and the events that Acts describes certainly occurred within the next few years.

According to Acts (10:2–3) Cornelius was "a religious man, and he and his whole family joined in the worship of God." The centurion, his family, and at least one of the soldiers under his orders (10:7) had no doubt learned of the Jewish God from the Jews of Caesarea. Cornelius offered prayers to this God several times a day. Because of his prayers and his charity to Caesarea's Jews, an angel came in a vision to

Cornelius, urging him to send for Saint Peter. Peter, the head of the Christian community in Jerusalem, was preaching at the time among the Jews in the coastal city of Joppa (modern Jaffa), not far south of Caesarea. Miraculously, a vision came to Peter as the messengers of Cornelius were approaching:

*He saw a rift in the sky, and a thing coming down that looked like a great sail-cloth. It was slung by the four corners, and was being lowered to the ground. In it he saw creatures of every kind, whatever walks or crawls or flies. Then there was a voice which said to him, "Up, Peter, kill and eat." But Peter said, "No, Lord, no: I have never eaten anything profane or unclean." The voice came again a second time: "It is not for you to call profane what God counts clean." This happened three times; and then the thing was taken up again into the sky.**

*Quoted from *The New English Bible with the Apocrypha* (New York: Oxford University Press, 1970), pp. 160–61.

Peter puzzled about the meaning of this vision until the messengers arrived. It then became clear that God required him, a pious Jew who observed all the dietary laws and did not eat or socialize with Gentiles, to bring news of Jesus to Cornelius and his household. They were the "creatures of every kind" in the vision. Peter returned with the messengers to Caesarea, stayed for some time in the house of Cornelius, and preached to the centurion, his family, and friends. The Holy Spirit came upon the Gentiles, and they spoke in tongues. Cornelius and many in his household received baptism (Acts 10:3–48).

The Cornelius episode illustrates Caesarea's importance as a seedbed of primitive Christianity. The crowded, alien, and intense social universe of the city definitely encouraged conversion. Caesarea had made Cornelius lonely, like any man who lived far from his native city and the familiar gods and goddesses of his childhood. It had also brought him into daily contact with new social groups and devotions that might fill the empty places in his life, especially with the Jews. Cornelius discovered that the Jews had a sense of community and a sturdy faith, but many of their laws were barriers against his conversion. Then a miracle occurred. Men came to Caesarea who were indeed Jews but who seemed willing to eat with Gentiles and to admit them to the full fellowship of their faith. The development seemed equally "miraculous" to Peter's companions:

The believers who had come with Peter, men of Jewish birth, were astonished that the gift of the Holy Spirit should have been poured out even on Gentiles. (Acts 10:45)

There was reason for their astonishment. If the events in his house changed Cornelius' life, they proved equally momentous in the life of the young church. It was apparently at Caesarea, even before Saint Paul began his career, that Christianity became universal.

Caesarea had other roles to play in the history of the primitive Christian church. The provincial governor, Felix, kept Saint Paul there for two years under house arrest (58–59), until the next governor, Festus, tried him and sent him on appeal to Rome (p. 111). With its busy port and ready access to sea routes, the city offered Paul, although an unwilling guest, the ancient equivalent of air-mail communication with the churches he had established in Asia Minor, Macedonia, and Greece. Certainly he wrote letters to them from Caesarea, and some of them may be among the epistles that survive (e.g., Philippians). According to a later tradition, Philip's daughters transmitted accurate knowledge of the early days – perhaps some of the material in the Acts of the Apostles – and modern scholars even suspect that the accounts of Jesus' life in the Gospels took shape in part at Caesarea.

After Saint Paul and the Acts of the Apostles, nothing is known of the Christians of Caesarea from either literary sources or archaeology for a century and a half. This is not surprising. At least the Jewish part of the Caesarea community must have suffered heavily in the massacre that preceded the outbreak of war in 66, when, according to Josephus, twenty thousand Caesarean Jews lost their lives. In any case, from the end of the first century to the first decades of the third, Christianity remained a small sect competing against other religions for converts. It achieved only modest success – less, perhaps, than the religions of Mithras, Jupiter Dolichenus, Artemis of Ephesus, Zeus Serapis, and Isis, all attested at Caesarea during this period. Then, early in the third century, the number of Christians in the Roman Empire began to grow dramatically, and soon the towering genius of Origen brought Caesarea's Christians once again onto history's stage.

Origen was born in Alexandria, the metropolis of Egypt. He embraced the ideal of Christian asceticism with such fervor that he performed self-castration, an act of dubious appropriateness in the church's eyes. He devoted himself to scholarship with even greater intensity. As a teacher and author, Origen undertook to interpret Christian scriptures and doctrine in terms of Platonism, the dominant philosophy of the ancient world. His fame and independence of mind led him into conflict with his ecclesiastical superior, the bishop of Alexandria, but also brought him an invitation to take up residence in Caesarea, which he accepted in 231.

In the two decades that followed, Origen turned Caesarea into a university town. The city already had a reputation for its "sophists," teachers of rhetoric and

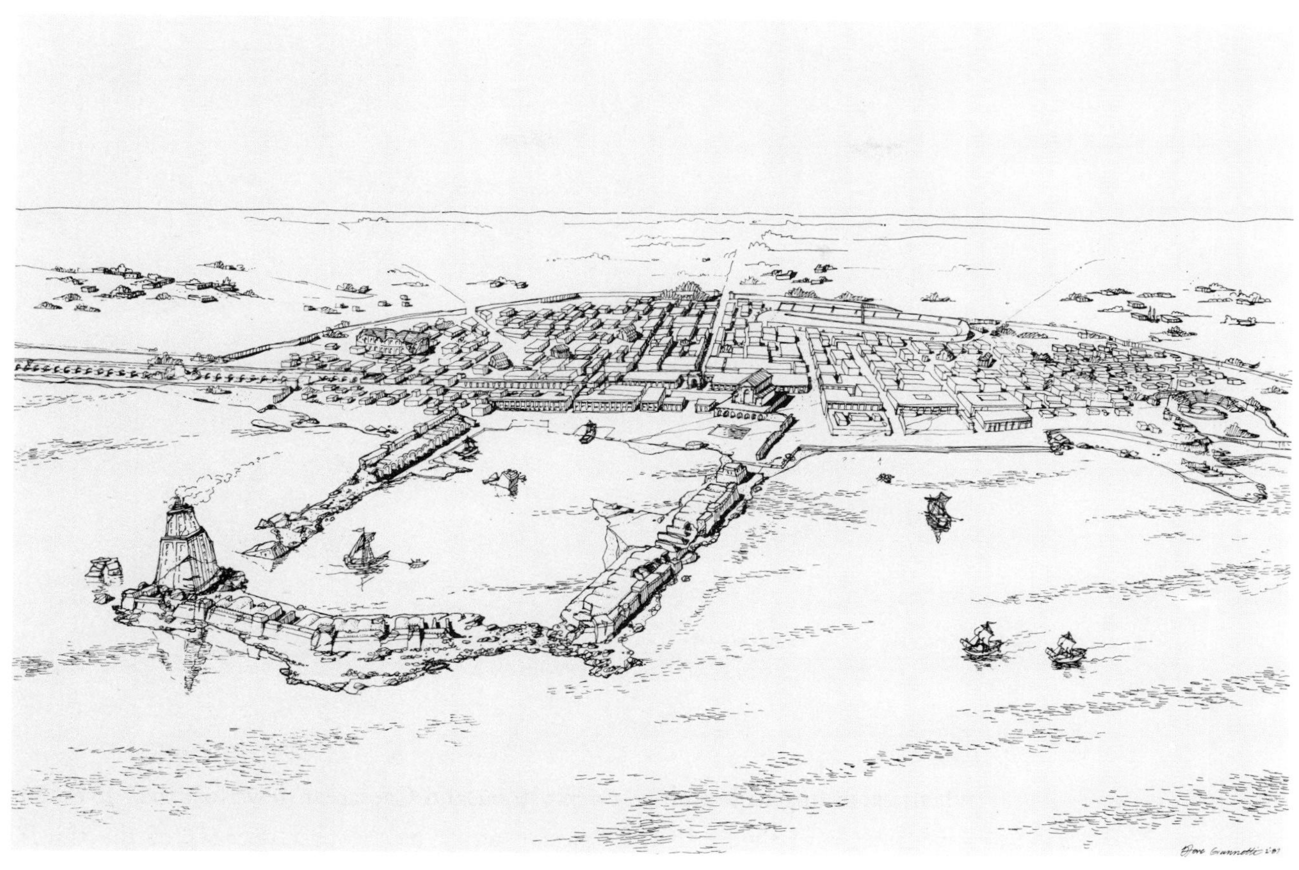

the pagan classics who could equip a young man with the kind of learning he needed to be a success in urban society. Origen added Christian learning and advanced research. He wrote a number of his theological and apologetic works at Caesarea, and there he completed the Hexapla, an immense critical edition of the Old Testament with the text arranged in six parallel columns: Hebrew, Hebrew in Greek letters, and four different translations into Greek. Because a work of such size could not circulate widely, serious Bible scholars had to come to Caesarea to use it. Origen attracted many pupils, some of whom became prominent theologians in the Eastern Roman Empire.

Figure 110. Byzantine Caesarea about 550 C.E., hypothetical perspective view looking east. Stephen Giannetti drawing.

In 250–51 the Roman emperor Decius ordered the persecution of Christians throughout the empire, including Palestine. Origen was arrested, imprisoned, and tortured on the rack. His tormenters hoped to force him to abjure Christianity by sacrificing to pagan gods. Origen survived the ordeal with his faith intact, but died a few years later as a result of his injuries. He left as a legacy to his adopted city the

Figure 111. Internal face of Caesarea's Byzantine wall, exposed in 1974 in JECM's area H.1 just east of the hippodrome. View toward the east. George Whipple photo.

rich library of pagan and Christian books that he had assembled while writing his own works. Caesarea's library later reached an estimated size of thirty thousand volumes.

The emperor and his men attacked Christians again in the Great Persecution of 303–13. In Caesarea many died as martyrs ("witnesses") for their faith. The toll was especially heavy in the capital of Palestine because the Roman governor had his headquarters there, and he was the official charged with enforcing imperial decrees against Christians. Hence Christians taken into custody elsewhere were delivered to Caesarea in chains to be tried in the governor's court. Procopius, for example, the first Christian of Palestine to die in this persecution, was arrested in Scythopolis (Beth Shean), where he had held the minor clerical positions of reader and exorcist for the Christian community. If the accused refused to sacrifice on pagan altars, they were beheaded, burned, cast into the sea, thrown to bears in the amphitheater, or, in the case of women, delivered to the brothel keepers. Of course, the authorities hoped to avoid making additional martyrs, so they ordered the torturers to ply their craft energetically, to persuade victims to perform the necessary sacrifices to pagan gods or the emperor. Those who refused and suffered death also included the priest Pamphilus. A native of Caesarea, this man had devoted his family's great wealth to putting in order and expanding Origen's library. Pamphilus had also used the library, along with his own learning and personal magnetism, to educate another generation of pupils in the Christian school of Caesarea.

Among the pupils of Pamphilus none achieved greater fame than Eusebius. A native of Caesarea and a scholar by temperament, Eusebius found happiness in his native city among the books of Origen and Pamphilus. Before the turn of the third century, he had written his *Ecclesiastical History*, the first history of the Christian church, explaining the inexorable advance of Christianity from apostolic times to the eve of victory in his own day. In 311, when the Great Persecution was near an end, he wrote *On the Martyrs of Palestine*, an eyewitness account of the suffering in Caesarea, and over the following three decades he brought the *History* and the *Martyrs* up-to-date and wrote other books that ranked him among the foremost apologists and theorists of the early church.

In the *Martyrs*, amid lurid accounts of suffering and martyrdoms, Eusebius included a few brief vignettes, derived from his own experience, of life in early fourth-century Caesarea. People still crowded the city's marketplace and bath-houses, as in other eastern cities, to shop, cleanse their bodies, and to mingle and catch up on the latest gossip. Unmarried women for the most part kept modestly to their homes, as was traditional in Greek and Near Eastern society – although they would emerge for a spectacle, like the corpse of a martyr washed up on the shore. In his palace the governor of all of Palestine, now entitled *praeses* ("president"), sat on his tribunal, surrounded by bodyguards and attendants, hearing lawsuits or trying criminals. Obviously the big man in the city, he could order his officers (centurions and tribunes) to canvass the neighborhoods and rouse people to assemble at the pagan temples and perform sacrifice. Apparently most did so willingly. During pagan religious festivals the governor presided over chariot races in the circus, witty and licentious performances in the theater, and beast combats in the amphitheater that had, in starring roles, bears, leopards, and condemned Christians. Caesarea's citizens flocked to performances and applauded enthusiastically. Generally Eusebius presents a flourishing Roman provincial capital that was not much different from what it had been a century or two earlier. Despite growing numbers and impressive intellectual, moral, and religious achievements, the Christians still occupied the fringes of urban society.

From Rome to Byzantium

In his writings Eusebius made it clear that he expected sudden, miraculous change, and he was not disappointed. Far from his own city, on October 26, 312, the warrior-emperor Constantine defeated his rival Maxentius at the Milvian bridge just north of Rome, thus winning a civil war. Convinced that the Christian God had contributed to his victory, Constantine began immediately to patronize the Christians, brought persecution to an end, and in time made Christianity his own religion. Expediency as well as conviction induced many in high society to embrace the new faith, and within a century Christianity had become the official religion of the empire. In 324, meanwhile, Constantine had founded a new capital on the Bosporus, Constantinople, on the site of the ancient city Byzantium. Over the next decades Constantinople emerged as the New Rome, an eastern capital for the empire to complement the old one on the Tiber. Eusebius and his city also played a role in these dramatic developments. It was the Christian scholar of Caesarea who contributed most to the ideological side of the new Christian empire. Immensely heartened by the phenomenon of a Christian emperor, Eusebius argued that God had appointed Constantine to rule over the earth, just as he had engendered Christ to reign in heaven. Thus we can say that in Caesarea as well as in Constantinople the world of Byzantium was born.

From *Byzantium* historians and archaeologists give the name "Byzantine" to the Christianized Roman Empire with its capital in the East. They refer to the era

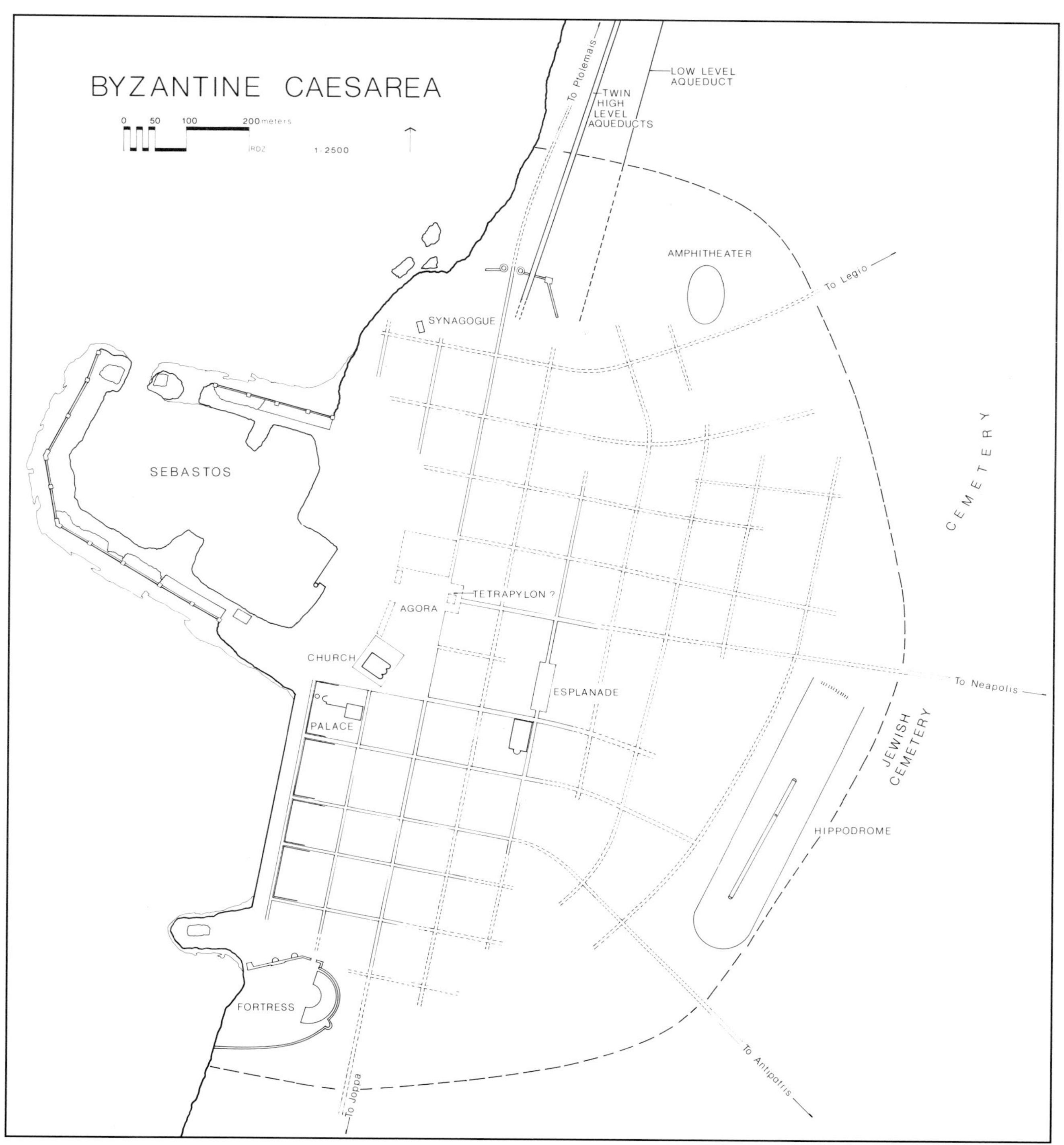

Figure 112.
Urban plan of Byzantine Caesarea about 550 C.E., based on archaeology and literary sources.
Robin Ziek drawing.

from roughly 324 to 640 C.E. as the Byzantine period and classify objects dating to it as Byzantine. But "Byzantine" is misleading. It suggests that the period from 324 to 640 differed essentially from the preceding centuries. It evokes the conventional notion that this entire era was one of cultural impoverishment, religious intolerance, declining city life, and the collapse of frontier defenses before the onslaught of foreign barbarians – developments that brought a precipitous end to ancient Mediterranean civilization.

This conventional wisdom goes back to the British historian Edward Gibbon (d. 1794), who blamed Christianity – its intolerance and otherworldliness, specifically – for Rome's decline and fall. The assessment has received reinforcement in the twentieth century. The noted Russian historian of antiquity, Michael Ivanovich Rostovtzeff (d. 1952), argued that a many-faceted crisis in the third century struck a blow to ancient civilization from which it never recovered.

It is an analysis, however, that fails on several counts. In the first place, Byzantine culture had a large Roman component. In fact the Byzantines called themselves Romans (*Rhomaioi* in medieval Greek) until the fall of Constantinople to the Turks in 1453. Second, Christianity, born in the world of antiquity, was just as much an ancient religion as Judaism, Mithraism, or the worship of Artemis of Ephesus. Above all, the Mediterranean world was still a world of cities in the fourth, fifth, and sixth centuries. If we accept the conventional wisdom of Gibbon and Rostovtzeff, and add to it the notion of Aristotle and Lewis Mumford that cities are the principal creators and transmitters of culture, we should find, *ipso facto*, that urbanism in the Roman Empire declined rapidly as Christianity became the dominant religion. While some cities did contract in size and prosperity, especially in Italy and the West, the material remains of cities in the eastern part of the Roman Empire present a contradictory picture. From excavations we know that most cities in Asia Minor, Syria, Palestine, Egypt, and even Arabia reached the height of prosperity just when the conventional wisdom would have predicted decline. A part of the Roman world was rising when it should have been falling. Moreover, despite significant changes, by and large these cities preserved the style of urbanism and the culture they had inherited from the classical Greek and Roman past.

This was definitely the case at Caesarea. In fact, one of the most important results of archaeological research there is the discovery that the city flourished during the Byzantine period as never before. Part of the evidence is a new city wall, first discovered by aerial photography (figs. 1, 52) and then explored by archaeologists from both the Italian Mission and JECM. The wall would not have been much of an obstacle to attackers because its builders did not expend much time or money

on its construction. It was only 2.5 meters thick, of mortared rubble faced with local stones about 0.90-meter long and 0.55-meter high (fig. 111). It had both round and square towers and monumental gates, one of which Israeli archaeologists from IDAM excavated in the winter of 1986 inside Kibbutz Sdot Yam. What is remarkable is the amount of urban space within the wall. It extended in a semicircle 2,500 meters long from sea to sea, enclosing an area far larger than the projected Herodian fortifications (fig. 112; cf. fig. 50). As for the new wall's date, the Mission proposed the Byzantine period in general, based on ceramic evidence, while JECM tentatively specified the fourth or fifth century, based on pottery from their trenches H.1–3, dug between the back wall of the circus and the Byzantine wall.

Figure 113.
Wall and semicircular tower of Caesarea's kastron, *a fortress built in the sixth century in the city's southwestern quarter. The fortress incorporated the Herodian-Roman theater's outer* cavea *walls on its eastern flank. Excavated by the Italian Mission in the early 1960s. Looking southeast.*
Aaron Levin photo.

Despite its modest defensive capability and mediocre construction, this wall proves that Caesarea's population had grown substantially since the Roman period. If it had not, there would have been no need to enclose such a large area within the fortifications. On the other hand, the existence of the wall confirms the view that in the fourth, fifth, and sixth centuries the threat of foreign attack and of violence inspired by religion recommended that the authorities refortify the city. Similarly, after the Roman theater had fallen to ruin, its outer *cavea* walls were integrated into the defenses of the *kastron*, a fortress built in the sixth century within the line of the Byzantine fortifications (figs. 51, 112). The impressive battlements of the *kastron* (fig. 113) most likely protected the provincial governor and his men from a citizen body that was disorderly and prone to violence.

Figure 114.
Bag-shaped amphora of a type common at Caesarea, used in homes and shops for liquid and dry commodities. This example dates to the fifth or sixth century C.E. Height 44.0 cm. Found at Akko. Now in the Museum of Ancient Art, Haifa.
Aaron Levin photo.

Figure 115.
Byzantine cook pot, common kitchenware at Caesarea in the sixth or earlier seventh century C.E. Height 21.4 cm. Found by JECM in area C.21. IDAM collection, at DIAR.
Aaron Levin photo.

Figure 116.
Dish or shallow bowl, fine tableware of a type common at Caesarea during the Byzantine period. Diameter 25.2 cm. It belongs to the general category known as late Roman fineware, which developed from the popular red-slipped wares of the Hellenistic and Roman periods (cf. fig. 45). This bowl, which has a dolphin stamped in the center and traces of black slip on the rim, is form 3 of the tableware called Late Roman C, manufactured in the fifth and sixth centuries. From an unknown site within the area of ancient Palestine, now in the Museum of Ancient Art, Haifa.
Aaron Levin photo.

Figure 117. *Ceramic oil lamps from the Byzantine period, all typical of Caesarea. At the lower left and center are the so-called candlestick lamps of the fifth and sixth centuries, 10.8 and 10.1 cm long respectively, the example at lower center with a molded inscription in debased Greek: "The light of Christ shines beautifully for all." The lamp at the upper center, 12.0 cm long, was made in Africa in the fourth or early fifth century and has a red slip and a lion on its upper body. The lamp at the right, 14.7 cm in length, dates from the sixth or earlier seventh century and has a bearded head on its discus. Provenance of the last example JECM's area C.21, of the other three unknown but in the area of ancient Palestine. Lamp at right IDAM collection, at DIAR, others DIAR collection.*
Aaron Levin photo.

Figure 118. *Glass vessels typical of Byzantine Caesarea. Left: stemmed goblet used for wine or as a lamp, height 8.6 cm, unknown provenance, now in the Israel Museum. Center: double cosmetic tube, 19.9 cm high (with handle), found in Israel in a tomb, now in the IDAM collection. Right: rounded jar with short neck, 9.0 cm high, found in Israel in a tomb, now in the IDAM collection.*
David Harris photo, Israel Museum.

Figure 119. Bronze coin of the Emperor Constantius II, who reigned 337–361. Diameter 2.1 cm. Found in JECM area C.36. The obverse (pictured here) shows the emperor facing left, wearing the diadem and paludamentum *(military cloak), and holding a globe in his right hand. The legend reads D(ominus) N(oster) CONSTANTIVS P(ius) F(elix) AVG(ustus) and means "Our lord Constantius, faithful and fortunate Augustus." IDAM collection, at DIAR.*
Aaron Levin photo.

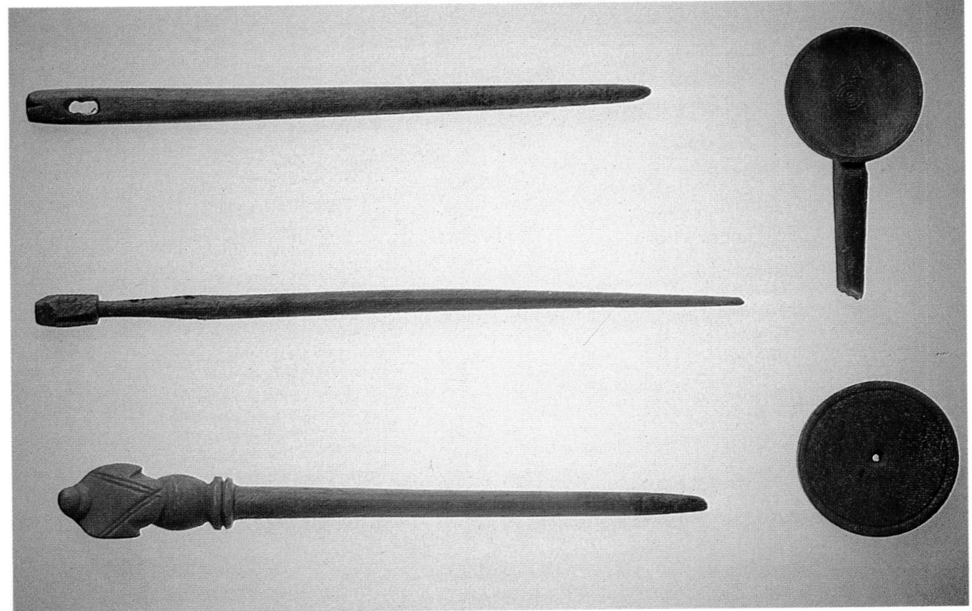

Figure 120. Group of bone objects found by JECM in areas A.1, A.3, and G.4: two hairpins, a cosmetic spoon, a sewing needle, and a disk, perhaps used to decorate furniture. Length of the cosmetic spoon 4.3 cm. These objects are typical bone instrumenta domestica *found at Caesarea, from either the Roman or the Byzantine period. IDAM collection.*
Aaron Levin photo.

There is other evidence for an increasing population. Even the casual visitor to Caesarea is struck by the vast numbers of potsherds that seem to blossom from the soil everywhere. Although the statistical study of Caesarea pottery is in its infancy, it appears that the bulk of the sherds date from the Byzantine period, with two or three types of amphora prevailing: common bag-shaped amphoras, storage jars used in homes and shops for storing liquid and dry commodities (fig. 114), and what are sometimes called Gaza amphoras (fig. 138). The latter are cigar-shaped vessels in which the wines produced in the region of Gaza were shipped all over the Mediterranean world in the fourth, fifth, and sixth centuries. The frequency of sherds from these vessels suggests not only a dense population within the city during Byzantine times, but lively commercial and industrial activity as well. Also commonly found both on the surface and in excavations are sherds of Byzantine cooking pots, tableware, glass vessels, and oil lamps, and coins from the period (figs. 115–19). In short, the site's material culture can be dated overwhelmingly to the period from the fourth century to the early seventh.

The same is true of building remains. Every archaeological team that has excavated at Caesarea has encountered, in every part of the site, the ruins of Byzantine domestic, commercial, and industrial structures. Usually the ruins are foundations and two or three courses of wall built of rectangular ashlars of the local *kurkar* sandstone. Sometimes the mortar that held the wall together still exists, and

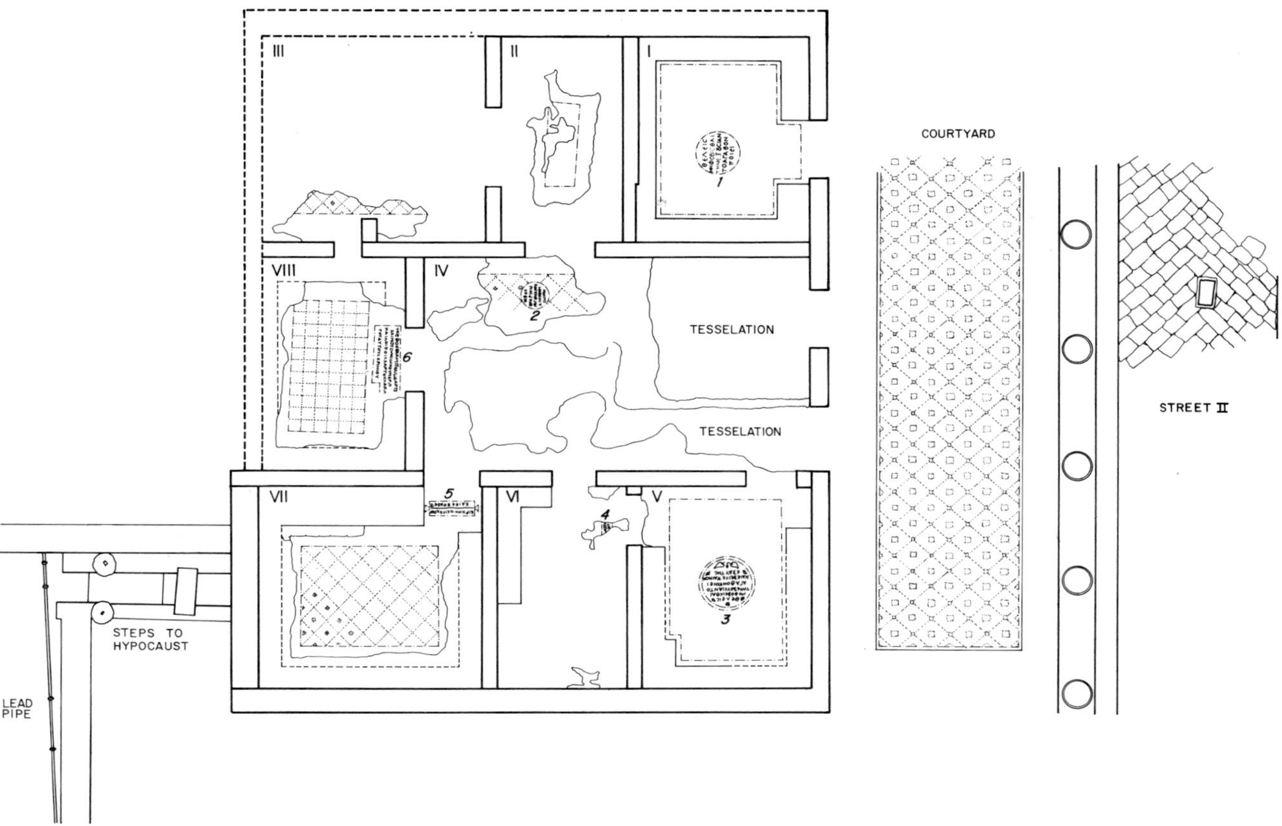

Figure 121.
The archives building discovered by JECM in field C. Its seven rooms opened onto an entrance court, accessible from one of Caesarea's colonnaded streets. Among the inscriptions in its mosaic floors, one (number 6 in the drawing) identifies the building as the office where the provincial governor's tax department kept its records, while another (numbers 1 and 3, cf. fig. 122) cautioned the city's inhabitants to obey the governor.
Tom Wilkinson drawing, courtesy of JECM.

traces of plaster adhere to the vertical faces. Often, plastered floors and mosaic pavements survive, the latter either plain or decorated with simple geometric patterns. Occasionally the plan of a building is evident. In area G.5, for example, to the north of the Crusader fortifications, JECM excavated part of the peristyle of a Byzantine house dating to the fifth century, including the stylobate (the foundation for a colonnade) and a mosaic pavement. In the west-central sector of the Crusader city, close to the sea, the Hebrew University team headed by Netzer and Levine uncovered part of a large Byzantine building with several wings, at least 38 by 40 meters in size, with cisterns in the basement and at least one story above the ground floor. The excavators identified it as a public building, the residence of a merchant or official, or a warehouse. In JECM's field C, just to the south of the Crusader fortifications, a Byzantine stratum extended over all of the thirty-six areas the team excavated. The best-preserved structure in field C is the so-called archives building (fig. 121). Consisting of seven rooms arrayed around a central court, it was the office where accountants of the imperial governor's tax department kept their records. Two

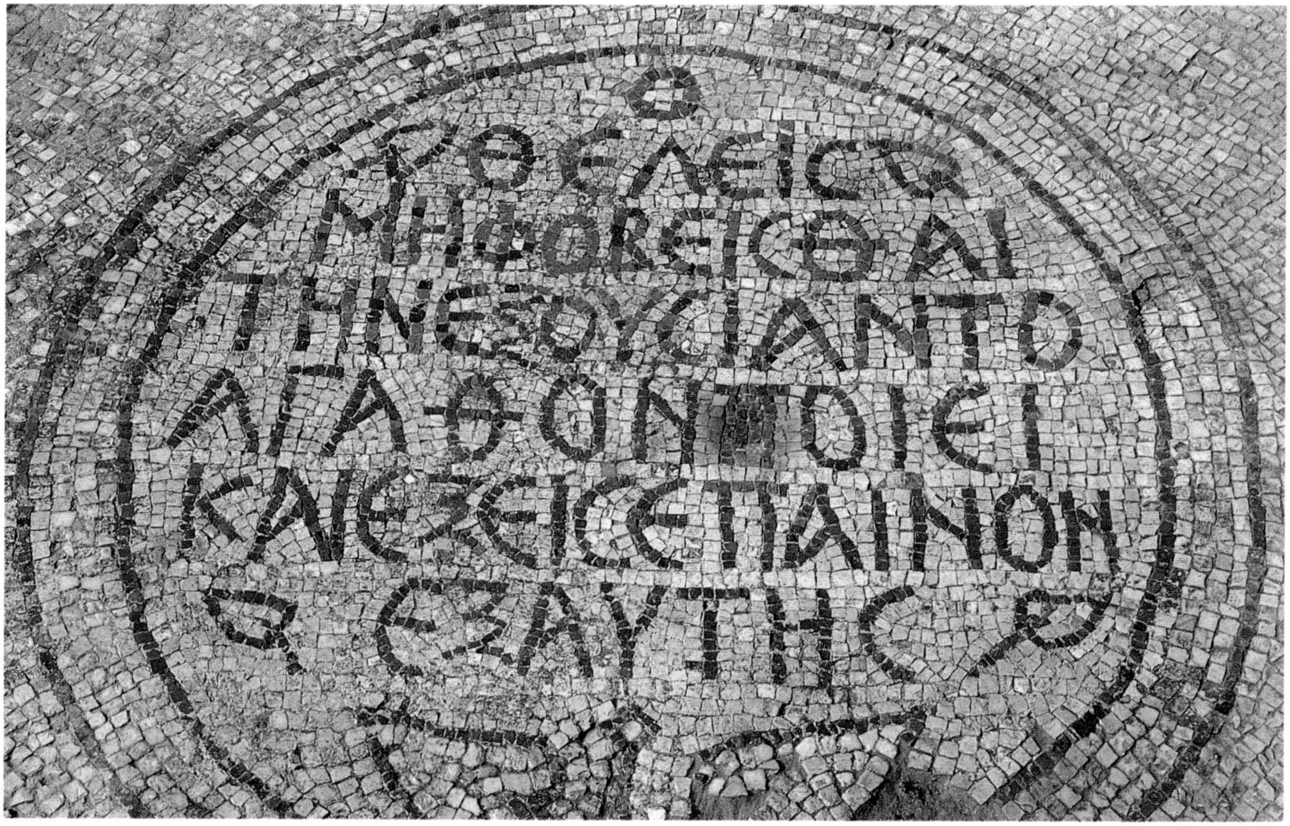

Figure 122.
Personification of Spring, fragment of a mosaic pavement found by JECM in C.25, now mounted on a panel 0.7-m high and 1.48 m wide. Spring is depicted as a beautiful winged woman holding a basket of flowers (to her left). The elaborate border with double guilloche (interlaced bands) is also preserved. The same pavement, perhaps on the floor of a dining or reception room, would have contained images of all four seasons (cf. fig. 124). Collection of IDAM.
David Harris photo, Israel Museum.

Figure 123.
Inscription set into the mosaic pavement of one of the rooms in the Archives building (number 3 in fig. 121). The Greek text is from St. Paul's Letter to the Romans (13:3): "If you would not fear the authority [i.e. the governor], do good and you will receive praise from it."
Paul Saivetz photo.

Figure 124.
Personification of Winter, fragment of the same mosaic pavement as fig. 122, mounted on a panel 74.5 cm. high and 81.0 cm wide. The winged woman who represents the season holds a plant stalk in her right arm. Collection of IDAM.
David Harris photo, Israel Museum.

inscriptions set into the mosaic pavements of this building (fig. 123) reminded those who entered it of their duty to the government by quoting Christian scripture: "If you would not fear the authority, do good and you will receive praise from it" (Romans 13:3).

Also in field C, not far from the archives building, JECM archaeologists discovered fragments of an exceptionally beautiful mosaic pavement created in the fifth or sixth century. What survives is part of its border and the personifications of two of the four seasons of the year, spring and winter (figs. 122 and 124). An outstanding work of art, the pavement decorated the floor of what must have been a lavishly appointed dining or reception room belonging to one of the richest men in Caesarea. The proximity of the archives building suggests that the room may have been in one of the governor's palaces.

Another indication that the population of Byzantine Caesarea increased is that the city both maintained and expanded its water-supply system. Along the existing

Figure 125. Vaulted low-level aqueduct that brought water from a dam and reservoir north of Caesarea, constructed in the fourth or early fifth century. In the background, the twin high-level aqueduct. View looking north. Aaron Levin photo.

Figure 126.
Stone-built dam on the Crocodile River (Nahal Tanninim) north of Caesarea. Although not dated archaeologically, the construction of this structure can reasonably be associated with the low-level aqueduct (fig. 125) built in the fourth or early fifth century. The aqueduct received its water from the reservoir created by this dam and another farther to the north (fig. 42). View looking south.
John Oleson photo.

aqueduct line, the settling of bridge piers into sand or soft marshland threatened the flow of water and had to be countered with buttressing (fig. 85) and siphoning pipes. A literary source reports that work of this type was still going on in the sixth century. In addition, either the authorities or private benefactors financed the construction of a new aqueduct line, the so-called low-level aqueduct. Covered by a masonry vault, this channel had a capacity more than six times that of the two high-level channels Herod and Hadrian had built (fig. 125). The new aqueduct brought water from a stone dam on the Crocodile River (Nahal Tanninim) 5.0 kilometers north of the city (fig. 126). This dam and a second one 1.6 kilometers farther north (fig. 42) raised the water level high enough to supply Caesarea and formed a reservoir 496 hectares in area in the low-lying ground to the northeast of the city (dubbed "Lake Caesarea" by the archaeologists). The JECM team extracted ceramic evidence from beneath the low-level aqueduct that dates it to the fourth or early fifth century C.E. Even if some of its capacity was for irrigation and industry

Figure 127. The mill area at the Dam on the Crocodile River north of Caesarea. The stream of water coming through the millrace (channel from upper left to lower right) drove an undershot wheel supported on stone pillars on either side of the race. The pillars also supported the gearing that drove the mills.
Vytenis Gureckas drawing, courtesy of CAHEP.

rather than for the city's fountains and private water lines, its existence in the Byzantine period demonstrates increased water needs for a growing population.

Byzantine engineers knew how to exploit the water behind the dam for industrial purposes. Just south of the dam, several channels and an area for machinery cut into the rock testify to the existence of ancient mills that would have ground flour for the inhabitants of Caesarea. The surviving machine area sits astride a sluice channel, or millrace (fig. 127). Four stone pillars supported an upright, undershot mill wheel above the millrace, and, through gearing, the wheel probably drove two sets of millstones.

Based on the space available within the Byzantine city's new walls – the density of habitation, the water supply, and the large volume of material-culture remains – archaeologists and historians estimate a population of about one hundred thousand during the Byzantine period, making Caesarea one of the larger cities in the empire. If this figure is anywhere near correct, the population would have filled the urban space within the new wall, and there would have been suburbs beyond the line of the Byzantine fortifications.

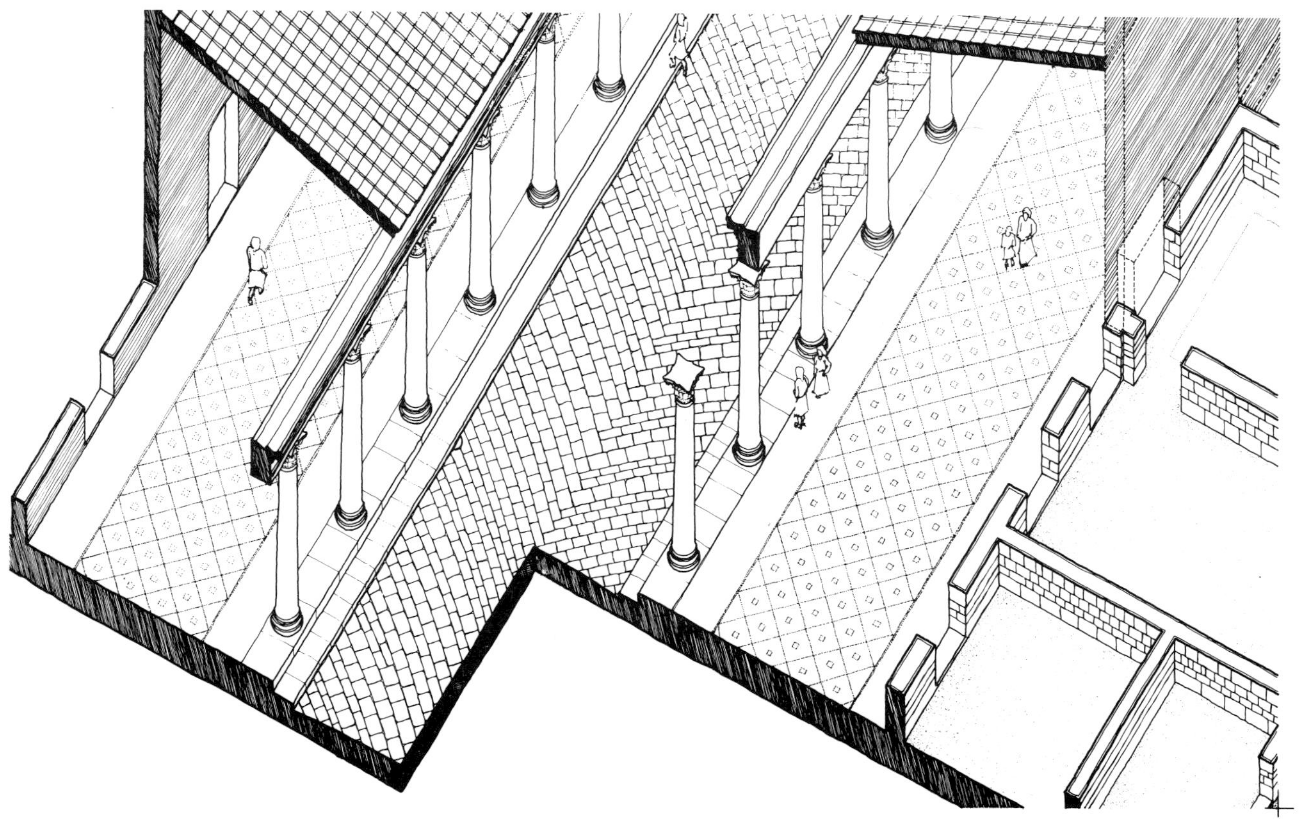

Figure 128. Reconstruction of street II from the Byzantine period, the portion just in front of the archives building (cf. figs. 112, 121). On either side of the street, colonnades supported roofs over the sidewalk, in this case paved with mosaic. Houses, shops, and public buildings opened onto the sidewalks – in this case the archives building (in the foreground). The structure was similar to that of streets built about 200 in Sebaste (fig. 66).
JECM drawing.

Not only did Caesarea's population increase during the Byzantine period, but the forms of urbanism, both material and social, remained what they had been in preceding centuries. For example, nothing characterized the classical city in the eastern Mediterranean region more universally than paved streets laid on a grid plan. Hellenistic and Roman engineers often laid sewer channels beneath the streets and provided walkways flanking the main thoroughfares. The walkways frequently were colonnaded and roofed and gave access to public buildings, shops, and private dwellings. Streets of this type existed in abundance at Caesarea. In one sector JECM archaeologists have excavated enough remains to reconstruct the superstructure of one street – JECM's street II, located in field C just south of the Crusader fortifications (fig. 128).

Caesarea's grid system of paved streets with sewers beneath them went back to King Herod, as Josephus relates. The surviving capitals from street colonnades were carved mostly in the time of the Severan emperors at the end of the second century and the beginning of the third (pp. 133–34). Thus far, however, nearly all of the actual street pavement uncovered dates from the Byzantine period. JECM has exposed enough street segments to the north, east, and south of the Crusader fortifications to reconstruct much of the Byzantine street plan (fig. 112). Street II, for example, a major north–south thoroughfare in the zone to the south of the Crusader city, was surfaced or resurfaced in the third century C.E. with limestone paving stones quarried some distance from Caesarea. After three centuries or so of use, the authorities laid down a new pavement on this street, in about 525–50, but the street crews first graded the roadbed extensively and installed new paving stones as much as 1.50 meters higher than their third-century predecessors. This presumably brought the new pavement nearer to the floor level of the sixth-century buildings that had been constructed on the debris of buildings from Roman and Herodian times. In addition, at least one east–west street, street 4, was paved for the first time during the sixth century. It consisted of carefully dressed limestone and local sandstone blocks laid in a slight camber, or arch, to facilitate drainage, and a sewer manhole and access shaft that permitted workmen to clean a sewer line beneath the street. JECM eagerly explored such sewers, which have revealed the same sturdy and careful construction as the streets themselves (fig. 129). Clearly, the quality of sixth-century street and road engineering at Caesarea had declined little since the heyday of the second century.

Besides streets, other constituents of the classical city similarly remained part of the urban scene in Byzantine Caesarea, although significantly modified and expanded. Citizens still thronged the original marketplace to purchase goods and exchange news, but there was at least one additional public square in the Byzantine city. Literary sources mention not only the *agora* but a place called the *pedion*, or Campus Martius, that was used for military parades. JECM found part of an open square paved with stone slabs in its field B, to the east of the Crusader fortifications, with what may have been a civil basilica, a public hall for the lawcourts, opening onto it (fig. 112). At some point, the city received its magnificent *tetrapylon*, one of its most famous landmarks. This was a monumental quadruple arch over the intersection of two of the main streets, which archaeologists may someday find in the vicinity of the eastern gate of the Crusader city (fig. 112). Caesarea's amphitheater still existed in the time of Eusebius, when it was the setting for Christian martyrdoms, but both it and the theater fell into ruin not long after because the Christian empire suppressed the bloody and licentious performances formerly held in them. The immensely popular chariot races, however, continued to be held in the city's circus until the sixth century.

One feature of Caesarea's urban landscape changed dramatically, or at least underwent conversion. With or without official approval, Caesarea's Christians

Figure 129. JECM volunteer emerges from a sewer manhole during exploration of street II south of the Crusader fortifications.
Kenneth Holum photo.

demolished the temples or rebuilt them as churches and brought an end to pagan sacrifice. This did not mean, however, that the Caesareans would lack divine protectors to "stand before" their city, because they dedicated their churches to powerful saints and martyrs, holy men and women who dwelled in heaven and could intercede with Christ and God the Father on the city's behalf. In some cases the churches possessed the holy bones and other relics of the saints and martyrs, making them present physically, as statues had earlier embodied the presence of gods and goddesses in the city.

King Herod had erected his temple to Rome and Augustus on a man-made platform overlooking the harbor – Caesarea's grandest temple in the most conspicuous position in its urban landscape. In the Byzantine period an important church succeeded Herod's temple on the same spot, after the temple had been razed and its stones, stained with the pollution of pagan sacrifice, taken far away. In 1961 Avraham Negev uncovered the foundations of a Byzantine church there, on the Herodian platform to the northeast of the thirteenth-century Crusader church. We are uncertain about which church this was, but a good candidate is the *martyrium*, the martyr church, of Saint Procopius, known from literary sources. This saint, whom Eusebius mentions, had died a martyr's death at Caesarea in the Great Persecution and thereafter became a mighty patron of the city's inhabitants. The custom arose of naming children for him, both male and female, to guarantee his

Figure 130.
Marble capital, Corinthian order, height 66 cm, found in 1961 by Avraham Negev during excavations on the Herodian temple platform. The Christian cross shows that this ancient capital was carved or recarved during the Byzantine period. It is one of eight that Negev located amid what he identified as the foundations of a large Byzantine church. Now at Caesarea, courtesy of IDAM.
Aaron Levin photo.

protection over them. The names Procopius and Procopia abounded all over Palestine, but especially at Caesarea.

Christian churches blossomed in other parts of the city as well. Because we have not yet been able to identify their ruins, a few pieces of architectural sculpture are virtually all that we have of Caesarea's churches (fig. 130). The literary sources mention nine other Christian *martyria* and holy places in the city or just outside its walls. Saint Cornelius, the centurion who welcomed Saint Peter to Caesarea, had a *martyrium*, as did Saint Philip, the first leader of Caesarea's Christians, and his four virgin daughters; Saint Pamphilus, Eusebius's martyred teacher; Saint Euphemia, a female martyr from near Constantinople; and Saint Anastasius, executed for his beliefs early in the seventh century. The literary sources also mention two churches dedicated to Saint Mary, the Mother of God; one dedicated outside the walls to the Holy Apostles; and another dedicated simply "to Christ." Presumably many more churches than those were scattered across Caesarea's urban landscape in the Byzantine period. In this way the city put on a Christian face without abandoning

*Figure 131. Limestone pillar with marble Corinthian capital, from the Roman period. Height 3.0 m. In the sixth century Flavius Euelpidius and Elias ordered an inscription, visible in the photo, cut in Greek on the surface of the pillar, recording that they had built a public hall (*basilica*) and the steps of the neighboring* Hadrianeum *(formerly the temple of Hadrian). Now in the courtyard of the Caesarea museum.*
Kenneth Holum photo.

traditional urban forms. Christianity insinuated itself into the fabric of classical urbanism at Caesarea.

We can safely claim, therefore, that those who assumed responsibility for urban design and the maintenance of public facilities thought themselves to be heirs of a tradition from the classical past, even after they had embraced Christianity. The Byzantine Caesareans remind us of Marcus Flavius Agrippa in the Roman period, who financed public buildings with his own resources. They thought it was their obligation to do so, and they expected recognition in the form of statues and inscriptions in public places. This attitude definitely lived on undiminished in the fifth and sixth centuries.

In an inscription cut into a small stone from the eastern gate tower in the new Byzantine wall, Flavius Procopius Constantius Alexander, the "admirable count and former governor" of the province, proclaimed himself builder of the wall "from its foundations." An imposing limestone pillar with a beautifully carved Corinthian capital (fig. 131), now on display in the Caesarea Museum, records that in the sixth century, Flavius Euelpidius, the "most magnificent count," and Elias, the "most distinguished father of the city," financed both a public hall with a marble and mosaic pavement and the steps of the neighboring Hadrianeum (the ancient temple of the Emperor Hadrian converted to secular use). In JECM's field C, south of the Crusader fortifications, a man named Andreas, the "most-glorious proconsul" who was "devoted to building," made unspecified additions to a public building late in the sixth century or early in the seventh, perhaps at the very end of Byzantine Caesarea.

These inscriptions illustrating continuity with the classical past also reveal important changes. In the first place the language is uniformly Greek. By the fourth century the use of Latin had virtually ceased for public and private inscriptions, and most likely only a few imperial bureaucrats could still speak and write the ancient language of Rome. In that part of the world, it was the Greek tongue that carried Roman culture into the Middle Ages. Also striking in the inscriptions is the proliferation of pompous titles and honorary epithets that the Byzantines liked to use. Caesarea's greatest citizens fell all over one another in their eagerness to rank as *lamprotatos*, "most distinguished," as Elias did. *Lamprotatos* meant not only local prominence but that the local man had entered the imperial aristocracy, as a member – theoretically at least – of the senate of Constantinople or Rome. Better yet, one could become *peribleptos*, "admirable," or *megaloprepestatos*, "most magnificent," or even *endoxotatos*, "most glorious," the highest distinction of all. These distinctions meant that the Caesarean had served the emperor as a provincial governor, general, or prefect, or in a similarly lofty position and had earned preeminence in urban society. Caesarea's old aristocracy, composed of local landholders who were *decuriones*, members of the local senate, had disappeared into the lower classes, and a new aristocracy of imperial senators occupied the pinnacle of urban society. In Byzantine times the aristocracy was small, and there was less room at the top.

The inscriptions make it clear that men like Elias and the others not only governed the empire, but ruled Caesarea as well. In their day imperial aristocrats were the "godfathers" of urbanism, returning to their native cities to dominate the rest of the inhabitants. At Caesarea there is no further mention of the institutions of Roman municipal government – of the "two men," the municipal senate, and the municipal treasury mentioned in the Marcus Flavius Agrippa inscription. In the fourth, fifth, and sixth centuries, it was the imperial governor of Palestine, the "most glorious count and proconsul," who saw to the municipal affairs of Caesarea with the help of his officials and soldiers. He was most often probably a native of the city

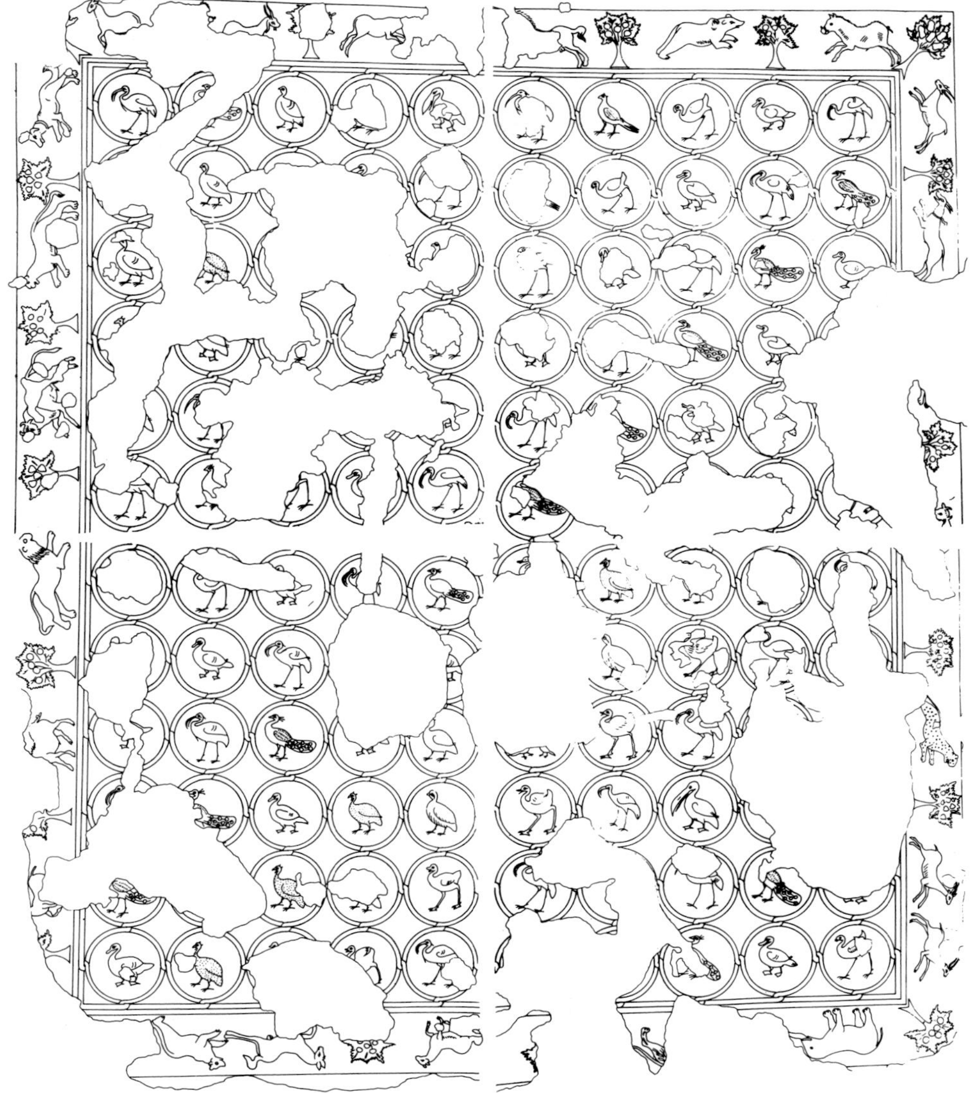

Figure 132. Drawing of a large mosaic pavement, 11.5 × 13.4 m, found in 1950 in the northeastern suburbs of Byzantine Caesarea. The central panel (carpet) consisted of 120 medallions, each containing one of eleven species of bird. Ronny Reich of IDAM identified them as: flamingo, peacock, purple gallinule, pelican, pheasant, crowned guineafowl, partridge, ibis, two kinds of duck, and one uncertain species. The surrounding frame had twenty-four species of mammal, of which Reich identified eighteen: hound, elephant, bear, ibex, boar, bull, buffalo, horse, lion and lioness, panther or leopard, tiger, antelope, sheep, goat, and three horned animals. North to left. IDAM drawing.

or the province. At his side stood a few prominent citizens – men like Elias who had received or assumed the title "father of the city." Purely honorific, this title indicated great wealth, success in the emperor's service, a record of urban patronage – and consequently, the power to exercise leadership in the local community.

Godfathers like Elias or the more impressively named Flavius Procopius Constantius Alexander either already possessed vast estates in Caesarea's territory or acquired them during their terms of office. This was another phenomenon of the

Figure 133. Southwestern corner of the large mosaic pavement uncovered in Caesarea's northeastern suburb (fig. 132). In the border, the elephant, a tree functioning as a divider, and a horned animal, perhaps a gazelle, are visible. The bird in the medallion is a purple gallinule. North to right. Paul Saivetz photo.

Figure 134. Plan of the Byzantine bath complex, JECM field E, excavated in 1976 and 1978, dated to the late Byzantine period, ca. 550–640. In this drawing south is at the top, and there is no scale (but cf. fig. 135). The bath is small in scale and unusual in design, but contains the same facilities that had characterized the Roman bath for centuries: cold, warm, and hot water baths, known to the archaeologists by their Latin names as frigidarium, tepidarium, *and* caldarium *respectively. The* praefurnium *was a furnace room, the* piscina *a fish tank.* Ken Smith drawing, courtesy of JECM.

Byzantine period, the concentration of the city's land and wealth in a few hands. Generally such men of wealth lived outside the city walls in sprawling villas in the open country. Excavations have revealed some of the luxury in which they lived. In 1950 Shmuel Yeivin examined the remains of a mosaic floor accidentally uncovered by the Israeli army on a ridge to the northeast of the city. The main pavement was large, 11.5 by 13.4 meters, with a central panel, or carpet, of 120 medallions. A bird is depicted in each medallion, representing a total of eleven different species (fig. 132). Surrounding the central panel is a frame with images of twenty-four different species of mammal (fig. 133). Yeivin originally identified the pavement as part of a church, but it almost certainly decorated the peristyle courtyard of a luxury villa. Other remains in the vicinity, including rooms with mosaic pavements and an *exedra*, a semicircular alcove, confirm this identification. Apparently, the owner of the villa had a taste for exotic animals, one that had long characterized wealthy urban Graeco-Romans, and thus had created, in effect, a zoo and aviary.

Not far to the north of this villa, the Italian Mission briefly explored a small building that proved to be one of the most exciting finds made at Caesarea. In 1976 and 1978 JECM completely excavated the building, demonstrating that it had not been a Christian baptistry, as the Italians had proposed, but a luxuriously appointed, Roman-style bath dating from the end of Caesarea's Byzantine period, about 550–640 (figs. 109, 134–35). Despite its late date the bath had facilities that

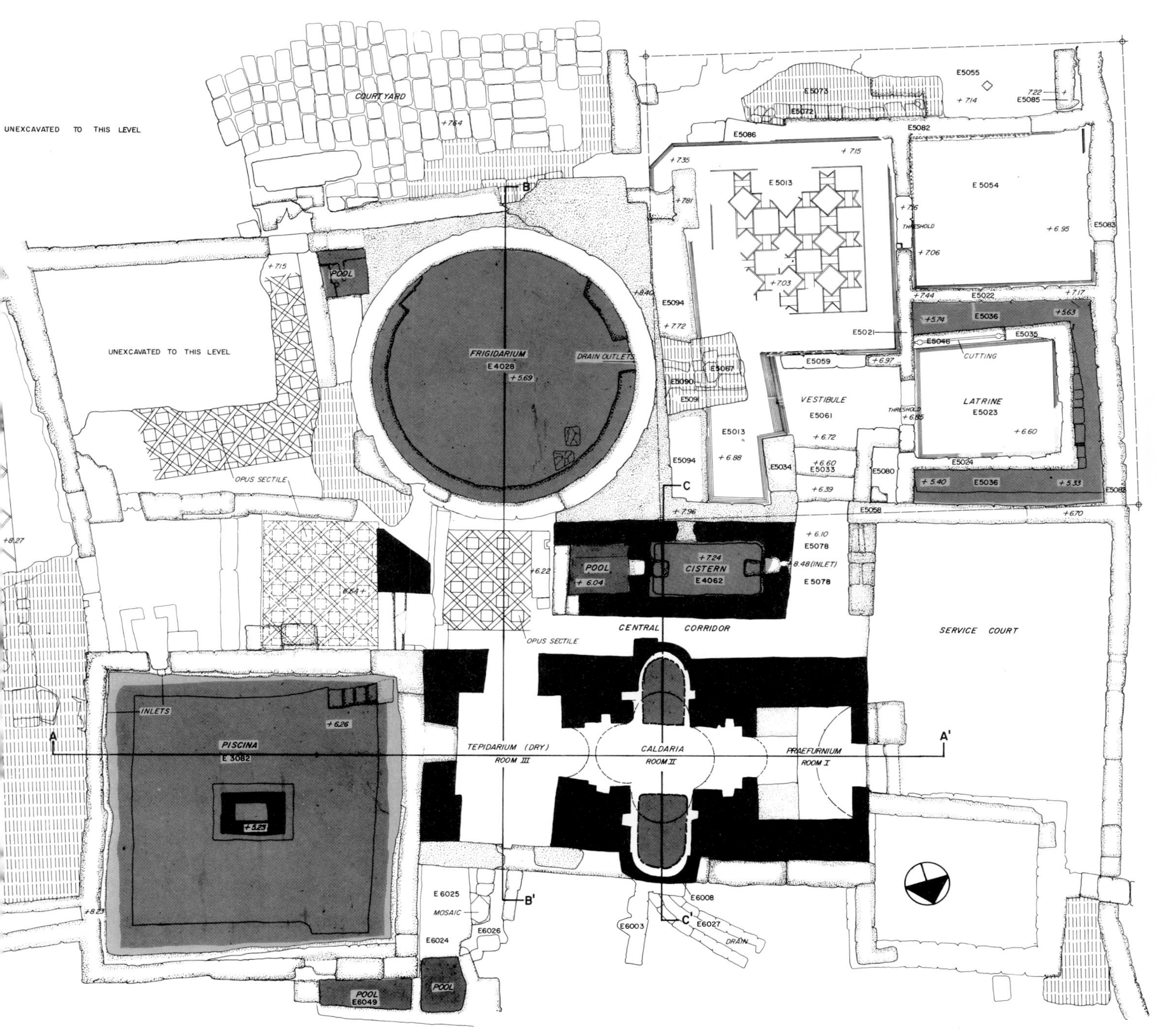

UNEXCAVATED TO THIS LEVEL
COURTYARD
FRIGIDARIUM
E4028
DRAIN OUTLETS
POOL
UNEXCAVATED TO THIS LEVEL
OPUS SECTILE
E5013
E5054
E5055
E5073
E5072
E5085
E5086
E5082
E5083
THRESHOLD
E5094
E5022
E5036
E5021
E5035
E5046
CUTTING
E5059
E5067
E5090
VESTIBULE
E5061
LATRINE
E5023
E5024
E5034
E5033
E5080
E5058
C
CISTERN
E4062
8.48 (INLET)
E5078
CENTRAL CORRIDOR
SERVICE COURT
OPUS SECTILE
INLETS
PISCINA
E 3082
A
A'
TEPIDARIUM (DRY)
ROOM III
CALDARIA
ROOM II
PRAEFURNIUM
ROOM I
B
B'
C'
E 6025
MOSAIC
E6024
E6026
E6003
E6008
E6027
DRAIN
POOL
E6049

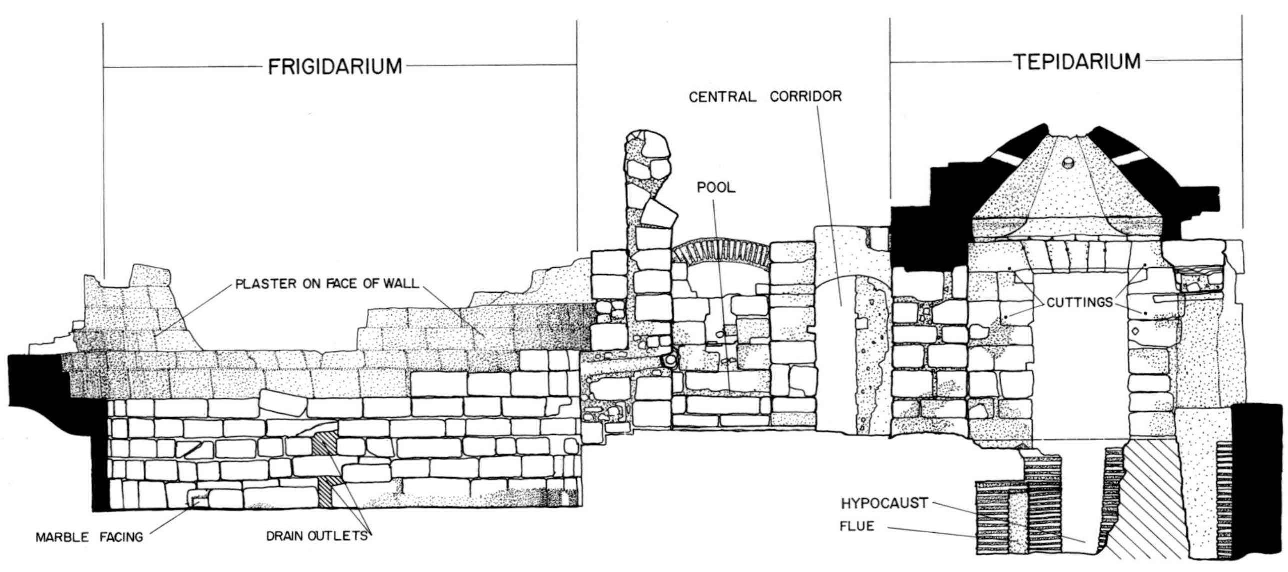

Figure 135.
Section B–B′ through the Byzantine bath complex, JECM field E, north to right. The hypocaust (lower right) brought heat from the furnace beneath the tepidarium, *the warm bath.*
Ken Smith drawing, courtesy of JECM.

had been traditional since Republican Roman times. On its periphery were service and access courts, a latrine, and several rooms paved with marble floors in *opus sectile*. The bathers undressed in those rooms, received massages, had attendants read to them, conversed with their friends, or otherwise relaxed before and after the bath. To the northeast, a *piscina*, or "fishpond," preserved live, fresh-water fish for the bathers' dinner. The actual bath began in the *caldaria* ("hot baths"), which were brought to high temperature by a fire in the *praefurnium* ("furnace room"); it was continued in the warm and dry *tepidarium* and ended with a plunge in the cold water of the *frigidarium*. Apart from its date, what is surprising about this bath is its small size. The *tepidarium*, for example, measures only about 2 by 4 meters. Apparently, the building did not serve the public – to do so it would have had to be larger. It probably belonged to another of the luxury villas built on the high ground to the northeast of Caesarea. Like the aviary mosaic, the bath reflects the life-style and tastes of the aristocracy that ruled Byzantine Caesarea.

Drawings of the Byzantine bath (figs. 134 and 135) illustrate how an excavation team's architect contributes to recording the buildings found and conveying the results of excavation to other archaeologists. The twin objectives are accuracy and visual effect. Figures 134 and 135 are a plan – a bird's-eye view – of the ruins of the bath and surrounding structures exactly as the archaeologists found them and a section – a view of a vertical slice – of the bath on the line labeled B – B′ on the plan. The architect prepared preliminary versions of each in pencil on graph paper at the site, using a string grid and meter tape to guarantee accuracy. Later, in the drafting room, he transferred the drawings in ink onto mylar, a drafting film. By combining solid inking, stippling with a pen point, a dotted overlay, and various line weights, he rendered the masonry walls, mosaic and *opus sectile* floors, solid masses of structure, and tanks and pools. After the archaeologists approve the drawings, the architect adds the locus numbers, elevations above sea level, and labels for the main structures and any of their divisions whose functions have been identified.

Despite the wealth of the new aristocrats of Byzantine Caesarea, some of the city's needs surpassed their resources. As in the Roman period, the emperor, now dwelling in Constantinople, acted to reinforce his reputation as the leading patron of urbanism. A case in point is Caesarea's harbor facilities. The south bay still served as a fair-weather anchorage from which goods could be on- and off-loaded using lighters, but the pounding surf, vast quantities of silt, and tectonic subsidence of the coastal shelf had seriously damaged Sebastos, Herod's artificial harbor basin. The archaeological evidence indicates to some that it declined rapidly or was even abandoned by early in the second century (pp. 141–42). Others, however, insist that Sebastos remained in service throughout the Roman and Byzantine periods, and that further excavation in the harbor will reinforce their interpretation. There is already some evidence in their favor. CAHEP found a large number of late sixth-century coins beneath the sea floor just outside the harbor entrance, which might mean that Sebastos was still in use. Sailors or stevedores might have lost the coins within the harbor basin, and the current would then have carried them seaward out through the entrance. In addition, CAHEP has identified from concentrations of pottery at least two shipwrecks from the fourth century or later within the harbor basin. The ships must have sunk just as they neared their berths, after having struck submerged rubble from harbor structures that had succumbed to the surf or coastal subsidence. This evidence suggests that Herod's harbor was in use but in bad condition.

The Byzantine Emperor Anastasius (491–518) stepped into the breach. The rhetorician Procopius of Gaza, a contemporary of Anastasius, delivered an oration about 502 in which he praised the emperor for supporting urbanism. Procopius describes vividly how the inhabitants of Caesarea watched helplessly from the shore as ships bringing the goods they craved struck subsurface ruins and sank within the harbor. The emperor ordered restoration work, perhaps the addition of some superstructure on the submerged portions of the breakwaters, so that once again Sebastos functioned well (fig. 110). "The city welcomes ships with confidence," Procopius relates, "and she is filled with all the necessities."

The excavation of Caesarea Maritima over the last few decades has elucidated one of history's conundrums: the "decline and fall" of the Roman Empire. What archaeologists have found at Caesarea is that, despite the profound and dramatic changes it brought, the Christianization of the empire did not, as Gibbon once argued, mean the end of antiquity. The ruins of cities like Caesarea are testimony that the ancient world flourished for centuries under the aegis of Christianity, called, in the region of ancient Palestine, the Byzantine period. Yet archaeologists have also found that beneath a prosperous facade decay had set in by early in the seventh century.

One kind of decay is evident in the so-called Byzantine esplanade, one of Caesarea's more picturesque ruins (fig. 136; cf. figs. 112 and 82). Late in the sixth century, an unknown benefactor devoted his wealth to paving and embellishing an open courtyard in the city's east-central sector. The design he chose is classical. At the courtyard's northern end a triple archway gave access to a room probably roofed with a vault in the Roman fashion. To dignify the setting the colossal statues of two emperors were placed facing each other across the esplanade, just outside the triple arches: probably Hadrian on the east and a later, unidentified emperor on the west. Close inspection, however, reveals important anomalies. The statues were antique pieces. That is, they were carved in the second and third centuries, and they had probably already lost their heads and other members by the time the sixth-century builders installed them in the esplanade. Reuse of the statues indicates that, late in the sixth century, urban design at Caesarea was nostalgic and antiquarian – a look back at the classical past, to a world that was slipping away. Also instructive is the slipshod way in which the builders installed the two statues: they used makeshift bases and odd bits of stone to prop the statues up where parts of the original fabric were missing. There is no sign of the discipline and care that had once characterized Greek and Roman construction, although it is visible in Caesarea's paved streets. Declining standards in other – but not all – sixth-century buildings confirm that Caesarea's inhabitants no longer held to all of the principles of classical urbanism.

Figure 136. Caesarea's Byzantine esplanade, east of the Crusader fortifications, looking north (cf. fig. 112 for the location). At the northern end of a paved courtyard, two statues reused from the Roman period flank the the triple-arched entrance to a large building, in which a stairway leads to a higher level. An inscription at the base of the stairway indicates a late sixth or early seventh-century date for the complex.
Aaron Levin photo.

The Prosperity of Byzantine Caesarea

When an ancient observer like Procopius of Gaza accounted for the prosperity of a city, he limited his vision to rich and powerful patrons like the emperor and the senatorial aristocracy who gave the city its buildings and frequently its operating capital. Modern economists, and sometimes policymakers as well, properly focus on the needs of the urban population as a whole, on employment opportunities for bureaucrats, clerks, laborers, educators, craftsmen, and merchants. Generally, archaeologists and urban historians, the modern observers of ancient cities, attempt a broad view and rely on the material evidence from excavations to support it.

Caesarea prospered during the Byzantine age because she remained a provincial capital. The governors named in inscriptions did use their own wealth to ornament the city with new buildings, but they also had at their disposal a large staff of bureaucrats (*officiales*) – possibly as many as four hundred – to collect taxes, administer justice, keep order, and generally promote the interests of the cities in the

Figure 137.
Gold solidus, *of Phocas, who reigned 602–10. Diameter 2.2 cm. The obverse (pictured here) has a facing bust of Phocas wearing the imperial diadem and* paludamentum. *The legend reads D(ominus) N(oster) FOCAS PERP(etuus) AVG(ustus), "Our lord Phocas, ever Augustus." The emperor's costume and the legend (in Latin) had changed little since the time of Constantius II (fig. 119). Coins like this one came to Caesarea for use in paying the salaries of men on the governor's staff. Museum of Ancient Art, Haifa.*
Aaron Levin photo.

province. Those bureaucrats in charge of accounting for the taxes collected would have worked in the archives building JECM excavated in field C. In the sixth century the governor stationed at Caesarea received the large sum of twenty-two pounds of gold annually, in the form of 1,584 gold coins called *solidi*, or subdivisions of the *solidus* (fig. 137), with which to pay his staff. Salary, however, was only part of a bureaucrat's income, because it was perfectly legal for him to demand a bribe, or "gift" (*sportula*), from a provincial for his services – and in some cases the law even regulated the amount. Imperial officials, imperial soldiers who kept order, and men and women from other cities who came to sue or be sued in the governor's court filled Caesarea's streets and public buildings and contributed to Caesarea's economy.

Equally important to the city's prosperity was its role as a center of ecclesiastical authority. Because Caesarea was the provincial capital, her bishop ranked as the metropolitan of Palestine, superior even to the bishop of Jerusalem. The first known bishop of Caesarea, a man named Theophilus, held the post in 195, when he presided over a council of other bishops called to discuss the correct date of Easter. The historian Eusebius, bishop of Caesarea from about 314–38, tended toward heresy as well as scholarship. He was accused of Arianism, the doctrine that Christ was not "of the same substance" as God the Father and coeternal with him but somehow subordinate. Despite this aberration, in 325 the Council of Nicaea confirmed Caesarea's status vis-à-vis Jerusalem. It was not until the mid-fifth century that the Holy City was able to displace her as seat of the metropolitan bishop in the Christian Holy Land.

The prominence of her bishop and the consequent press of ecclesiastical business brought many visitors to Caesarea who had to be housed, fed, and entertained. More important, in the fourth and fifth centuries, bishops everywhere in the empire were accumulating enormous wealth, acquired from imperial gifts and the bequests of the faithful, which often made them the most powerful men in the cities. The presence of the imperial governor tended to keep Caesarea's bishop in check, but even so the latter commanded vast financial resources that he used to construct and ornament churches and support hospitals, orphanages, and other charitable institutions – all of which made him popular with the city's lower classes. Managing the bishop's property and institutions must have required a staff even larger than the provincial governor's – men like Johannes, son of Zalouphios, treasurer of the Martyr Church of Cornelius, attested in a literary text from the seventh century – and their upkeep helped maintain the prosperity of Caesarea's merchants and laborers.

Caesarea also attracted students, the sons of up-and-coming families, who hoped to make their way into government service and the upper ranks of society by acquiring an education in Greek rhetoric. They too brought capital into the city. Caesarea's city fathers offered professors the highest salaries, hoping to attract the most renowned sophists available. In the fifth century, for example, the philologist Orion, who wrote grammatical treatises, taught in Alexandria and Constantinople, two of the most prestigious university towns in the Eastern Empire, and then finished his career in Caesarea. In the sixth century the celebrated Procopius of Gaza was persuaded to come to Caesarea, after he had turned down both Antioch and Beirut. Despite a gigantic salary he soon left, however, out of loyalty for his native city. Of course, Caesarea could offer such men not only money but the opportunity to work in an unparalleled library. Among those who used it was the church father Saint Jerome, whose translation of the Christian scriptures from the original Hebrew and Greek into the Latin, known as the Vulgate, became the authoritative version of the Roman Catholic Church. Jerome consulted the works of Origen at Caesarea during a sojourn in the Holy Land between 385 and 392. He later remarked that the Hexapla he used there was the only copy of the work he had ever seen.

Outstanding pupils of Caesarea's sophists included Saint Gregory Nazianzen, a father of the Greek Christian church, in the fourth century, and in the sixth, Procopius of Caesarea, the last great author in the Greek tradition of historical writing. The latter, a scion of one of Caesarea's wealthy landholding families, bore the name of the powerful martyr whose bones rested in one of the city's principal churches. His education at Caesarea consisted of the study of rhetoric and exercises in imitating the speaking and writing style of classical Greek authors. In 527 Procopius left Caesarea to become the adviser and secretary of Belisarius, the emperor Justinian's leading general, and he spent the rest of his life on various military campaigns or in Constantinople. He wrote the *History of the Wars* on Justinian's campaigns against the empire's enemies – the Persians, Vandals, and Goths – adopting a favorable attitude toward the emperor's imperialist policies; the *Secret History* attacking Justinian and the empress Theodora for demonic cruelty and repression; and the *Buildings* praising Justinian once again for lavishing his money on construction projects in many parts of the empire. Consistent in this author's works, whether or not he was praising the emperor, was suspicion of the unbridled imperial autocracy that threatened the independence and prosperity of aristocrats like himself. His was an urban attitude, one that Procopius had brought with him from his native city to his career in the imperial service.

Figure 138.
CAHEP archaeologists, working in area D1, discover one of the so-called Gaza amphoras, a cigar-shaped vessel used (among other purposes) for transporting the popular wines of the Gaza region in southern Palestine to other parts of the Mediterranean world. Sherds of such vessels also occur commonly on the land site at Caesarea. Height of this example 61.0 cm. IDAM collection, at the Center for Maritime Studies, Haifa.
Harry Wadsworth photo.

Figure 139.
A potter's workshop like the one that existed at Caesarea in JECM's field C at the beginning of the seventh century. The clay was levigated, or refined, in basins. The potters shaped vessels on a potter's wheel or in molds and placed them in a kiln for firing. This hypothetical reconstruction is based on ancient pottery workshops found at Avdat in Israel's Negev Desert and Tell Abu Gourdan in Jordan.
Shorieh Talaat drawing.

Caesarea prospered during the Byzantine period in part because, as a center of government, education, and the church, she could offer employment. More than that, the city on the sea still was the market and distribution point for a large hinterland. Using wagons and pack animals, merchants still carried goods in bulk from Caesarea to outlying markets, following the network of paved Roman roads that the Byzantine authorities maintained and even expanded. Farmers and villagers from Caesarea's territory still visited her markets to sell agricultural products and purchase manufactured goods and commodities. Archaeologists have evidence that what was available in Caesarea's markets in Byzantine times often arrived by ship – lamps from Africa and jars of the famous Gaza wine (figs. 117, 138). An active import and export trade kept Caesarea's harbor busy and employment high, making the refurbishing of the harbor a suitable object of the emperor's generosity.

The proximity of a bustling market also encouraged local manufacture. Excavation has turned up evidence that Caesarea was an industrial center as well as a seaport and distribution point. In JECM's field C, for example, just to the south of the Crusader fortifications, the archaeologists found evidence of the production of

Figure 140.
Group of lamp molds, top and bottom pieces, and associated lamps found in JECM area C.21 and C.19 adjacent to it. The molds are of soft limestone, the largest measuring 13.7 cm long, and all date from the late sixth or earlier seventh century. The potter pressed clay into the molds with his fingers, allowed the top and bottom pieces to dry separately, and then fastened them together with slip – clay in solution – before firing. Objects are upper center and lower right DIAR collection, others IDAM collection, at DIAR.
Aaron Levin photo.

ceramic goods in area C.21 from the late sixth and early seventh century. Area C.21 and the vicinity provided a large number of soft limestone lamp molds (both tops and bottoms), molds for more exotic objects like cosmetic boxes and horse figurines, wasters (fragments of imperfectly made objects), and a huge dump of both broken and complete vessels (figs. 140 and 141). The "factory's" equipment has disappeared, but it would have been relatively simple: basins for washing and levigating clay, potters' wheels for shaping ceramic vessels, molds for lamps and other objects, and a kiln for firing (fig. 139). In two seasons of excavation, the archaeologists extracted more than two thousand buckets of pottery from trench C.21 – mostly sherds of cook pots, transport amphoras, and storage jars – that may have been both the factory's waste and part of its inventory.

Although it is clear that trade and industry contributed much to Caesarea's economy, as they had in Herodian and Roman times, they do not necessarily account for the dramatic *expansion* of the city's economy in the Byzantine age. Years ago, the late Israeli archaeologist and art historian Michael Avi-Yonah assembled evidence – mainly the density of Byzantine pottery and building remains – that during the Byzantine period the population grew and the economy expanded all over Palestine. If the population of the country as a whole reached its peak for antiquity in Byzantine times, then Caesarea would have had to expand to meet the demand for goods and services.

Figure 141.
Mold for stylized horse and for horse and rider, 18.4 and 13.2 cm wide respectively. Carved in soft limestone with incised saddle, bridle, and harness. The function of the figures made from these molds is unknown, but they may have been toys. Avraham Negev found the molds in 1961 south of the Crusader fortifications, presumably in the same sector where JECM later found evidence of a potter's workshop. Thus they probably date from the later sixth and earlier seventh centuries, like the lamps and molds in fig. 140. IDAM collection.
Aaron Levin photo.

Avi-Yonah made another point: that the economy of ancient Palestine had expanded because the Roman Empire embraced Christianity. What had been a forgotten province in a remote corner of the world suddenly became the Christian Holy Land. Shortly after 312, pilgrims of both sexes, all ages, and from various levels of society began to set out on the roads and sea lanes for Jerusalem. Whether fashionable ladies or humble monks, they felt compelled to visit the places named in the Christian Bible to relive in authentic settings the events that had brought their own salvation. They came in large numbers, bringing money. Some stayed, but many returned home to encourage others to undertake the same arduous but rewarding journey. At the same time emperors and other wealthy men and women showered benefactions on the Holy Land, building and decorating churches and founding monasteries, hospitals, and hostels and endowing the inmates generously. An influx of men and women, of capital, and of a new kind of tourism – Christian pilgrimage – created prosperity in Byzantine Palestine.

Caesarea brought in a rich harvest from the Holy Land phenomenon and the new tourism. It was in the middle of the sixth century, when the emperor Justinian was diverting huge sums of gold to construction projects in Jerusalem and the rest of Palestine, that Caesarea's city fathers refurbished and expanded the city's paved streets (pp. 175–76). Perhaps Justinian's benefactions created an economic upswing that indirectly helped finance the street project in Caesarea. More directly, Caesarea

Figure 142. Pewter ampulla (pilgrim flask), made in Jerusalem about 600 C.E., now at Dumbarton Oaks, Washington, D.C. Diameter 4.7 cm. Pilgrims carried flasks like this one home with them from the Holy Land, filled with oil made holy by contact with the bones of martyrs or other holy objects. This one, for example, may have contained some of the oil that burned in the lamp in Christ's tomb. On its reverse (pictured here) two women approach the empty tomb from the left, as in Luke 24:1, while Christ observes them from the right. The tomb appears as it did in Constantine's Resurrection Church in Jerusalem, with open gates and behind them, at the entrance to the burial chamber, an oil lamp on a stand.
Photo courtesy of Dumbarton Oaks.

had its own Christian history and Christian holy places, so pilgrims included it in their itineraries and brought large sums of tourist money into the city. In the early fourth century, the anonymous Pilgrim of Bordeaux (in Gaul) visited the "bath of Cornelius the centurion, who had performed many deeds of mercy." Later in the same century, Saint Jerome's spiritual friend Paula saw the "house" of Cornelius, the church of Christ, and the house of Philip, with the chamber of the four virgin prophetesses. In the sixth century, Antoninus of Piacenza (in Italy) visited the churches of Pamphilus, Procopius, and Cornelius, "from whose bier I took a blessing." Apparently, Antoninus had removed a bit of wood or stone from the platform on which the saint's relics rested because he believed that it would secure the saint's protection for him. At Caesarea and elsewhere archaeologists have found evidence for such souvenirs – sherds of the so-called pilgrim flasks, ceramic vessels that contained oil consecrated by contact with the bones of the saints or other holy objects. Flasks in metal also exist, richly decorated with images of the Holy Land (fig. 142).

Most often, however, pilgrims went to Caesarea because it was one of the Holy Land's principal ports of entry and exit or, if they followed the land routes, it was a way station on the road to Jerusalem. In 326, for example, the empress Helena, mother of Constantine, arrived in the Holy Land on a journey that became a model and inspiration for all later Holy Land pilgrimage. During her sojourn in Jerusalem,

Figure 143. Ship graffito on a stone, 65 cm wide, beneath the Church of the Holy Sepulcher, drawn there about 330 C.E. by pilgrims from the western Mediterranean to show their means of conveyance to the Holy Land. The Latin inscription reads, Domine ivimus, *"O Lord, we have come."*
Zev Radovan photo.

the empress presided over the destruction of the city's main pagan sanctuary, the temple to Jupiter that Hadrian had built. Beneath the ruins an empty tomb was discovered that Helena and other Christians immediately recognized as Christ's tomb. Within a few years Constantine ordered the construction of a magnificent church on the site – the forerunner of the present Church of the Holy Sepulcher – to commemorate the resurrection. Even as the work proceeded, other, less exalted pilgrims arrived from the most distant parts of the empire to view the empty tomb and share in the religious enthusiasm that Helena's discovery had created. Archaeologists recently found evidence of those pilgrims in excavations beneath the Church of the Holy Sepulcher (fig. 143). Among the substructures of the old pagan temple, on a stone that was covered by Constantine's church, someone had sketched a crude image of their ship, which must have been dismasted during its perilous voyage, and inscribed beneath it, in Latin, a terse remembrance of their visit: *Domine ivimus*, "O Lord, We have come." Over the next centuries, other vessels like it would arrive, bringing thousands of pilgrims from all over the empire, many of whom docked at Caesarea. The Holy Sepulcher ship is testimony to the traffic that must have kept Caesarea's harbors in business until the very end of antiquity.

Still, it would not be fair to credit Byzantine Caesarea's well-being entirely to Christianity, because the city still boasted large non-Christian minorities. The last material evidence for paganism that can be dated (although only roughly) is the

Caesarea Cup (figs. 5 and 6). This object was probably created in the second quarter of the fourth century to commemorate the birthday of the city goddess, or Tyche, in a pagan festival. Nevertheless, paganism did survive well into the Byzantine period. The sophists, for example, who taught rhetoric on public salaries, used pagan texts and probably still avowed paganism in the fifth century, until several generations after the last pagan temple had succumbed to the fury of Christian mobs. Members of two non-pagan minorities proved to be far more tenacious: the Samaritans and the Jews. In their legislation, the Christian emperors adopted a hostile attitude toward these groups, calling Judaism, for instance, a "savage and abominable sect." The state, however, had neither the resources nor the will to carry out systematic persecution, and in fact frequently protected synagogues from attacks by Christian zealots. For their part, the Jews and Samaritans, and the few surviving pagans, experienced what modern sociologists call marginality, minority status in a culture that was hostile or at best indifferent to their own. Like marginal minorities in modern cities, Caesarea's Jews and Samaritans labored with special devotion and skill to participate in the prosperity that life in a flourishing city had to offer.

Samaritans, children of Israel who insisted that God's holy mountain was not Zion in Jerusalem but Gerizim in Samaria, flourished in many parts of Palestine and were a very large minority in Caesarea and its territory. In his *Secret History* Procopius relates that Christians owned Caesarea's land – "the finest farmland in the world," he calls it – but those who farmed it, the peasant farmers or *coloni*, were Samaritans. In excavations within the city, archaeologists have collected amulets inscribed with passages from the Samaritan scriptures and especially Samaritan lamps. *Menorot*, seven-branched candlesticks similar to Jewish ones, decorate the lamps, as do inscriptions quoting Samaritan scripture. The "ladder" patterns on the lamps are thought to represent a staircase on Mt. Gerizim that once led to the Samaritan altar of sacrifice and to their temple (fig. 144). A significant number of Caesarea's Samaritans entered the imperial service. A rabbinic text reports that the governor's staff was composed mainly of Samaritans. One of them, a man named Faustinus, even won the position of governor for himself, after he converted to Christianity, and later managed all of the emperor's estates in Palestine.

After the massacre of Caesarea's Jews in 66, when twenty thousand are said to have lost their lives (p. 75), the city had only a small Jewish presence. At the close of the second century C.E., Jews moved to the city in large numbers, probably attracted by its economic opportunities. In the third and fourth centuries, prominent rabbis, including Rabbi Hoshaya, Rabbi Abbahu, and Rabbi Isaac Napaha, taught and issued legal decisions at Caesarea that contributed much to both the

Figure 144. Fourth-century ceramic oil lamp, 6.6 cm in length, found in JECM area C.10. The menorah, *or seven-branched candlestick, and the ladder pattern decorating the nozzle identify this as a Samaritan lamp, used by one of Caesarea's major religious minorities. Now in the IDAM collection.* Aaron Levin photo.

Jerusalem and Babylonian Talmuds. The rabbis' humbler brethren played a role in Caesarea's economy. Ancient sources mention Jews in many trades – goldsmith, shopkeeper, potter, fish merchant, baker, and weaver. One Caesarean Jew was an "engineer," perhaps responsible for the city's aqueducts, and at least one is known who served on the governor's staff.

The two Talmuds and other rabbinic literature provide us with precious details of the daily life of Caesarea's Jews in the late Roman and Byzantine periods, but archaeology also has a contribution to make. Twenty-six Jewish gravestones, completely or partially preserved, have turned up at Caesarea, most of them from a Jewish cemetery from the fifth and sixth centuries. It is located east of the city, just outside the line of the Byzantine wall (fig. 112). Within the city, north of the Crusader fortifications and hard by the sea, Israeli archaeologists have excavated a synagogue that had been used during the fourth, fifth, and sixth centuries. The excavators identified its plan as a broadhouse type, 9 meters wide and 18 meters long, east–west. They discovered column capitals embellished with the *menorah* and mosaic pavements. Although small in scale, the synagogue was decorated lavishly by the community that prayed there. Several inscriptions were set into the mosaics, including one recording that "Beryllos, Son of Justus, administrator and head of the synagogue, laid the mosaic floor of the triclinium with his own funds." Beryllos was one of the wealthy Jews of Caesarea who typically took responsibility

Figure 145. The Caesarea list of priestly courses, from the Byzantine synagogue north of the Crusader fortifications. Two marble fragments, 14.5 and 15.5 cm high, still exist, and a third was found, published, and lost again. The inscription has been completed with the aid of Jewish liturgical poetry. It lists Jewish priestly families and their native towns in order of their service in the Temple cult in Jerusalem. IDAM collection.
Drawing and photo courtesy of IDAM.

for the community and its facilities. Near the synagogue the Israelis found fragments of a marble slab on which the list of twenty-four priestly courses was inscribed (fig. 145). These courses were the priestly families that, while the Temple stood, went up to Jerusalem by courses, or in turn, to officiate over the Temple cult. In the Byzantine period the Jews of Caesarea prayed on each sabbath that these families might return to their "places" – that the Temple and its cult might be restored.

At the very beginning of the Byzantine period, Eusebius of Caesarea wrote about a revealing incident. In November or December 309, he claims, at the height of the Great Persecution, "most of the columns that support the public porches emitted tears, as it were, drop by drop, although the weather was clear, the air was calm, and there was no sign of a rainstorm." Presumably, Eusebius and the people of Caesarea had witnessed a natural phenomenon, condensation forming on the columns of Caesarea's colonnaded streets (fig. 128), but Eusebius did not doubt that they had seen a miracle. Like other Christians he believed that the columns wept because the state was torturing and murdering men and women who confessed Christ. Significantly, the city's Jews rejected the interpretation but not the miracle, insisting that the occasion for the tears was the death of Rabbi Abbahu, which had occurred at the same time. The Samaritans rejected the arguments of both rival religions and responded sarcastically that the columns were not weeping but "only perspiring." In the following weeks and years debate over this incident continued in Caesarea's streets and public places. Despite the threat of persecution, the teeming city still was a place in which rival marginal groups could assert their claims against one another.

This atmosphere persisted well into the Byzantine age, permitting Caesarea's Jews and Samaritans to make their contribution to the city's vibrant cultural and economic life. By the end of the fifth century, however, and especially during the sixth, the Christian Empire became militant in its attitude toward religious minorities. The emperor Justinian (527–65) renewed neglected laws forbidding Jews to build synagogues, fill government positions, teach, and own Christian slaves. The Samaritans fared even worse; they were deprived of their synagogues altogether. Justinian also meddled in Jewish internal affairs, by requiring the Jews, for example, to use the scriptures in Greek rather than Hebrew. The first forced conversions to Christianity are recorded during the reigns of Justinian and his successors.

The Samaritans of Palestine responded to renewed oppression by rebelling three times (in 484, 529/30, and 555), venting special fury against what they perceived to be the source of their oppression – the city of Caesarea. In the third revolt, in 555, they attacked and burned Caesarea's churches, including Saint Procopius's, and murdered the governor and plundered his palace. The emperor responded with a military force that crushed the revolts, executing the Samaritan leaders and slaughtering or enslaving thousands of men, women, and children. Without their peasant farmers, the estates in Caesarea's territory, including what Procopius calls "the best farmland in the world," soon lay waste, and the city's economy declined. Caesarea's Jews, meanwhile, bided their time. Their patience was rewarded, for in the next century, a new people and a new religion arose that would rescue them from oppression.

CHAPTER 6

Caesarea Under Muslim Rule: "A Beautiful City . . . on the Greek Sea"

Figure 146. CAHEP's area S, excavated in 1986. Basins (upper right) with tesselated floors, each 1.5 × 2.3 m, may have been settling basins for use in producing olive oil. View toward the north. Mark Little photo.

"The Roman Empire did not die a natural death," wrote André Piganiol, "it was assassinated." With these words the noted French historian of the Christian empire framed a challenge to Edward Gibbon that shifted the blame for the empire's demise from such internal problems as Christian otherworldliness, intolerance, and the bureaucratization of the state to attacks that came from beyond its frontiers. In the West defense against the Germans and other northern barbarians imposed crushing financial burdens that the cities and the aristocracy could no longer sustain. From the fourth century to the sixth, the attackers gradually dismembered the empire and depopulation reduced the cities, except for Rome and a few others, to villages.

In the East, meanwhile, the emperor's soldiers generally held the Euphrates front against the Sassanian kings of Persia, Rome's enemy on that flank, until the seventh century. Then, in a breathtakingly short time, a new military and imperial people overwhelmed both the Sassanians and Rome. Early in the seventh century, the prophet Muhammad (d. 632) unleashed the vitality of the Arabian peninsula, of flourishing merchant cities in the Hejaz and of the Bedouin who lived in tents on the desert's fringes. By 641 the earliest caliphs ("successors") had destroyed the Sassanians and driven Rome's armies from most of the Levant. Henceforth, the emperor would rule from Constantinople over Asia Minor and his remaining European possessions.

In the Levant these developments brought an end to the urban civilization of classical antiquity. The eastern cities, however, unlike those in the West, did not decline and disappear. Scholars have sometimes assumed incorrectly that invading

Muslim armies typically demolished ancient cities. The truth is that the experience of Byzantine religious intolerance and the burdens of taxation frequently induced urban populations to open their gates to the invaders, who most often accepted a city's submission gratefully because it permitted them to collect the same taxes the old rulers had. The Muslim commanders invited Christian and Jewish inhabitants to embrace Islam. If they refused, they were reduced to *dhimmi* status, membership in protected but inferior religious minorities.

Nonetheless, the Muslims, many of whom had lived in cities for centuries, created their own essentially new style of urbanism. Shops invaded the ancient colonnaded streets, slowly reshaping the monumental open vistas into the narrow lanes of the medieval Islamic market (*suq*). Dwellings soon crowded the formerly open marketplace of the classical city. The Muslims bathed almost as enthusiastically as the ancient Romans, but in smaller, more intimate settings. The great prayer hall, or mosque, became the chief public building on the new cityscape. Many ancient cities prospered in their new guise, and the Muslims built new ones. The Umayyad dynasty of caliphs (661–750) made Damascus their capital, erecting its celebrated Great Mosque, while the Abbasids (750–1258) founded Baghdad, the fabulous round city on the Tigris River in Iraq, scene of *The Thousand and One Nights*.

At Caesarea the Muslims did indeed "assassinate" classical urbanism, both by violent and destructive conquest and by creating a new Muslim world in which the ancient city-on-the-sea ceased to function as a major seaport. Within a century or two, Caesarea became only a coastguard station on what Muslims called the Greek Sea and a market town for a still-rich agricultural hinterland. Even so, King Herod might have been pleased with the smaller but still prospering city, now of the Muslim type, that carried the name of his old foundation into the Middle Ages.

The Persian and Muslim Conquests

In 614 a Persian army invaded Palestine and conquered its cities, including Caesarea, holding them until 627–28, when the emperor Heraclius at last succeeded in driving Persia's forces back to their capital, Ctesiphon (near later Baghdad). The Persians had persecuted Caesarea's Christian inhabitants and turned its public buildings, including the governor's palace and a jail in the city's *kastron*, to their own use. JECM archaeologists and others who have excavated at Caesarea have assumed that when the Persians took Caesarea in 614 they sacked it and put many of its buildings to the torch. As evidence JECM cites the discovery in its fields A, B, and

C of what the archaeologists call destruction layers – strata containing architectural debris, charcoal, and other evidence of violent destruction and burning. The destruction layers held pottery and coins consistent with an early seventh-century date and were covered by new construction, of Byzantine type, that may be the rebuilding of the city after Heraclius freed Palestine from the Persian menace. Some archaeologists, however, question a Persian destruction of the city. A literary source reports that the people of Caesarea capitulated without a fight, "begging for peace and humbly bending their necks in obedience." Moreover, one archaeologist's destruction by hostile attack is another archaeologist's accidental conflagration. It is not easy to distinguish between the two.

Only six years after Heraclius expelled the Persians, the first Muslim army invaded Palestine. The ninth-century Arabic chronicler al-Baladhuri reports that the general 'Amr ibn al-'As, who would later conquer Egypt, first besieged Caesarea in 634. He and other generals continued the siege intermittently for seven years, until Mu'awiya, later the founder of the Umayyad dynasty of caliphs, finally stormed the city in 640 or 641. Thus Caesarea held out after the battle of the Yarmuk River (636), in which the Arabs decisively defeated the army of Heraclius, and even after the fall of Jerusalem (638). She was able to resist because of her fortification walls, the large garrison the emperor had left to defend her, and because she could easily be resupplied by sea. When the Muslims failed to take the walls, a Jew named Joseph led them into the city through a "conduit" in which "the water reached a man's waist," according to al-Baladhuri. This conduit may have been a sewer channel, but more likely the chronicler refers to the city's low-level aqueduct.

Again JECM archaeologists found destruction layers from the time of the Arab conquest. The layers, widely reported in fields A, B, C, H, and K, included sixth- and seventh-century coins and potsherds that might date to about the middle of the seventh century. Burned pottery, charcoal, lumps of melted glass, and soot-blackened soil indicate conflagration. The team assumes that concentrations of building rubble – including broken and fallen building stones, bits of marble and mosaic floor paving, and fragments of marble architrave blocks and column capitals – point to a coordinated effort to plunder and destroy at least some parts of the city. Here we have a strong case. The literary sources do attest a siege. The length of that siege and the fact that this was the enemy's capital support the archaeologists' interpretation. The victorious Muslims very likely craved revenge and therefore unleashed special fury against Caesarea. Even so, it is unlikely that one of the relatively small Arab armies could have destroyed much of the city even had it wanted to.

Nevertheless, the Muslim conquest did bring a precipitous end to classical urbanism at Caesarea – because the Caesareans abandoned their city. During the siege many must have left by ship, and in the years and decades that followed thousands more must have taken to the road as refugees, slowly making their way to friendly territory. The Arabic literary sources make it clear that Caesarea was seriously depopulated in the century after the conquest, and the reason is not difficult to find. Although many Christians, Jews, Samaritans, and pagans willingly embraced Islam, many also declined conversion or life under Islam as part of a dhimmi minority. Most of the wealthy Caesareans probably left, including the landholding aristocracy, as did some of the common people – the craftsmen, day laborers, and peasant farmers. The city's poorer inhabitants would have lacked the movable wealth to make flight a possibility.

The new geopolitical situation further depressed Caesarea's economy. The Mediterranean, once a highway teeming with ships that united the lands on its shores, now separated the Muslim south and east from emerging Europe to the north and west. The Muslims called it the Greek Sea because the hostile navy of the Greek-speaking Roman emperor in Constantinople controlled it. Although neither commerce nor the pilgrim traffic ever ceased completely, Arab ship captains ventured across the Mediterranean at their peril. After the conquest few ships, other than coastal traders, called at Caesarea's harbor. Those who lost their livelihoods as a result further swelled the stream of refugees leaving the once proud city.

The archaeological evidence, especially from JECM trenches in Caesarea's southwestern zone (fields C, K, L, M, and N; fig. 16), confirms the depressing picture of seventh-century depopulation. JECM found virtually no indication above the destruction layers that anyone repaired ruined buildings or constructed new ones. In fact, within a century or two, the people of Caesarea seem to have abandoned the entire zone to the south of the Crusader fortifications. They used the area once occupied by dwellings, commercial and industrial enterprises, and government headquarters to bury the dead. The earliest human burials JECM has excavated in this zone probably date from the first centuries after the conquest (pp. 221, 224–26). More than 350 burials have already been found in what is only a small percentage of the zone's total area, indicating that this part of Caesarea became a vast burial ground.

Equally pervasive in the southwest zone is evidence of what archaeologists call robbing. Those who still lived in Caesarea used the area as a gigantic quarry, robbing the stones from the walls of ruined buildings for reuse. As sand and new topsoil accumulated over the ruins, they dug "robber trenches" to reach, for example, the stylobates on which the Roman and Byzantine builders had set the columns of their

Figure 147. Ceramic oil lamp found at Caesarea, 9.3 cm long, with Greek letters on its nozzle that spell (in reverse) the name Elias (Elijah). This is a Christian lamp that potters continued to manufacture after the Muslim conquest and well into the Umayyad period. IDAM collection.
Aaron Levin photo.

colonnaded streets. The hard but easily worked limestone from these stylobates made excellent doorsills and pavements. Even more precious were the marble column shafts and capitals, and the inscribed slabs and forests of statuary that had once honored prominent citizens and urban patrons of Roman and Byzantine Caesarea. Frequently the marble fell victim to the lime-burner's kiln, where it was burned to secure the lime needed to make mortar and fertilizer. In the zone south of the Crusader fortifications, the archaeologists found evidence for this type of robbing – marble fragments, lumps of lime, and the remains of the kilns themselves. The robbing that has victimized the site through the centuries, down to the modern era, very likely began shortly after the Muslim conquest.

Despite this evidence for destruction and depopulation, the material culture of Caesarea from the conquest period speaks for a high degree of continuity with the past. In the decades after the conquest, local potters, some of whom probably chose conversion or dhimmi status rather than flight, continued to make the familiar bag-shaped storage jars (fig. 114), but with higher rims. Sherds of the Roman-style red-slip fineware turn up in Islamic strata at Caesarea into the eighth century. Archaeologists believe that some of the Byzantine lamps that display Christian inscriptions or symbols were still manufactured in the Umayyad period (fig. 147). Caesarea's Muslim rulers had neither the ability nor the desire to enforce new tastes in consumer goods on their subjects. In fact, they too embraced continuity. The earliest coins from Muslim mints in the newly conquered territories copied Byzantine types, including imperial portraits, Greek legends, and even the Christian cross (fig. 148). Not until about 698, by which time the Umayyads had firmly established themselves, did Caliph 'Abd al-Malik introduce purely Islamic types that respected the Muslim prohibition against human and animal images (fig. 149).

Figure 148.
Bronze coin, called a fals, *1.3 cm in diameter, struck in the seventh century by one of the first Muslim caliphs. To encourage public acceptance of these coins, the mint imitated the* follis, *large bronze coins issued by the last Byzantine emperors. The reverse (pictured here) includes even the Christian cross. Found at Caesarea in JECM's area G.7. IDAM collection, now at DIAR.*
Aaron Levin photo.

The Emergence of Muslim Caesarea

Caesarea – which became known in Arabic as Qaisariyah – quickly took on some importance for the Muslim conquerors. Caliph Umar, second in succession from Muhammad, ordered Mu'awiya, then governor of Syria and Palestine (al-Filastin), to rebuild Caesarea's fortifications, along with those of the other coastal cities to the south, Arsuf (ancient Apollonia), Jaffa (Joppa), Ascalon, and Gaza. These became what the Arabs called *ribatat* (singular *ribat*) or coastguard stations. Mu'awiya tried to attract soldiers to settle in Caesarea and the other *ribatat* by offering them the houses and probably the land of the Christians who had fled, and for those soldiers he built Caesarea's first mosque. The soldiers were to man watchtowers, looking for movements of the Byzantine fleet offshore. They could communicate with the other *ribatat* by signal fire if landings were attempted. As a *ribat* Caesarea also provided a haven for the population in the countryside in case of enemy attack.

Apparently the Arabs did not rush to repopulate Caesarea, despite Mu'awiya's efforts. In general, the Arabs preferred the desert to the dampness and lush vegetation in Caesarea's hinterland. According to one source, even Mu'awiya, when he became caliph in 661, ordered one of his deputies to find him some estates, but "not in the swamps of Caesarea." Hence Mu'awiya had to bring in volunteers from other lands, especially from Persia. There was another attraction to service in a *ribat* or other frontier city. Muslims considered such service to be a special form of devotion and those who died fighting the infidel in such a place won fame as martyrs. *Ribatat* did offer an occasion for this type of sacrifice. In about 685 the Byzantines sacked Caesarea and razed its mosque. They even appear to have held on to the city for a few years, until, in 690, Caliph 'Abd al-Malik recaptured it, rebuilt its mosque, and renewed its garrison. In 975 the Byzantine emperor John I Tzimisces marched south from Syria toward Jerusalem, conquering Caesarea briefly along the way. Similar attacks may have occurred in the intervening centuries that the chronicles do not mention.

Mu'awiya appears to have established a different kind of city at Caesarea. With a new population, a new religion, and a dramatically different reason for existing, Muslim Qaisariyah hardly resembled its Roman and Byzantine predecessor. Although there is no evidence that he claimed the distinction, Mu'awiya deserves recognition with Strato, Herod, Vespasian, and Hadrian as a founder of Caesarea.

Despite its precarious situation, Caesarea appears to have flourished in the time of the Abbasid caliphate (after 750), especially under several dynasties of breakaway Muslim rulers of Egypt, the Tulunids (877–905), Ikhshidids (941–69), and Fatimids (969–1070). During this period several Muslim travelers visited the city and recorded favorable impressions of it. In 985 al-Maqdisi, a native of Palestine who wrote in Arabic, expressed enthusiasm for Qaisariyah's agricultural wealth:

> *On the coast of the Greek sea, there is no city more beautiful, nor any more filled with good things: plenty has its well-spring here, and useful products are on every hand. Its lands are excellent, and its fruits delicious; the town is also famous for its buffalo-milk and its white bread. To guard the city there is an impregnable fortress, with a well-founded wall encircling it. The drinking water of the inhabitants is drawn from wells and cisterns. Its Great Mosque is very beautiful.*

Two generations after al-Maqdisi's visit, in 1047, the Persian Nasir-i-Khusrau similarly found Caesarea

> *a fine city, with running waters and palm-gardens, and orange and citron trees. Its walls are strong, and it has an iron gate. There are fountains that gush out within the city. The Great Mosque is a beautiful edifice. Seated in its courtyard, one may enjoy a view of the sea which is exceedingly pleasant.**

To judge from these texts, the descendants of the early Muslim military settlers had brought Caesarea's rich fields back into production. As in Roman and Byzantine times, the city's well-to-do landowners once again enjoyed a luxurious life.

The texts also permit us to reconstruct part of the urban plan of Muslim Caesarea (fig. 150). The courtyard in which Nasir-i-Khusrau could sit and enjoy a view of the sea must have been situated on the vaulted platform on which Herod had built his temple to Rome and Augustus long before. Once a city's sacred topography has been established, it tends to remain the same, despite cultural and religious changes. A careful reading of the texts gives us other information: in 985 water is

Figure 149.
Bronze fals, *1.8 cm in diameter, struck at al-Ramla in ancient Palestine ca. 698–750. The obverse (pictured here) has a palm tree within a circle and surrounding it an Arabic legend reading: "There is no God but Allah." After the currency reform of the Umayyad Caliph 'Abd al-Malik, about 698, the Muslims adopted coin types that accorded with Muslim prohibitions against graven images. Found in JECM area G.9. IDAM collection, now at DIAR.*
Aaron Levin photo.

*Translations of Arabic and Persian texts by Guy Le Strange (adapted), quoted in Harry W. Hazard, "Caesarea and the Crusades," *Studies in the History of Caesarea Maritima*, ed. Charles T. Fritsch, The Joint Expedition to Caesarea Maritima, vol. I (Missoula, Montana: Scholars Press, 1975), pp. 79–80.

Figure 150.
Urban plan of Muslim Caesarea in the tenth century. As this plan makes clear, little is known about Caesarea in this period.
Robin Ziek drawing.

drawn from "wells and cisterns," but in 1047 it is "running water" that "gushes out." The city's Fatimid *amir* ("governor") may have brought one of the ancient aqueducts back into operation, probably the low-level channel that had once brought water from the dam and reservoir to the north. Finally, it is striking that both travelers emphasized the city's defenses, which included both a powerful citadel and encircling the city, a fortification wall with an iron gate.

Archaeology has contributed some important details to Muslim Caesarea's urban plan. No trace of the citadel has been found, presumably because it stood on the site of its Crusader successor (fig. 150; cf. fig. 170). More is known about the fortification wall. City dwellers, including the Muslim urbanists, ordinarily buried their dead outside the city walls. Thus, JECM's discovery of a cemetery in fields C and K makes it likely that the southern wall of the Muslim city passed to the north of the cemetery, perhaps on the line of the later Crusader fortifications (fig. 170). Moreover, two major stages in the construction of the Crusader fortifications have long been apparent to archaeologists. The Hebrew University team headed by Lee Levine, Dan Bahat, and Ehud Netzer has found evidence that the earlier phase went back as far as the early Arab period, perhaps to Mu'awiya himself. Whatever the exact date of the fortifications, it appears that the built-up area of Muslim Caesarea corresponded to that of the Crusader city, and that it was therefore a far smaller city than Roman and Byzantine Caesarea.

The Hebrew University team exposed a number of Fatimid-period houses in the city's northwestern quarter. Built over the ruins of poorer Abbasid dwellings, these houses had rooms walled with sandstone ashlars and opening onto paved courtyards. A certain amount of care and expense went into the doorsills, fashioned from ancient marble columns, and the ubiquitous wells and cisterns (the latter fed by ceramic pipes), indicating that their owners possessed some wealth. The Fatimid and Abbasid houses extended over the line of one of Byzantine Caesarea's streets, confirming that the Muslims generally ignored the ancient broad, open streets in favor of narrow, winding lanes. They created an urban environment more crowded and intimate than the city's classical predecessor.

Archaeological excavation has also produced indications that Caesarea was always a commercial and industrial center, even in the depressed period after the Muslim conquest. In 1986 CAHEP examined a series of six rectangular basins that the Hebrew University team had discovered adjacent to a sea wall of the great harbor basin (figs. 146 and 150). The floors of the basins are cream-colored mosaic pavements with circular depressions in one corner. They may have been settling basins for the production of olive oil. In construction, although perhaps not in

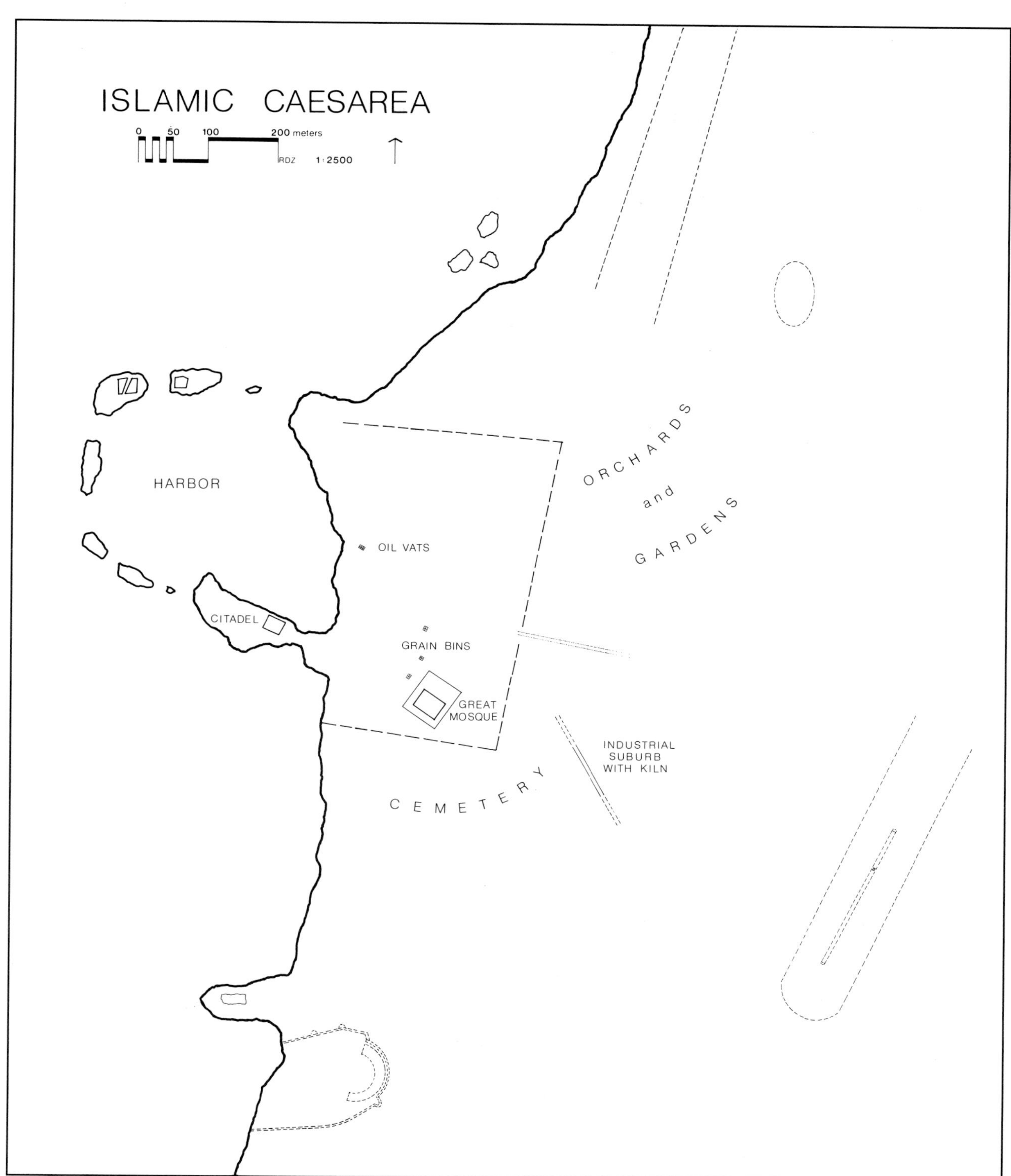
ISLAMIC CAESAREA
0
50
100
200 meters
RDZ
1:2500
HARBOR
CITADEL
OIL VATS
ORCHARDS
and
GARDENS
GRAIN BINS
GREAT
MOSQUE
INDUSTRIAL
SUBURB
WITH KILN
CEMETERY

Figure 151.
Bronze objects found by JECM in Islamic levels: at the upper left an ankle bracelet, 7.9 cm in diameter; at the lower left, a pen point, 6.1 cm long; and to the right a shallow container for pouring – its spout is missing – 11.9 cm long. Depending on the alloy and soil conditions, bronze objects found in archaeological trenches acquire a brown or light green patina or heavy oxidation. Object at lower left DIAR collection, others IDAM collection, at DIAR.
Aaron Levin photo.

Figure 152.
Ceramic oil lamps, length 9.8 cm (left) and 9.6 cm (right), found by JECM in areas B.6 and B.10, the Muslim industrial area in the east central sector of the site. This lamp, probably manufactured in Caesarea in the ninth century, was a pentagonal variant of the Muslim spur-handled form (fig. 155) that was descended in turn from certain forms of Byzantine lamp (e.g. fig. 147). DIAR collection.
Aaron Levin Photo.

Figure 153.
Glass vessels typical of Muslin Caesarea. Left: ribbed bottle, ninth- or tenth-century, 10.1 cm high, Israel Museum. Front center: small eighth-century bottle, 8.1 cm high, of Byzantine form with a new type of applied decoration, Israel Museum. Right: eighth-century bottle, 11.1 cm high, IDAM collection. Provenance of the bottle at left Beth Shean, of the others unknown.
David Harris photo, Israel Museum.

function, these basins recall the Islamic "grain bins" that Avraham Negev discovered earlier in front of Herod's vaulted temple platform. CAHEP dated the basins, from ceramic evidence, to the Umayyad period, making it likely that in the eighth century small ships still carried some agricultural commodities from the great Herodian harbor. Even if stormy seas and tectonic action had practically destroyed the breakwaters, they could still have protected a few coastal traders calling at Caesarea's docks.

In the southernmost vault of the Herodian platform, Negev found a thick layer of iron slag, charcoal, and ashes from the early Muslim period, and in front of the platform – above what had been the inner harbor of Strato's Tower and Herodian Caesarea – more slag, ashes, and large pieces of copper, indications of a metal industry. In Caesarea's soils, iron implements rarely survive intact, but JECM did uncover bronze objects in its trenches that may be of local manufacture (fig. 151).

Figure 154.
Ceramic water flask from the Umayyad period, suitable for suspending from a saddle. Height 23.5 cm. This vessel belongs to the class of white ware pottery manufactured in the seventh and eighth centuries C.E. It has typical molded decoration in geometric forms. Found at Ramla, now in the IDAM collection.
Aaron Levin photo.

Figure 155.
Ceramic oil lamps with high spur handle, common during the Umayyad and Abbasid periods of Muslim Caesarea. The almond shape and the rinceau *(vine scroll) decoration were descended from Byzantine and classical models. The example on the left, 10.9 cm long, is of unknown provenance. The miniature on the right, 4.2 cm long and found in JECM area C.5, may be a merchant's sample or a child's toy. Lamp at left, DIAR collection, at right IDAM collection, at DIAR.*
Aaron Levin photo.

Outside the Muslim city to the east, in field B, JECM excavated an industrial suburb that was active in Abbasid times. It included a furnace, a storage vault, a well, numerous crude buildings that probably were used by the craftsmen as both workshops and dwellings, and a paved street leading toward the city and the harbor. The team also found huge, well-stratified deposits of pottery, lamps, and glass. Among the likely products of this industrial area were pentagonal, spur-handled lamps from the ninth century that probably were manufactured in Caesarea (fig. 152).

Even before the close of the Umayyad period in 750, artists and craftsmen like those who worked in this industrial suburb had begun to shed their reliance on classical models in favor of the abstract designs that characterize Islamic art. The glassblowers began with Byzantine forms but used new varieties of applied decoration (fig. 153). Umayyad potters decorated their whiteware bowls, cups, and flasks with incised or molded geometric or floral designs (fig. 154). The typical Umayyad-Abbasid lamps found at Caesarea (fig. 155) continue a Byzantine form and the rinceau (vine scroll) motif inherited from classical art, but by Abbasid times the same lamp appeared with a dark-green glaze (fig. 156). For archaeologists, brightly

Figure 156.
Ceramic oil lamp with spur handle, 9.5 cm long, said to come from Caesarea, now in the Museum of Ancient Art, Haifa. This lamp, of the type in fig. 155, has a rich green glaze.
Aaron Levin photo.

Figure 157.
Ceramic bowl (repaired, large fragment missing), 24.4 cm in diameter, probably dating from the ninth century. Decorated in green, cream, and light brown glaze with a partridge or other game bird in a field of flowers. Found in JECM's area B.6, now in the DIAR collection.
Aaron Levin photo.

Figure 158.
Muslim treasure from ca. 1090, found in a ceramic jar in the southern vault of the Herodian Temple platform. Height of the jar 10.3 cm. The treasure consists of a woman's jewelry in gold, silver, and semi-precious stones. The gold necklace is made up of nine beads and ten spacers executed in filigree work and granulation. The silver objects – an amulet, two cylindrical amulet cases, and earrings – are decorated in niello with figures and calligraphy quoting the Qur'an. Collection of IDAM, displayed in the Israel Museum.
David Harris photo, Israel Museum.

colored and glazed sherds – above all else – identify Islamic levels. A splendid example is a bowl, probably Abbasid in date, that JECM found in the industrial suburb to the east of Muslim Caesarea (fig. 157). The decoration on this bowl, glazed inside in rich green, light brown, and cream, includes a partridge or other game bird walking in a field of flowers. The exuberant decoration on the piece makes the red-slipped Roman and Byzantine finewares seem dull.

No archaeological find from Caesarea better evokes Muslim art and culture than the hoard of jewelry that Negev discovered in the southern vault of the Herodian temple platform (fig. 158). The objects in this hoard date from about 1090 C.E., and, to judge from their costliness and elegance, must have belonged to the favored wife or concubine of one of Caesarea's merchants or landowners. The jar that contained the jewelry is splashed with a green and yellow glaze that typifies the more expensive Fatimid pottery. The gold necklace is strung with nine large "beads" exquisitely decorated with geometric and vegetal patterns in filigree and granulation, the work of a skilled goldsmith. The patron who ordered them must have been wealthy. The lesser objects in the collection, silver earrings and amulets and necklaces of semiprecious stones, demonstrate their owner's refined taste.

An inscription in Kufic, the Arabic script of the Abbasid and Fatimid periods, decorates one of the amulets. Such inscriptions, quotations from the *Qur'an*, the holy book of Islam, were to protect the amulet's owner: "Say he is Allah, the One! Allah, the eternally Besought of all!" This amulet did its owner no good. Danger persuaded her to conceal her jewelry in its jar and flee. She did not return after the danger had passed. It is very likely that the danger was the Crusader armies that besieged her city in 1101, slaughtering its inhabitants and ushering in a last, violent era in the history of Herod's city.

CHAPTER 7

Caesarea Under Crusader Rule: A European City in the Holy Land

Christian pilgrims from Europe continued to visit the Holy Land even after it had passed into Muslim hands, and many of them went through Caesarea. The bronze reliquary cross found in the sea to the south of the Crusader fortifications and dated to the Fatimid or Crusader periods may have belonged to one of them (fig. 160). In it was a fragment of the true cross or some other holy relic. Traffic to Palestine from the West increased in the tenth and eleventh centuries, in part because the Fatimid rulers of Jerusalem, who stood to make a healthy profit, generally welcomed pilgrims. The Muslim Caesareans had a good dose of Europeans in 1064–65, when a horde of about seven thousand German pilgrims stopped in their city on the long road to Jerusalem. Soon, wayfarers of a different type would arrive.

Figure 159.
The eastern Crusader gatehouse, interior of the thirteenth-century structure looking south. Visible are the trough for watering horses in the southwest corner of the hall, the Gothic vaults that roofed the structure, and the doorway in the western wall that gave access to the city.
JECM photo.

In November 1095, at Clermont in southeastern France, Pope Urban II delivered a sermon before a church council that has been called the most effective speech in all history. He directed the energies of Christian Europe, especially the Franks of France and the Low Countries, against the "wicked Saracens" who held the Holy Sepulcher and other Christian holy places in Jerusalem and elsewhere in Palestine. Christians – high-born and low; men, women, and even children – took up the cry "*Deus vult*" ("God wills it") and by the spring of 1097, 150,000 warriors had gathered in Constantinople, wearing the sign of the cross, poised for the First Crusade against the Muslims. The reasons for this dramatic development were complex. Pope Urban had tapped deep reservoirs of religious zeal, as well as the universal hope that henceforth Christians would rule the holy places, but the appeal of the crusade was also materialistic. Historians see the Crusaders as Europe's first

Figure 160.
Bronze reliquary cross, 9.0 cm high, found in the sea at Caesarea, now in the Caesarea Museum. The cross consists of two pieces, hinged at the top and closed at the bottom with a clasp, that enclosed a relic, perhaps a fragment of the True Cross. On the front piece (pictured here) there is an image of the crucified Christ with angels in medallions above and below and the Virgin Mary and St. John to the left and right. On the back piece Mary is surrounded by medallion images of the four evangelists, and there is a Greek inscription calling Mary "Mother of the Most High." The pose of Christ on the cross and of the other figures suggests a date in the eleventh or twelfth centuries, but similar objects were common from the sixth century on.
Danny Friedman photo.

imperialists. Among the leadership were many who had responded to Urban's call because they were the younger sons of princely Frankish families. Legally deprived of the right to inherit the family domains, they needed to find land elsewhere. These young men transplanted a European population, the European feudal system, and European culture, along with their warlike and boorish manners, to the Near East. They also remade Caesarea into a medieval European town.

In the spring of 1099, the Crusader army, led by Godfrey of Bouillon and three other commanders, arrived at a marsh north of Caesarea, presumably the waters backed up by the dam on the Crocodile River. While they were encamped, a Frankish hawk intercepted a carrier pigeon bearing a dispatch from the Muslim ruler of Acre to the amir of Caesarea. The writer warned of the "doglike race, the stupid, contentious, and undisciplined mob" that had just passed through his territory and urged the amir to do them whatever harm he thought appropriate. At the outset it looked as though the amir had decided against that, for early in the next year he signed a treaty with Godfrey purchasing immunity from attack, for a monthly tribute of five thousand bezants (gold coins). The amir then honored Godfrey at Caesarea with a sumptuous banquet. The guest died after the banquet. It was rumored that he had been poisoned.

On Christmas Day in 1100, in Bethlehem, the Franks crowned as their king Godfrey's brother, Baldwin I. The new ruler, entitled king of Jerusalem, renewed the treaties with Caesarea and other coastal cities but immediately reneged by engaging ships from Genoa, the great Italian merchant and naval power, to help him capture the cities by force. On May 2, 1101, Baldwin's army and the Genoese fleet appeared at Caesarea. The king ordered his men to cut down the luxuriant orchards that surrounded the city, to give the army maneuvering room, and to construct stone-throwing catapults and siege towers for attacking the city's 30-foot high defensive walls.

Before these could be readied, however, a Genoese named William Embriaco led an assault that drove the "soft and effeminate" defenders from the walls and conquered the city. The Muslims took refuge in the Great Mosque, "in an elevated position . . . where once had existed a temple of marvelous workmanship built by Herod in Honor of Augustus Caesar," hoping that the Crusaders would spare a holy place. They did not. The attackers saved only the amir, the *qadi* (or religious leader), and a few rich merchants for ransom. The Franks and their allies slaughtered the men, burned the corpses in order to reveal bezants that might have been swallowed, and sold the women into slavery. A Frankish eyewitness, Fulcher of Chartres, later described the carnage with obvious delight:

> *. . . it sometimes happened when one of our men struck the neck of some Saracen with his fist that from ten to sixteen bezants would be ejected from his mouth. The women also shamelessly hid bezants within themselves in a way that was wicked and which is more shameless for me to tell.**

The scene may explain the haste of the Muslim woman who, in the last days before the attack, concealed her jewelry in a jar beneath the Herodian temple platform. It also reports accurately both the wealth of the Muslim city and the nature of those who would next rule Caesarea.

The victorious Franks acquired a city that was virtually intact but emptied of its previous inhabitants. All that was necessary was to purify the Great Mosque, previously a church, according to medieval sources, and rededicate it as the cathedral of Saint Peter, who had originally brought Christianity to Caesarea. A Frank named Baldwin became the first Crusader archbishop. The Genoese, as a reward for their services, received one-third of the city and of the territory extending several miles outside the walls. They also received an extraordinary hexagonal cut-glass cup

*Fulcher of Chartres, *A History of the Expedition to Jerusalem 1095–1127*, trans. Frances Rita Ryan (Knoxville: The University of Tennessee Press, 1969), pp. 154–55.

they thought was of emerald that had been found in the Great Mosque. Believing the cup to be the Holy Grail, they took it to Genoa, where it still forms part of the San Lorenzo Cathedral treasure. Some of the Genoese, probably merchants, remained. Other Europeans, mainly from the Low Countries, made up the rest of the population. Any Muslims who survived the fall of the city had fled. The Jewish traveler Benjamin of Tudela, who visited Caesarea in about 1162, counted ten Jews and two hundred Samaritans living there.

The Franks turned Caesarea into a European-style feudal principality. By 1110 King Baldwin of Jerusalem had granted Caesarea as a fief (a feudal estate) to a Frank named Eustace Granier, who ruled the city as its "lord," a title he would bequeath to his descendants, male and female, until the end of Crusader Caesarea. The authority of the lord or lady extended roughly to the limits of Caesarea's ancient territory – to about one hundred villages in the countryside in which Arab peasants tilled the soil. Caesarea's ruler commanded a body of knights. Twenty-five of them lived from the produce of the ruler's domain lands, while the archbishop and the merchants of the city each provided for another fifty. These knights formed Caesarea's garrison and also fought at the side of the king of Jerusalem in his wars with the Muslim enemy.

Feudal Caesarea prospered until 1187, when Saladin (Salah al-Din, "rectitude of the faith"), ruling as sultan ("he with authority") for the Abbasid caliph, defeated the Crusader armies at the Horns of Hattin above the Sea of Galilee. His lieutenants seized Caesarea and, without their chivalrous master's authorization, destroyed the cathedral and killed or captured most of the inhabitants. To make them useless to the enemy, Saladin leveled at least part of the fortifications of all the Crusader cities that he captured. One of them was Caesarea, which thereafter, although taken and retaken several times, lay mostly desolate for nearly forty years. The lords and ladies of Caesarea received little benefit from their fief during this period, and neither they nor the titular archbishop lived for long in the city.

In 1228 Germans who had arrived with the Fifth Crusade set to work rebuilding Caesarea's walls, and the city experienced a final brief instant of reconstruction and prosperity. In 1251–52, the French king Louis IX, known as "Saint Louis," salvaged the Sixth Crusade, marred when he failed to take Egypt, by completing work on the magnificent fortifications that still dominate the site. A papal legate granted a pardon (remission of sins) to all who labored on the walls, so Louis took part in person. "Several times," his biographer relates, "the blessed king carried stones to the top [of the wall] upon his shoulders." This episode preceded the end of Crusader Caesarea by fewer than fifteen years.

The Archaeology of Crusader Caesarea

The European inhabitants of Crusader Caesarea cooked their dinners in locally made cook pots that have "elephant ear," or "bootstrap," handles. They represent the last phase of a native ceramic tradition as old as the city (fig. 161, cf. figs. 47, 115). Similarly, the "saucer lamps" typical of the Crusader period belong to an eastern Mediterranean form produced between the seventh and fifteenth centuries (fig. 162). When dinner was served, the Franks and Genoese preferred to eat it from dinnerware decorated in what archaeologists call the sgraffito technique, designs the potter incised before applying a transparent glaze (fig. 163). A large deposit of this dinnerware turned up in one of CAHEP's trenches. It was first produced in Muslim lands in the ninth century and by the eleventh formed part of the repertoire of medieval Byzantine workshops. Caesarea's Europeans clearly developed a taste for the products of the eastern craftsmen, most of them presumably Muslim, with whom the local merchants did business. In this limited sense at least, the Europeans began to absorb the culture of Islam and of Oriental Christianity.

On the other hand, the coins that identify Crusader layers at Caesarea have included billon (low-grade silver) pieces struck in Italy or the Iberian Peninsula and two remarkable, early twelfth-century dinars inscribed in Arabic with verses from the *Qur'an* and struck in southern Spain by mints of the Muslim Almoravids who had their headquarters in Morocco (fig. 164). A Crusader Caesarean had dropped the Almoravid coins within vault 1 in JECM's field C, which in the Crusader period apparently served as a charnel house. To judge from the coins, travelers and commerce moved with relative ease between West and East and between Muslim territory and the Crusader states during this energetic period in Mediterranean history.

Because JECM limited its excavations to sectors outside of the fortifications, it has gathered relatively little information about the urban environment in which Crusader Caesareans lived. The team has learned much more about the Caesareans themselves, because they buried their dead in cemeteries outside the walls. In the southwest zone, especially in fields C and K, JECM archaeologists have excavated more than 350 human burials, ranging in date from the seventh or eighth century to the nineteenth and even the twentieth. Sometimes grave goods help date a burial, as did a bronze, upside-down "Saint Peter's" cross that had belonged to one of the twelfth or thirteenth century inhabitants of Caesarea (fig. 166). More often, however, it is burial practices that enable archaeologists to estimate a date.

Figure 161.
Ceramic cook pot (restored) with strap handles, 20.0 cm high, found in CAHEP's area I1. Decorated with splashes of brown glaze on the shoulder. This form of cook pot had been in use since the eighth century, but this example comes from a twelfth- or thirteenth-century layer. IDAM collection, at the Center for Maritime Studies, Haifa.
Danny Friedman photo.

Figure 162.
Group of lidded saucer lamps, made of ceramic, diameters 7.3–8.0 cm. Such lamps were used widely in Syria and Palestine from the seventh century to the fifteenth. The examples shown here, from JECM areas B.8, C.14, and C.32, date from the tenth and eleventh centuries, perhaps into the beginning of the Crusader period. In the twelfth- through fourteenth-century variant, the juncture between the lid (the lamp's domed upper part) and the saucer (the lower part) occurs deeper in the saucer. Lamp at center, DIAR collection, others IDAM collection, at DIAR.
Aaron Levin photo.

Figure 163.
Ceramic tableware (restored) from Caesarea's Crusader period, found by CAHEP in area I1. Left: bowl, 19.5 cm in diameter, decorated in the sgraffito *technique with a design of leaves. Center: bowl, 21.0 cm in diameter, perhaps manufactured in Syria, decorated with white glaze and abstract designs in lustrous brown. Right: plate, 21.0 cm in diameter, decorated in* sgraffito *like the bowl on the left but with green instead of yellow glaze. IDAM collection, in the Center for Maritime Studies, Haifa.*
Danny Friedman photo.

Figure 164.
Gold dinar of the Almoravid dynasty of southern Spain and Morocco, 2.5 cm in diameter, found by JECM in area C.8. On the reverse (pictured here) the marginal legend, in Arabic, dates the coin to 1106/7 and identifies Malaga, Spain, as the place where it was minted. The central legend reads, "The Imam 'Abd Allah, the Commander of the Faithful." It reveals that the Almoravids recognized the spiritual authority of the Abbasid caliph (called here imam, *legitimate successor of Muhammad) in Baghdad. Now in the IDAM collection.*
Aaron Levin photo.

Figure 165.
Glass beaker, 10.3 cm high, provenance unknown but of a type that occurs in Israel in late Crusader contexts. Date thirteenth or fourteenth century. Originally ornamented with enameling in red and blue, of which only faint traces survive. Such beakers also occur in European churches, indicating that they may have served as pilgrim vessels for soil from the Holy Land. Now in the Israel Museum.
David Harris photo, Israel Museum.

Figure 166.
Bronze cross, 3.0 cm high, found in association with a burial in JECM's area C.5. The position of the loop for hanging shows that this is an upside-down or "St. Peter's" cross, so named because of the tradition that St. Peter had been crucified upside down. The wearer of the cross must have been devoted to St. Peter, to whom the cathedral of Crusader Caesarea was dedicated. Now in the collection of IDAM.
Aaron Levin photo.

The study of burial practices belongs to a branch of archaeology known as mortuary archaeology. It is practiced by physical anthropologists, who are among the specialists working at Caesarea. The site's burials have revealed, for example, that both Muslims and Crusaders buried their dead in stone-lined pits (fig. 167). They typically dug a deep grave in the ruin-filled field south of the city and lined the bottom with flat stones set on edge. After laying in the corpse, they covered it with flat stone cappers and then filled the grave with earth. What distinguishes the Crusader burials from the Muslim ones is the skeleton's position. Typically, the Muslim skeletons lie on their right side, extended or semiflexed, with their feet to the east and the skull facing south toward Mecca, the direction of prayer in Islam. In Christian burials the skeleton lies on its back, fully extended, its feet to the east, its arms folded across the chest, and its skull slightly elevated, often on a stone "pillow" (fig. 167). This position too had religious significance, for Christians expected that, on the day of judgement, the risen Christ would appear in the east, like the rising sun.

Sometimes mortuary archaeology has surprising results. In 1982 JECM excavated a grave in field C that contained the poorly preserved skeleton of a Crusader wearing scale armor of thin bronze plates originally attached to a leather backing. Examination of the skeleton showed that it was a female, the remains of a woman

Figure 167.
Crusader burial found in JECM area C.5, looking west. The corpse was placed in a stone-lined pit, with the head to the west and slightly elevated. Remains of walls visible in the photograph date from the Byzantine period.
JECM photo.

Figure 168.
Head of a bearded man, 19.5 cm high, carved in marble, said to be from Caesarea. Long mistaken for a Hellenistic or Roman image of Zeus, this head has recently been identified as a Crusader work that once decorated a corbel. A European probably carved it, under the influence of local tradition in Palestine. Now in the Museum of Ancient Art, Haifa.
Aaron Levin photo.

whom the archaeologists immediately dubbed "Joan of Caesarea." A search of the literary sources has revealed that women did on occasion wear armor and engage in combat against the hated Saracens, not because they coveted the male role, but as a demonstration of piety.

Studying the skeletons is the task of a branch of physical anthropology, human skeletal biology. The work begins with the painstaking recovery of the skeletal material, for which archaeologists need extreme patience and special instruments – paintbrushes and flattened and pointed wooden tools – to remove the soil adhering to the skeleton without damaging the bones and teeth. At Caesarea this is a special problem because human bone tends to disintegrate in the site's damp soil. Recovering all of the skeleton's bones is not an easy assignment when, as sometimes occurs, the skeleton is of a fetus buried with the corpse of its mother.

The analysis of a skeleton begins in the field, with an effort to determine its sex and age at death, but the archaeologists quickly pack the bones for shipment to the anthropology lab, where they are measured, examined, and analyzed. As that work proceeds the anthropologists learn a great deal about the physical makeup of a population. From the more than 350 skeletons excavated, they will determine to which human groups members of the population belonged – whether they resemble more closely Mediterranean types or types characteristic of the Arabian Peninsula. Analysis of the bones will reveal patterns of longevity among males and females, whether the diet that the Caesareans typically consumed was a healthy one, and which diseases were prevalent. The skeletons speak volumes to the physical anthropologist about the causes of death among a population. Already noticeable in the field examination are signs of violent death – hack marks on the long bones of the arms and legs and indications of cranial penetration or fracture can mean that the person died in battle, perhaps against the Saracens, perhaps in private combat.

Caesarea's Crusader fortifications, like the bones of her inhabitants, evoke an era of violence and insecurity. Apart from the destroyed upper portions of the fortification walls, they stand today, Caesarea's most imposing ruins, much as they did when Saint Louis and his Crusaders completed them early in 1252 (fig. 169). In the early 1960s, under Avraham Negev's supervision, the Israeli National Parks Authority cleared the moats and reconstructed the eastern gatehouse. The fortifications measure about 650 meters north–south and 275 meters east–west. They enclose an area of about 12.2 hectares, far smaller than either the Byzantine or the Herodian and Roman cities. Originally walls protected the city on all four sides, but over the centuries the sea has carried away most of the western range of fortifications (fig. 170). The existing ruins represent the military architecture of

thirteenth-century Europe. A counterscarp, the vertical drop into the fosse, or moat, and a scarp that slopes upward (also called a glacis, or talus) hindered the enemy's approach to the walls, which stood about 10 meters high (fig. 171). The lower parts of sixteen rectangular towers survive, built into the wall. Opposite each tower is a recess in the line of the counterscarp that preserves the full width of the fosse. Loopholes that permitted the defenders to direct crossbow fire at the enemy pierced the masonry of the walls and towers. Entrance to the city was through gates in the northern, southern, and eastern walls, and an escape could be made from the fosse through posterns in the eastern wall, north of the eastern gate, and in the southern wall near the southeastern corner tower.

Figure 169. Caesarea's Crusader fortifications, completed by St. Louis in 1252, and the ruins of the Crusader city within. View looking north. Aaron Levin photo.

The building stones are relatively small ashlars cut from the local calcareous sandstone that was used in most of Caesarea throughout the centuries. The mortar in

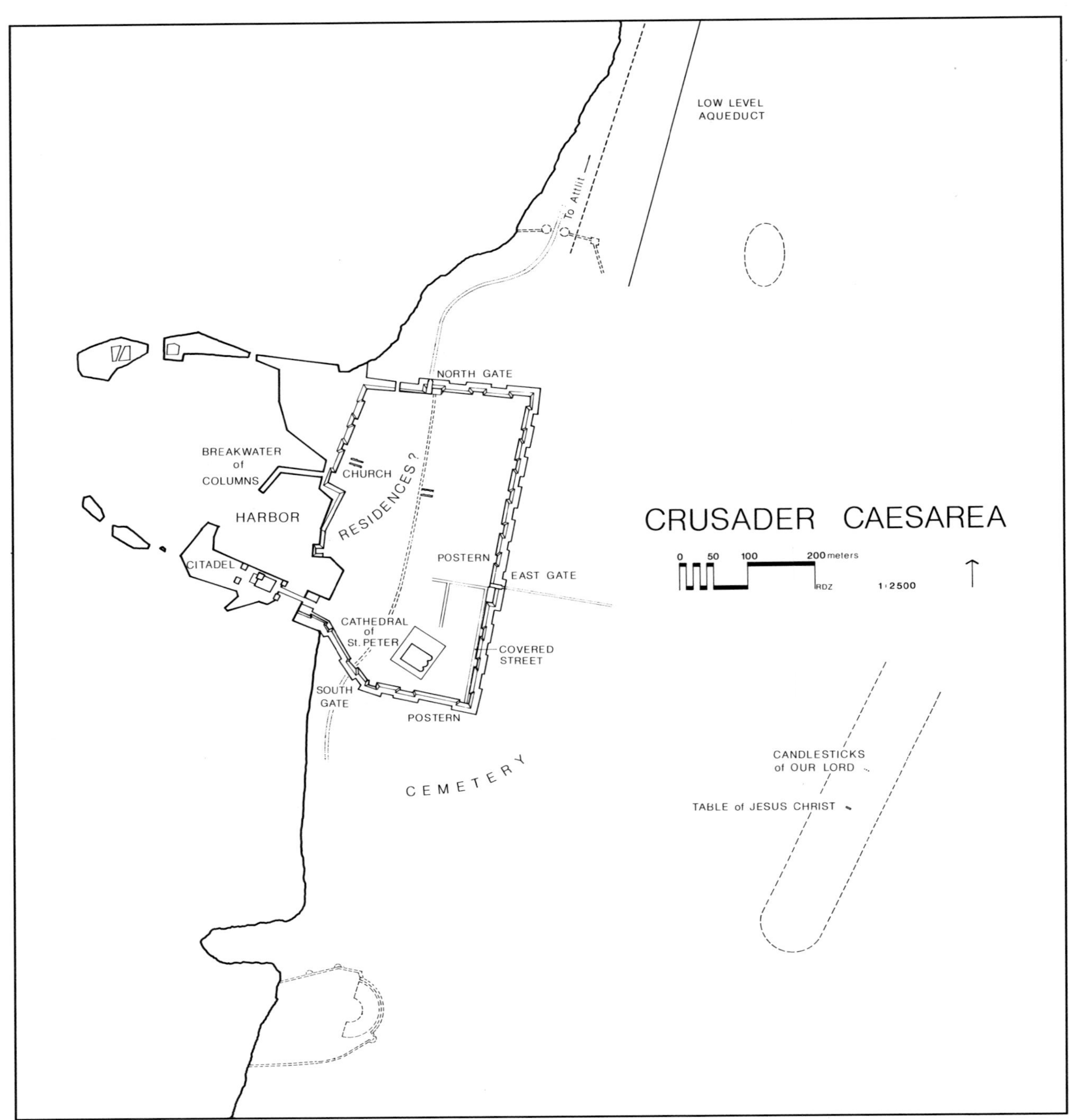

Figure 170.
Crusader Caesarea, urban plan ca. 1252, based on archaeology and literary sources.
Robin Ziek drawing.

Figure 171. The Crusader fortifications, eastern range, looking north. Little of the fortification wall survives above the scarp (glacis or talus) that protected the towers and the wall.
Aaron Levin photo.

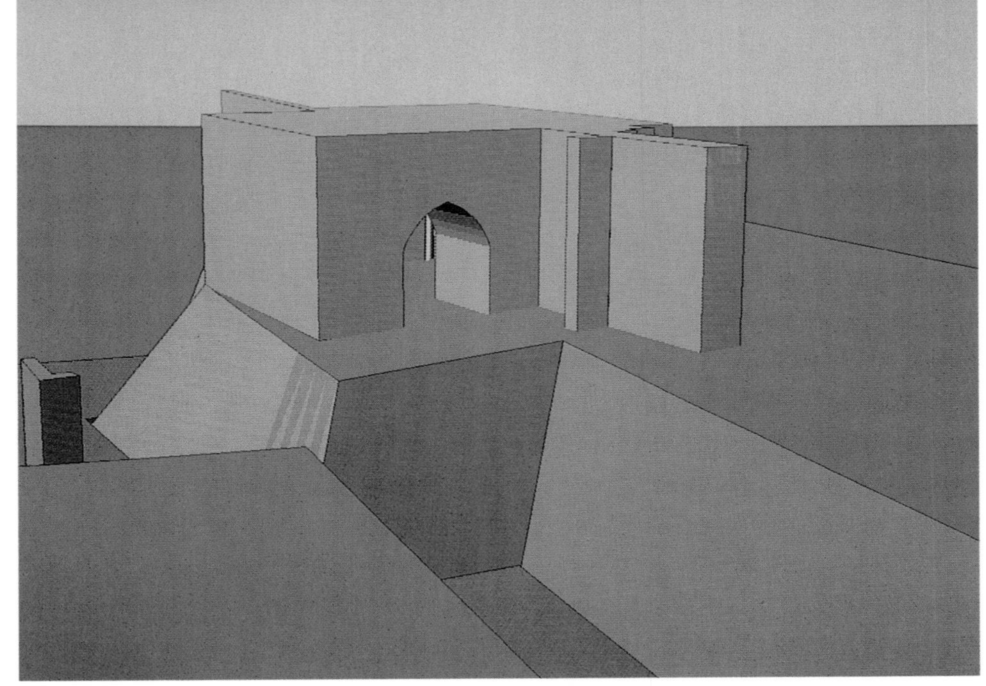

Figure 172.
The northern gate of the Crusader fortifications, computer reconstruction prepared at the University of Maryland School of Architecture. Architects working with CAHEP collected the data for the reconstruction and recorded it on a portable computer.
Stephen Sachs drawing.

the glacis differs from that in the preserved portions of the walls themselves, and the glacis was built against the wall but not bonded into it. Hence the outer defensive works (glacis, fosse, and counterscarp) should be dated to the reconstruction of 1251–52, and indeed their design reflects mid-thirteenth century European prototypes.

The northern and eastern gates belong to the indirect-access type normal in Crusader construction from the mid-thirteenth century. In the eastern gatehouse Negev found evidence of an earlier, direct-access gate. After Saint Louis, access to the city was from the north or east on bridges built over the fosse. A turn hard left (exposing the right, unshielded side) brought visitors to an iron grille and a heavy wooden door. Using the eastern gatehouse visitors entered a large hall, stone-paved and with a bench along the eastern wall. A well with a basin in the southwest corner may have been used for watering horses. The roof of the hall consists of three Gothic cross vaults with diagonal ribs that spring from corbels carved with vegetal motifs (fig. 159). Another doorway in the western wall led to one of the main streets of the town.

The northern gatehouse, although smaller, corresponds in design with the eastern one. Recently CAHEP and students and faculty from the University of Maryland School of Architecture used computers to study the design of this gatehouse. The advent of the microcomputer has profoundly affected archaeology in the last decade. Both CAHEP and JECM use a computer to record archaeological finds. Now CAHEP is applying this technology to architectural studies. With a portable computer the measurements of a building can be recorded in the field and brought to the archaeological lab on magnetic disks. Using a larger computer with enhanced graphics capability, architects create an image of a building in two or three dimensions on the computer's monitor, and, if the building is in ruins, explore various systems for restoring it. When the restoration is complete, the computer prints a drawing that corresponds in quality to one made by hand (fig. 172). For field archaeology the computer reduces the time spent on recording and retrieving data and even assists with interpretation.

If we enter Caesarea by the eastern gate we emerge from the gatehouse onto a Crusader street that leads westward. The street is paved with limestone slabs taken from a Roman street. Much of this city's fabric, like that of its Muslim predecessor, was created from spoils from the past – building stones, capitals, column shafts, fragments of architectural sculpture from Roman and Byzantine buildings. There are some indications that the street plan of the Crusader city, like the line of the fortification walls, corresponded with that of Muslim Caesarea. Similarly, a Crusader house to the south of the eastern gatehouse – several rooms built around two courtyards – actually goes back well into the Muslim period. Even the low-level aqueduct, which the Muslims had brought back into service, still brought water to Caesarea for irrigating the gardens and orchards, which, by the thirteenth century, had recovered from the devastation of the Crusader conquest. On the other hand, the Franks and other Crusaders gave their city a European flavor. For example, they built a roof on pointed arches over the street to the east of the Crusader house, between it and the fortification wall, in the European Gothic style (fig. 173).

On the rock promontory that once protected the southern harbor of Strato's Tower, which later formed part of the southern breakwater of Herod's harbor and which probably held the amir's citadel, the lords and ladies of Caesarea had their castle (figs. 170 and 178). A channel nearly 20 meters wide separated this fortress from the city and the land. The upper part of the donjon, or keep – a masonry tower that rose several stories – was destroyed late in the nineteenth century to make way for a building that now houses an artist's studio and one of Caesarea's restaurants. The Crusaders built a bastion with several towers surrounding the donjon, reusing many of the site's granite columns to give strength to the structure.

To the north there are more columns, lying side by side in the sea in a line that leads southwest from the shore (figs. 170, 174). Many of them lined Caesarea's colonnaded streets in Roman and Byzantine times, but either the Muslims or the Crusaders reused them to form a small breakwater. A few small boats could find

Figure 173.
Covered street along the eastern wall of the Crusader fortifications, view looking south. The Crusaders imported European Gothic architecture into Palestine and the Near East.
Aaron Levin photo.

shelter behind it from westerly and northwesterly winds, and probably from the prevailing southwesterlies as well, because portions of the Herodian south breakwater still protruded above the sea. This column jetty also protected the entrance to the main Crusader harbor, which was so small, according to one source, that it could accommodate only one vessel at a time. CAHEP discovered evidence of this harbor near the entrance to the Herodian inner harbor: the foundations of a square tower similar to those of the Crusader bastion rest on the sea bottom. Leading northward from the tower are some remains of a fortification wall, presumably the western fortification wall of the Crusader city (figs. 170, 175). The gap between the square tower and the city's southern fortification wall was the entrance to a small harbor

Figure 174.
Jetty of columns jutting into the sea from the shore within the Crusader fortifications. CAHEP dates this jetty, made of columns that had lined Caesarea's Roman and Byzantine streets, to the Crusader period and suggests that it functioned as a breakwater to protect Caesarea's small Crusader harbor (cf. figs. 170, 175).
Bill Curtzinger photo, © National Geographic Society.

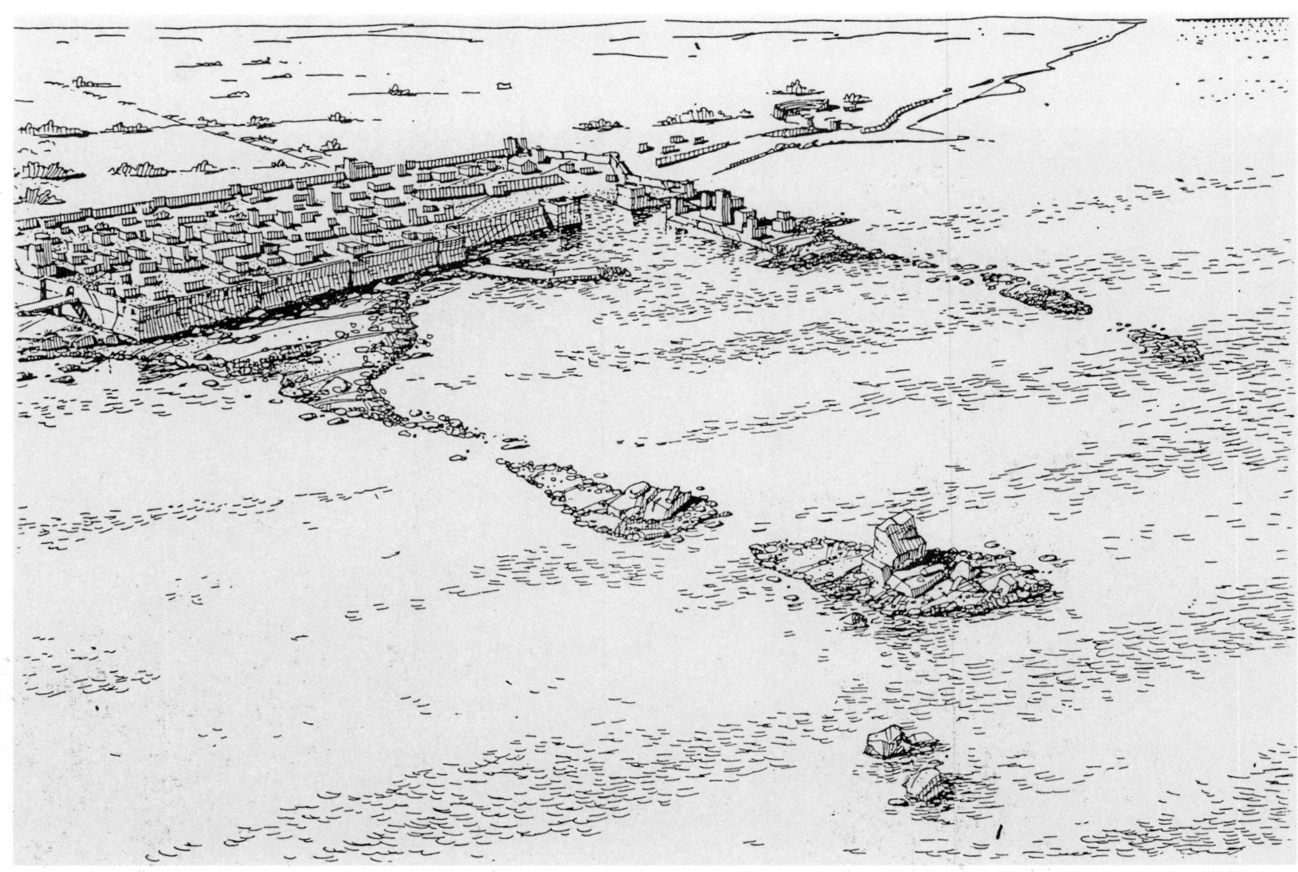

Figure 175. Crusader Caesarea, hypothetical perspective view in the thirteenth century.
Stephen Giannetti drawing.

basin that could be closed off with an iron chain to prevent the enemy from entering the city by ship. The modest size of the Crusader harbor makes it clear that neither Genoa nor any of the other prosperous Italian maritime cities were interested in developing Caesarea as a port.

Above the harbor, on the platform of vaults where Herod's temple to Roma and Augustus had once stood, rose the city's cathedral, dedicated to Saint Peter. Scholars generally associate the cathedral mentioned in the literary sources with the ruins of a triapsidal basilica near the southern end of the platform (fig. 176). This church is large enough, 24 by 27 meters, to have been the city's cathedral, but it seems to have been abandoned during construction, when its northern wall collapsed into the vaults below. More likely, the existing ruins are from the thirteenth century, perhaps from the time of Saint Louis, while the cathedral of Saint Peter stood further to the north and east. The latter church was destroyed in 1187 after Saladin's victory at the

Horns of Hattin. According to literary sources Saint Peter's had been the city's Great Mosque during the Muslim period, and earlier still a Byzantine church had occupied the site. The Crusaders even remembered that Herod's temple had once stood in the same position as their Saint Peter's cathedral. Herod's brilliant architectural conception of having the city's principal sanctuary dominate the harbor from a lofty platform was still honored in the medieval city.

Even so, the style of Crusader Caesarea's urbanism was European, the style of the Franks and Genoese – and others from France, the Low countries, and Italy. The Crusaders built with marble and stone spoils from antiquity on a plan inherited from the Muslims, but they brought their architecture with them from abroad. They ate from bowls of local manufacture, but they followed the feudal system and the social manners of Europe. King Herod would not have felt at home in the last version of his once grand city.

Figure 176.
Ruins of the unfinished Crusader church on the Herodian temple platform, looking southwest. Construction may have begun in the mid-thirteenth century, when St. Louis visited Caesarea, but ended abruptly when the north aisle collapsed into the vault below. The collapse is visible in this photograph. To the west of the central apse, a smaller apse is all that survives of a smaller, later church.
Aaron Levin photo.

Epilogue: Desolation and Development

On February 27, 1265, the Mamluk sultan Baybars, ruler of Egypt, brought an army, including stone-throwing artillery, to Caesarea and took the city with ease. His men swarmed over Saint Louis's walls and isolated Caesarea's knights in the castle, which contemporaries had considered impregnable. The defenders resisted for six days and then agreed to surrender on terms. In sharp contrast to the conduct of the Franks in 1101, Baybars spared their lives, and the Franks left Caesarea forever. In 1291 the next Mamluk sultan ordered Caesarea and the rest of the coastal fortresses destroyed to prevent the Europeans from gaining a foothold in the Levant again.

After 1291 natural processes of destruction took over. The sea, which had substantially eroded the breakwaters of Sebastos, went to work on the Crusader seaside fortifications. For centuries, Herod's artificial harbor had obstructed the coastal current, creating gigantic eddies that claimed the beach north of the city, cut the high-level aqueduct, and formed what the archaeologists now call the north bay (fig. 1). Herod's great work had another, even more damaging result. Huge amounts of sand piled up against the harbor and along the beach, and the wind slowly moved the sand inland. When the site was abandoned, and the orchards, gardens, and other vegetation that had once surrounded Caesarea no longer turned the sand into fertile topsoil, dunes began to drift into Caesarea's hinterland. Today they reach as far as 5 kilometers to the east. The same sand choked streams in the vicinity and the reservoir behind the dam north of the city, preventing runoff and creating pestilential swamps. The king who had willed Caesarea into being had an unwitting role in its destruction.

Figure 177. Engraving of Caesarea by W. H. Bartlett and C. Cousen, from 1842, 16.5 × 24.4 cm. View looking south from the shore toward the south Herodian breakwater. Ruins of Crusader citadel to the left, column jetty in the foreground. This copy is now at DIAR.
Aaron Levin photo.

Figure 178.
The southern breakwater of Herod's harbor, photographed by Félix or Adrien Bonfils of Beirut ca. 1885. On top of the breakwater stand the ruins of the Crusader citadel, on which the Bosnians who resettled Caesarea in 1882 built their government house. Also visible are a cafe and another, unidentified building of the Bosnian community. Félix Bonfils (d. 1885) and his son Adrien (d. 1929) were well-known French photographers of the Orient.
Photo courtesy of the Harvard Semitic Museum.

The land archaeologists at Caesarea dig through 1 to 5 meters of sand every time they excavate a trench. Virtually devoid of artifacts or other signs of human life, Caesarea's sandy blanket makes palpable the site's six-hundred-year desolation. During those six centuries pilgrims and other travelers from Europe who visited the site on their way to Jerusalem recorded their impressions. In 1334 a rabbi found a few Jews living there but no Samaritans. In about 1421 a visitor named Johannes Poloner saw swamps infested with crocodiles but no human beings. In the seventeenth century F. E. Roger, a Frenchman, lamented that there was only a village of Moors and seven or eight Jewish families. By the 1830s, according to J. Taylor and L. Reybaud, it was again "silent as a cadaver." Only a small population of bedouin, called "marsh Arabs," occupied the malaria-infested countryside nearby. The engravings that illustrated books by eighteenth- and nineteenth-century visitors to the Holy Land speak eloquently of Caesarea's desolation (fig. 177).

By the nineteenth century the Europeans' zest for travel and their interest in the Holy Land brought increasing numbers of travelers to the site, some of whom had a genuine scientific interest (p. 17), and in the nineteenth and twentieth centuries new settlers arrived. In 1882 the Ottoman Empire, which had ruled Palestine since the sixteenth century, gave land to the east of Caesarea to a small group of Muslim Turks, refugees from Bosnia. The Bosnians, fewer than one hundred persons in all, preferred to live by the sea, and with the help of a German architect laid out a small town within the ruined Crusader fortifications. The town included streets and alleys, a bakery, several mosques, and the house of a Turkish *mudir* ("governor"), built on the site of the Crusader citadel (fig. 178). Bosnians lived on the site until 1948. They brought the fields just outside the Crusader walls under cultivation again and had a prosperous business selling the building stones they quarried from the ancient ruins.

At the same time Jewish immigration from Europe was adding to the number of Jews already in the land. Early in this century Baron Edmond de Rothschild, of the French branch of the banking family, secured a concession from the Turkish sultan over a large tract of land between the Crocodile River, 4.0 kilometers to the north of Caesarea, and the Hadera River, which flows into the sea about 2 kilometers to the south. Baron Edmond founded a company called the Palestine Jewish Colonization Association (French acronym PICA), which purchased the Bosnian holdings and gradually became the proprietor of much of the land in and near Caesarea. PICA set about reclaiming fields from the dunes and swamps, in part by cutting a channel through the ancient dam on the Crocodile River with explosives. The Greek Orthodox Church also acquired title to part of Caesarea, including the

sites of the Herodian-Roman theater and the hippodrome. A Greek monk built the gateway that opens into the hippodrome from the north.

On May 2, 1940, a small group of Jews arrived at Caesarea from Haifa, some in horse-drawn wagons and others in a small boat. They planned to learn how to fish profitably in the sea. Within a few years the first permanent buildings of a farming and fishing collective named Kibbutz Sdot Yam, "Fields of the Sea," sprang up among the dunes, extending southward from the still-buried theater. Although commercial fishing did not bring great profits, the kibbutz flourished from agriculture, dairy herds, and the manufacture of quality furniture and marble floor tiles.

One of the first members of the kibbutz was Hannah Senesh, a young woman from Hungary who wrote poems in Hebrew. One of her poems gave voice to the Jewish refugees, like her, from Nazi-occupied Europe who were being landed at night secretly, illegally, in Caesarea's small harbor. The poem is called "To Caesarea."

Hush, cease all sound.
Across the sea is the sand,
The shore known and near,
The shore golden, dear,
Home, the Homeland.

With step twisting and light
Among strangers we move,
Word and song hushed,
Towards the future-past
Caesarea . . .

But reaching the city of ruins
Soft a few words we intone.
We return. We are here.
Soft answers the silence of stone,
We awaited you two thousand years.

Sdot-Yam, Caesarea 1941*

Along with other young Jews from Palestine, Hannah Senesh volunteered as a parachutist with the British Army during World War II. She was captured, tortured, and executed by the Nazis. She was twenty-three.

Muslim Bosnians and bedouin, Greek Christians, and Jewish entrepreneurs and kibbutzniks have all played a role in the modern revival of Caesarea. Located today within the territory of the State of Israel, Caesarea is part of the developing economy of a vibrant country. In 1954 PICA was dissolved and all of its property except for Caesarea was transferred to the State of Israel. The Caesarea Development

*From *Hannah Senesh: Her Life and Diary* translated by Marta Cohn. Copyright © 1972 by Nigel Marsh. Reprinted by permission of Schocken Books, published by Pantheon Books, a Division of Random House.

Corporation now develops parts of the site in equal partnership with the Israeli government. The organization has built more than four hundred homes on a large tract to the northeast of the Crusader city (fig. 1), and a luxury hotel with a renowned golf course occupies terrain, formerly sand dunes, to the east of the hippodrome. In the early 1960s, to attract tourists to the site, Israel's National Parks Authority cleared most of the old Crusader city of its modern buildings, and restaurants and shops opened in the former Bosnian buildings. The Old City, together with the area around the theater, is now part of Israel's extensive national park system. The Parks Authority restored the theater, which attracts large crowds to Caesarea during the summer for music and dance performances. Anastylosis, restoring ancient ruins, is a worthwhile investment: Caesarea is now the third most-visited archaeological site in Israel.

It is the job of the Israel Department of Antiquities and Museums (IDAM) to protect the archaeological realm of Israel's cultural heritage. IDAM is empowered to ensure that archaeologists examine all antiquities unearthed during construction work before new buildings cover them. New construction is sometimes even forbidden if it will limit the archaeologists' access to important ancient remains, such as exist beneath the entire zone within the line of Caesarea's Byzantine walls. At Caesarea archaeologists and developers have tried to work harmoniously together. Archaeology has promoted tourism and therefore makes a contribution to Israel's economy, and developers have contributed both money and services to archaeological excavation.

When archaeologists excavate they cooperate with IDAM by publishing the results of their work and by conserving the objects they remove from the soil and stabilizing exposed structures, for deterioration sets in very quickly. At Caesarea exposed walls have been consolidated with mortar and mosaic pavements have been reburied in order to protect them. When funds are available, excavating teams also undertake anastylosis to make the results of their work meaningful to the visitor.

Archaeology is a public discipline. It is involved not only with science, the humanities, and art but with local politics, economic planning, and the expenditure of large sums of public and private money. Caesarea's archaeologists are conscientious about fulfilling their obligations to IDAM, science, and the public, and they expect to work at Caesarea far into the future. Because CAHEP, JECM, and Israeli and other foreign teams have collectively excavated only a small fraction of the ancient site, there are still opportunities for volunteers to work under the hot sun or beneath the chilling sea, exploring the city that was King Herod's dream.

Bibliography

General

Avi-Yonah, Michael. *The Holy Land from the Persian to the Arab Conquest.* Rev. ed. Grand Rapids, 1977.

Blakely, Jeffrey. "A Stratigraphically Determined Date for the Inner Fortification Wall at Caesarea Maritima." In *The Answers Lie Below: Essays in Honor of Lawrence Edmund Toombs,* ed. Henry O. Thompson. Lanham, Md., 1984. 3–38.

Bull, Robert J. "Caesarea, Notes and News." *Israel Exploration Journal* 23 (1973): 260–62.

———. "Caesarea, Notes and News." *Israel Exploration Journal* 24 (1974): 280–82.

———. "Caesarea Maritima: The Search for Herod's City." *Biblical Archaeology Review* 8 (1982): 24–40.

———. "The Ninth Season of Excavation at Caesarea Maritima." *American Journal of Archaeology* 85 (1981): 188.

———, and Toombs, L. E. "Caesarea, Notes and News." *Israel Exploration Journal* 22 (1972): 178–80.

———, Krentz, Edgar, and Storvick, Olin J. "The Joint Expedition to Caesarea Maritima: Ninth Season, 1980." *Bulletin of the American Schools of Oriental Research, Supplement,* no. 24 (1986): 31–55.

Conder, C. R., and Kitchener, H. H. *Survey of Western Palestine.* Vol. 2. *Samaria.* London, 1882

Flemming, Nicolas C., Raban, Avner, and Goetschel, C. "Tectonic and Eustatic Changes of the Mediterranean Coast of Israel in the Last 9000 Years." In *Beneath the Waters of Time, Proceedings of the 9th Congress of Underwater Archaeology.* Austin, 1978. 129–65.

Fritsch, Charles T., and Ben-Dor, Immanuel. "The Link Expedition to Israel, 1960." *Biblical Archaeologist* 24 (1961): 50–59.

Frova, Antonio et al. *Scavi di Caesarea Maritima.* Rome, 1966.

Hamburger, Anit. "Gems from Caesarea Maritima." *Atiqot,* English Series, 8 (1968): 1–38.

Hohlfelder, Robert L. "Caesarea Beneath the Sea." *Biblical Archaeology Review* 8 (1982): 42–47.

———, Oleson, John P., Raban, Avner, and Vann, R. Lindley. "Sebastos: Herod's Harbor at Caesarea Maritima." *Biblical Archaeologist* 46 (1983): 133–43.

Holland, D. L. "The Joint Expedition to Caesarea Maritima, 1971." *American Schools of Oriental Research Newsletter* 1 (1971–72): 1–4.

———. "The Joint Expedition to Caesarea Maritima, 1972." *American Schools of Oriental Research Newsletter* 5 (1972–73): 1–4.

Humphrey, John H. "Prolegomena to the Study of the Hippodrome at Caesarea Maritima." *Bulletin of the American Schools of Oriental Research* 213 (1974): 2–45.

———. "A Summary of the 1974 Excavations in the Caesarea Hippodrome." *Bulletin of the American Schools of Oriental Research* 218 (1975): 1–24.

Kennedy, Hugh. "From *Polis* to *Madina:* Urban Change in Late Antique and Early Islamic Syria." *Past and Present* 106 (1985): 3–27.

Levine, Lee I. *Caesarea Under Roman Rule.* Leiden, Netherlands, 1975.

———. *Roman Caesarea: An Archaeological-Topographical Study.* Qedem: Monographs of the Institute of Archaeology, The Hebrew University of Jerusalem, no. 2. Jerusalem, 1975.

———, and Netzer, Ehud. *Excavations at Caesarea Maritima, 1975, 1976, 1979—Final Report.* Qedem: Monographs of the Institute of Archaeology, The Hebrew University of Jerusalem, no. 21. Jerusalem, 1986.

Lifshitz, Baruch. "Césarée de Palestine, son histoire et ses institutions." In *Aufstieg und Niedergang der römischen Welt,* ed. H. Temporini. Part 2, vol. 8. Berlin and New York, 1977. 490–518.

Negev, Avraham. *Caesarea.* Tel Aviv, 1967.

———. "The High Level Aqueduct at Caesarea." *Israel Exploration Journal* 14 (1964): 237–49.

———. "The Palimpsest of Caesarea Maritima." *London Illustrated News,* October 26, 1963, 684–86; and November 2, 1963, 728–31.

Olami, Ya'acov, and Peleg, Yehudah. "The Water Supply System of Caesarea Maritima." *Israel Exploration Journal* 27 (1977): 127–37.

Oleson, John Peter, Hohlfelder, Robert L., Raban, Avner, and Vann, Robert L. "The Caesarea Ancient Harbour Excavation Project (CAHEP): Preliminary Report on the 1980–1983 Seasons." *Journal of Field Archaeology* 11 (1984): 281–305.

Raban, Avner. "Caesarea Maritima 1983–84." *International Journal of Nautical Archaeology and Underwater Exploration* 14 (1985): 155–77.

Riley, John A. "The Pottery From the First Session of Excavation in the Caesarea Hippodrome." *Bulletin of the American Schools of Oriental Research* 218 (1975): 25–63.

Ringel, Joseph. *Césarée de Palestine, Étude historique et archéologique.* Paris, 1975.

Roller, Duane W. "The Wilfrid Laurier University Survey of Northeastern Caesarea Maritima." *Levant* 14 (1982): 90–103.

Toombs, Lawrence E. "The Stratigraphy of Caesarea Maritima." In *Archaeology in the Levant: Essays for Kathleen Kenyon,* ed. P. R. S. Moorey and Peter Parr. Warminster, England, 1978. 223–32.

Wiemken, Robert C., and Holum, Kenneth G. "The Joint Expedition to Caesarea Maritima: Eighth Season, 1979." *Bulletin of the American Schools of Oriental Research* 244 (1981): 27–52.

Chapter 1

Gersht, Rivka. "The Tyche of Caesarea Maritima." *Palestine Exploration Quarterly* 116 (1984): 110–14.

Ringel, Joseph. "The Harbour God of Caesarea Maritima." *Sefunim* 4 (1975): 22–27.

Wenning, Robert. "Die Stadtgöttin von Caesarea Maritima." *Boreas: Münstersche Beiträge zur Archäologie* 9 (1986): 113–29.

Will, Ernest. "La coupe de Césarée de Palestine au Musée du Louvre." *Fondation Eugene Piot: Monuments et mémoires* 65 (1983): 1–24.

Chapter 2

Foerster, Gideon. "The Early History of Caesarea Maritima." In *Studies in the History of Caesarea Maritima,* ed. Charles T. Fritsch. Bulletin of the American Schools of Oriental Research, Supplemental Studies, no. 19. Missoula, Montana, 1975. 9–22.

Hohlfelder, Robert L. "The Caesarea Maritima Coastline Before Herod: Some Preliminary Observations." *Bulletin of the American Schools of Oriental Research* 252 (1983): 67–68.

Joukowsky, Martha. *A Complete Manual of Field Archaeology.* Englewood Cliffs, New Jersey, 1980.

Levine, Lee I. "À propos de la fondation de la Tour de Straton." *Revue biblique* 80 (1973): 75–81.

———. "The Hasmonaean Conquest of Straton's Tower." *Israel Exploration Journal* 24 (1974): 62–69.

Martin, Roland. *L'urbanisme dans la Grèce antique.* 2d ed. rev., Paris, 1974.

Mumford, Lewis. *The City in History: Its Origins, Its Transformations, and Its Prospects.* New York, 1961.

———. *The Culture of Cities.* New York, 1970.

Roller, Duane W. "Hellenistic Pottery from Caesarea Maritima: A Preliminary Study." *Bulletin of the American Schools of Oriental Research* 238 (1980): 35–42.

———. "The Northern Plain of Sharon in the Hellenistic Period." *Bulletin of the American Schools of Oriental Research* 247 (1982): 43–52.

———. "The Problem of the Location of Straton's Tower." *Bulletin of the American Schools of Oriental Research* 252 (1983): 61–66.

Chapter 3

Flinder, Alexander. "A Piscina at Caesarea—A Preliminary Survey." *Israel Exploration Journal* 26 (1976): 77–80.

Gophna, R., and Kokhavi, M. "Notes and News: An Archaeological Survey of the Plain of Sharon." *Israel Exploration Journal* 16 (1966): 144.

Netzer, Ehud. *Greater Herodium.* Qedem: Monographs of the Institute of Archaeology, the Hebrew University of Jerusalem, no. 13. Jerusalem, 1981.

Oleson, John P. "Herod and Vitruvius: Preliminary Thoughts on Harbour Engineering at Sebastos." *Harbour Archaeology: Proceedings of the First International Workshop on Ancient Mediterranean Harbours, Caesarea Maritima 24–28.6.83,* ed. Avner Raban. British Archaeological Reports, International Series, no. 257. Oxford, 1985. 165–72.

Raban, Avner. "Josephus and the Herodian Harbour of Caesarea." In *Josephus Flavius: Historian of Eretz-Israel in the Hellenistic Roman Period,* ed. U. Rappaport. Jerusalem, 1982. 165–84. (in Hebrew).

Schalit, Abraham. *König Herodes: Der Mann und sein Werk.* Berlin, 1969.

Tsafrir, Yoram. "The Desert Fortresses of Judaea in the Second Temple Period." *The Jerusalem Cathedra* 2 (1982): 120–45.

Yadin, Yigael. *Masada: Herod's Fortress and the Zealots' Last Stand.* London, 1966; reprint, Jerusalem-Tel Aviv-Haifa, 1984.

Chapter 4

Avi-Yonah, Michael. "The Caesarea Porphyry Statue." *Israel Exploration Journal* 20 (1970): 203–8.

Bull, Robert J. "The Mithraeum of Caesarea Maritima." *Textes et mémoires* 4 (1978): 75–89.

Foerster, Gideon. "A Cuirassed Bronze Statue of Hadrian." *Atiqot,* English Series, 17 (1985): 139–60.

Hopfe, Lewis Moore, and Lease, Gary. "The Caesarea Mithraeum: A Preliminary Report." *Biblical Archaeologist* 38 (1975): 1–10.

Jones, A. H. M. *The Cities of the Eastern Roman Provinces.* 2d ed. by Michael Avi-Yonah et al. Oxford, 1971.

MacMullen, Ramsay. *Paganism in the Roman Empire.* New Haven and London, 1981.

Ward-Perkins, John B. *Roman Imperial Architecture.* 2d ed. Harmondsworth, England, 1981.

Chapter 5

Avi-Yonah, Michael. "The Caesarea Inscription of the Twenty-Four Priestly Courses." In *The Teacher's Yoke: Studies in Memory of Henry Trantham,* ed. E. J. Vardaman and J. L. Garrett, Jr. Waco, Texas, 1964. 46–57.

———. "The Synagogue of Caesarea, Preliminary Report." *Louis M. Rabinowitz Fund for the Exploration of Ancient Synagogues, Bulletin* 3 (1960): 44–48.

———. "The Economics of Byzantine Palestine." *Israel Exploration Journal* 8 (1958): 39–51.

Barnes, Timothy D. *Constantine and Eusebius.* Cambridge and London, 1981.

Ben-Zvi, I. "A Lamp With a Samaritan Inscription." *Israel Exploration Journal* 11 (1961): 139–42.

Broshi, Magen. "Excavations in the Chapel of St. Vartan in the Holy Sepulchre." *Israel Exploration Journal* 35 (1985): 108–28.

———. "The Jerusalem Ship Reconsidered." *International Journal of Nautical Archaeology and Underwater Exploration* 6 (1977): 349–52.

Cameron, Averil. *Procopius and the Sixth Century.* Berkeley and Los Angeles, 1985.

Claude, Dietrich. *Die byzantinische Stadt im 6. Jahrhundert.* Munich, 1969.

Dan, Yaron. *The City in Eretz-Israel During the Late Roman & Byzantine Periods.* Jerusalem, 1978 (in Hebrew).

Downey, Glanville. "Caesarea and the Christian Church." In *Studies in the History of Caesarea Maritima,* ed. Charles T. Fritsch. Bulletin of the American Schools of Oriental Research, Supplemental Studies, no. 19. Missoula, Montana, 1975. 23–42.

———. "The Christian Schools of Palestine: A Chapter in Literary History." *Harvard Library Bulletin* 12 (1958): 297–319.

Franken, H. J., and Kalsbeek, J. *Potters of a Medieval Village in the Jordan Valley.* Amsterdam, Oxford, and New York, 1975.

Frend, W. H. C. *The Rise of Christianity.* Philadelphia, 1984.

Hamburger, Anit. "A Greco-Samaritan Amulet from Caesarea." *Israel Exploration Journal* 9 (1959): 43–45.

Hohlfelder, Robert L. "Byzantine Coin Finds from the Sea: A Glimpse of Caesarea Maritima's Later History." *Harbour Archaeology: Proceedings of the First International Workshop on Ancient Mediterranean Harbours, Caesarea Maritima 24–28.6.83*, ed. Avner Raban. British Archaeological Reports International Series, no. 257. Oxford, 1985. 179–83.

———. "Caesarea Maritima in Late Antiquity: An Introduction to the Numismatic Evidence." *Ancient Coins of the Graeco-Roman World*, ed. W. Heckel and R. Sullivan. Waterloo, Ontario, 1984. 261–85.

Holum, Kenneth G. "Andreas *Philoktistes:* A Proconsul of Byzantine Palestine." *Israel Exploration Journal* 36 (1986): 61–64.

———. "Caesarea and the Samaritans." In *City, Town and Countryside in the Early Byzantine Era*, ed. Robert L. Hohlfelder. East European Monographs, no. 120, Byzantine Series no. 1. Boulder, Colo., 1982. 65–73.

———. "Fl. Stephanos, Proconsul of Byzantine Palestine." *Zeitschrift für Papyrologie und Epigraphik* 63 (1986): 231–39.

Hunt, E. D. *Holy Land Pilgrimage in the Later Roman Empire A.D. 312–460*. Oxford, 1982.

Krautheimer, Richard. *Early Christian and Byzantine Architecture*. 3rd ed. Harmondsworth, England, 1981.

Levine, Lee I. "R. Abbahu of Caesarea." In *Christianity, Judaism and Other Greco-Roman Cults, Studies for Morton Smith at Sixty*, ed. Jacob Neusner. Leiden, Netherlands, 1975. Part 4, 56–76.

Lieberman, Saul. "The Martyrs of Caesarea." *Annuaire de l'Institut de Philologie et d'Histoire orientales et slaves* 7 (1939–44): 395–46.

Negev, Avraham. *The Nabataean Potter's Workshop at Oboda*. Bonn, 1974.

Oleson, John Peter. "A Roman Water Mill on the Crocodilion River Near Caesarea." *Zeitschrift des Deutschen Palästina-Vereins* 100 (1984): 137–52.

Reich, Ronny. "On Some Byzantine Remains." *Atiqot*, English Series, 17 (1985): 205–13.

Siegelmann, A. "A Mosaic Floor at Caesarea Maritima." *Israel Exploration Journal* 24 (1974): 216–21.

Spiro, Marie. "Recent Mosaic Discoveries at Caesarea Maritima: Winter and Spring." *American Journal of Archaeology* 85 (1981): 319.

Sussman, Varda. "Moulds for Lamps and Figurines from a Caesarea Workshop." *Atiqot*, English Series, 14 (1980): 76–79.

Vann, Robert L. "Early Byzantine Street Construction at Caesarea Maritima." In *City, Town and Countryside in the Early Byzantine Era*, ed. Robert L. Hohlfelder. East European Monographs, no. 120, Byzantine Series, no. 1. Boulder, Colo., 1982. 165–98.

Yeivin, Shmuel. "Excavations at Caesarea Maritima." *Archaeology* 8 (1955): 122–29.

Chapter 6

El'ad, Amikam. "The Coastal Cities of Palestine During the Early Middle Ages." *The Jerusalem Cathedra* 2 (1982): 446–67.

Kaegi, Walter Emil, Jr. "Some Seventh-Century Sources on Caesarea." *Israel Exploration Journal* 28 (1978): 177–81.

Chapter 7

Benvenisti, Meron. *The Crusaders in the Holy Land*. Jerusalem, 1970.

Hazard, Harry W. "Caesarea and the Crusades." In *Studies in the History of Caesarea Maritima*, ed. Charles T. Fritsch. Bulletin of the American Schools of Oriental Research, Supplemental Studies, no. 19. Missoula, Montana, 1975. 79–114.

Jacoby, Zehava. "The Impact of Northern French Gothic on Crusader Sculpture in the Holy Land." *Il Medio Oriente e l'Occidente nell'arte del xiii secolo*. Atti del XXIV Congresso di storia del'arte, vol. 2. Ed. Hans Beltung. Bologna, 1982. 123–27.

Lamonte, J. L. "The Lords of Caesarea in the Period of the Crusades." *Speculum* 22 (1947): 145–61.

Prawer, Joshua. *The Latin Kingdom of Jerusalem, European Colonialism in the Middle Ages*. London, 1972.

Pringle, R. Denys. "Medieval Pottery from Caesarea: The Crusader Period." *Levant* 17 (1985): 171–202.

Runciman, Sir Stephen. *History of the Crusades*. 3 vols. Cambridge, 1951–54.

Setton, Kenneth Meyer, ed. *A History of the Crusades*. 4 vols. Madison, Wis., 1966–77.

Epilogue

Reifenberg, A. "Caesarea: A Study in the Decline of a Town." *Israel Exploration Journal* 1 (1950–51): 20–32.

Schumacher, G. "Recent Discoveries at Caesarea, Umm el Jemal, and Haifa," *Palestine Exploration Fund Quarterly Statement*, 1888: 134–41

Index

Abbahu, Rabbi, 196
death of, and miracle at Caesarea, 199
Abbasid caliphate, 202, 207
'Abd al-Malik, Caliph, 206
Acre, 218
Actium, battle of, 57
Acts of the Apostles, 109, 111
evidence of Caesarean Christianity in, 156-58
aerial infrared photography, 35, 37
agora (marketplace), 87, 176
Agrippa, Marcus Flavius, 118, 143
Byzantine Caesareans compared with, 179
Ahriman (god), 148
air bags, 96, 97
air lift, 96
air probe, 94-96
Akko, 44
Alexander, Flavius Procopius Constantius, 179, 181
Alexander Jannaeus, King of Judaea, 53
Alexander the Great, 26-27, 73
Alexandria, 26, 73, 158, 189
lighthouse at, 98
Origen in, 158
Alexandrion, 62
Altar of Burnt Offerings, 62
Amazons, 15, 16
American Schools of Oriental Research (ASOR), 19, 43
amphitheater, 82, 85-86
decline of, 176
'Amr ibn al-'As, 203
Anastasius, Byzantine Emperor, 185
anastylosis, 241
anchor, stone, 28, 30
Andreas, 180
Antioch, 72, 189
Christianity in, 155
Antipater, 55, 56
Antipatris (Aphek), 70
Antoninus of Piacenza, 194
Anu (god), 26
Aphek (Antipatris), 70
Apollo (god), 145, 153
Apollonia (Arsuf), 206
Apollonius, 30-31
aqueducts, 78-79, 127-29
Byzantine construction at, 172, 173
Muslim repair of, 208, 231
archaeology, 13, 16, 19, 21
architects in, 185-86
control in, 37
dating in, *see* dating
mortuary, 224-26
recording in, 38, 98
reporting in, 42-43
stratigraphic, *see* stratigraphic archaeology
typical day in, 19-20
underwater, 94-98, 137-41
volunteers in, 20-21
Archelaus, 108
architects, 184-85
archives building, 169, 170, 188
arena, 131
Arianism, 188
Aristotle, 26, 164
army, Roman:
in Caesarea, 112, 113
construction by, 129
worship of Jupiter Dolichenus popular in, 145
Arsuf (Apollonia), 206
Artemis (goddess), 145-47, 153, 158, 164
aryballos (oil jug), 93
Ascalon, 206
Aswan granite, 131
Atlit, 44
Augustus, Emperor of Rome, 22, 27, 56, 57, 69, 71, 73, 90, 142
on Herod, 55
Herod's meeting with, 57
temple dedicated to, 73, 88, 89, 113, 142
Avi-Yonah, Michael, 17, 43, 44, 127
on prosperity of Byzantine Caesarea, 192-93

Baghdad, 202
Bahat, Dan, 17
Bladhuri, al-, 203
Baldwin (Crusader archbishop), 219
Baldwin I, King of Jerusalem, 219
Caesarea granted as fief by, 220
balk, 33
Bar Kokhba, 124, 129
baths, 155
architect's reconstruction of, 184-85
Byzantine era, 182-85
Baybars, ruler of Egypt, 237
Bdellopotamos, 75
Bedouin, 201
Beirut, 189
Belisarius, 189
Benjamin of Tudela, 220
Beryllos, 197
Beth Shean (Scythopolis), 124, 161
bishops of Caesarea, 188
Bosnians, 238
Buildings (Procopius), 189
Byzantine esplanade, 187
Byzantium, 162
Crusader gathering in, 217

Caesarea, 271
al-Maqdisi on, 207
aqueduct system of, 78-79, 127-29, 172, 173, 208
aristocracy of, 75
Baybars' conquest of, 237
bishops of, 188
Byzantine aristocracy of, 180-82
Byzantine era population of, 174
Byzantine period in, 162-99
Byzantine reoccupation of, 206
as capital of Judaea province, 109
as center of ecclesiastical authority, 188
Christian destruction of pagan temples in, 176-77
Christianity in, 155-62
city wall of, *see* wall of Caesarea
coins minted at, 112-13, 114-15, 145
under Crusader rule, 217-35
as "daughter of Edom," 107-8, 109, 118, 133, 153
depopulation of, 204
dunes' advance on, 237
founding of, 11, 72-75, 155
gods and goddesses of, 142-53; *see also specific deities*
Greek used in, 180
Hadrian's visit to, 124
harbor of, *see* Sebastos (harbor)
Herod's considerations in founding, 73
history of, 22-23
imperial patronage of, 122-42
as industrial center, 191-92
Jewish claims on, 74
Jewish Wars and, 111-12
Josephus on, 72-74, 79
Latin used in, 111, 118, 180
modern revival of, 240-41
Mu'awiya on, 206
municipal institutions of, 75
Muslim name of, 206
under Muslim rule, 202, 203-15
Muslim siege of, 203
Nasir-i-Khusrau on, 207
official name of, 114
pilgrimages to Holy Land and, 193-94, 217
promoted to metropolis, 134
promoted to Roman colony, 113-14
prosperity in Byzantine era of, 187-99
religious syncretism in, 147-48
as *ribat,* 206
Romanization of, 108-21, 122
Roman troops in, 112, 113
Saint Paul in, 111, 155-56, 158
Saladin's conquest of, 220, 234-35
sea level at, 46-49
site map of, 18
six-hundred-year desolution of, 238
street plan of, 86
students in, 189
swamps in, 237, 238
territory of, 75-78
trade in Byzantine era of, 191
trade routes of, 137
Caesarea Ancient Harbour Excavation Project (CAHEP), 17, 19
basins examined by, 209, 211
computers used by, 230-31
diving volunteers of, 20-21
extent of Caesarea harbor determined by, 46-49
Herodian temple investigated by, 50
Josephus's descriptions confirmed by, 98
Sebastos explored by, 91-105
shipwreck investigated by, 137-41

statuette of Jupiter found by, 144, 145
wall of Caesarea discovered by, 49-53, 79, 82
Caesarea Cup, 13-15
as last evidence of paganism in Caesarea, 195-96
Caesarea Museum, 11
Caesarea's Tyche, 11-16, 74, 89, 142-43
on Caesarea Cup, 13-15, 196
on coins, 13, 112
Sebastos in statue of, 12, 16
caldaria, 184
Calderini, A., 17
Campus Martius (*pedion*), 176
Canadian Social Sciences and Humanities Research Council, 21
Caracalla, Emperor of Rome, 133, 143
carbon 14 dating, 38, 39
carceres, 131
cavea, 131
ceramicists, 135, 136-37
ceramic loom weights, 117
ceramic shards, 41-42, 43-44
chariot racing, 131, 133
Chorseos River, 75
Christianity, 155-62
in Antioch, 155
in Caesarea, 155-62
Constantine's conversion to, 162
decline and fall of Roman Empire and, 164, 186
Eusebius as apologist for, 161
as official religion of Roman Empire, 162
persecution of, 161
Persian persecution of, 202
prosperity of Byzantine Caesarea and, 193-95
churches, 177-79
on site of Christ's Tomb, 195
see also specific churches
Church of the Holy Sepulcher, 195
Cicero, Marcus Tullius, 142
circus, *see* hippodrome
Circus Maximus, 131
cities:
Aristotle on, 26, 164
founded by Alexander, 26-27
Mumford on, 25, 26, 107-8, 184
origins of, in ancient times, 55
Pausanias on, 74, 79
as prestigious to Roman emperors, 122
as religious communities, 142
requirements for, 74, 78-79
City in History, The (Mumford), 25*n*
Cleopatra, Queen of Egypt, 57
Clermont, 217
coins:
Caesarea's Tyche on, 13, 112-13, 142-43
of Constantius II, 168
of Crusader Caesarea, 221, 223
dating and, 41, 79, 112
Hadrian's visit to Caesarea on, 124
in Muslim Caesarea, 206
Serapis and Demeter on, 145
solidi, 188
struck at Caesarea, 112-13, 114-15, 145
computers:
CAHEP use of, 230-31
pottery sherd charts and, 136-37
concrete, hydraulic, 101
Conder, C. R., 17, 18
Constantine I, Emperor of Rome, 162
Constantinople, *see* Byzantium
Constantius II, Emperor of Rome, 168
cook pots, 221, 222
Cornelius, 156-57, 158, 178
counterscarp, 227
Crema, L., 17
Crocodile River, 29-30, 173, 238
dam on, 173, 174, 218
Crusader fortifications, 17, 23, 44, 226-31
glacis of, 230
northern and eastern gates of, 230
reconstruction of, 226
Crusaders:
burials of, 224
Caesarean harbors under, 231-34
castle of, 231
women as, 224, 226
Crusades, 217-19, 220
as imperialist, 217-18
Ctesiphon, 202
cults, public, 144-53
Culture of Cities, The (Mumford), 25*n*
cyma kantheros, 43
Cypros, 62, 69

Daliyya, Nahal, 75
Damascus, 202
Darius, King of Persia, 26
dating, 38, 41, 42, 79
carbon 14, 38, 39
coins and, 41, 79, 112
pottery sherds and, 136
of Sebastos concrete, 101
David, King of Israel, 26, 27
Dead Sea, 62, 64
Decius, Emperor of Rome, 159
decuriones, 118, 180
Demeter (goddess), 145, 153
dendrochronology, 41
dhimmi, 202, 204
Diocaesarea (Sepphoris), 124
Dionysus (god), head of, 143-44
dive raft, 94
divers, 20-21
techniques used by, 94
urinatores, 105
Dome of the Rock, 59, 60
Doq, 62, 69
Dor, 53
Drusion, 98-99
Drusus, 90
duumvir, 118

Ecclesiastical History (Eusebius), 161
Edom, 107
Elias, 179, 180, 181
Embriaco, William, 219
endoxotatos, 180
Ephesus, 145, 147, 164
Epic of Gilgamesh, The, 26
Erech (Uruk), 26
Euelpidius, Flavius, 179, 180
Eusebius, Bishop of Caesarea, 161, 177, 188
Caesarean life described by, 161-62
Constantine endorsed by, 162
on miracle at Caesarea, 199

Fatimids, 207
Felix, Antonius, 111, 158
Festus, Porcius, III, 158
field supervisors, 37
fortification wall, 208
Foster, Gideon, 17
frigidarium, 184
Frova, A., 17
Fulcher of Chartres, 219
funerary relief, 116

Gaza wine, 191
Gerasa (Jerash), 124
German barbarians, 201
Gibbon, Edward, 164, 186, 201
Gilgamesh, 26
glass vessels, 118
Byzantine, 167
Crusader, 224
millefiori, 79, 81
Muslim, 211
Godfrey of Bouillon, 218
gods and goddesses, 142-53
personal, 143-44
see also specific deities
Granier, Eustace, 220
granite, Aswan, 131
gravestones, Jewish, 197
Great Mosque, 202, 219
Great Persecution, 161, 177
Greek, 180
Gregory Nazianzen, Saint, 189
Hadera River, 238
Hadrian, Emperor of Rome, 78, 207
Caesarean aqueducts expanded by, 127
Caesarea visited by, 124
porphyry statue of, 127
statue of, 123, 124, 125
temple dedicated to, 143, 180
urban projects of, 124
Hadrianeum, 125, 127, 180
ha-kotel ha-ma'aravi (the Western Wall), 59, 60
Haram esh-Sherif, 59-61
Hebrew University of Jerusalem, 17
Hejaz, 201
Helena, Empress of Rome, 194
Heraclius, Byzantine Emperor, 202, 203
Hera of Argos, 73
Herodian-Roman theater, 23
Herodian temple, 46, 49-50
Negev's excavation of, 49-50
Herodion, 62
palaces in, 66-67, 69-70
Herod the Great, King of Judaea, 11, 17, 28, 142, 207, 235
Augustus on, 5
Augustus's meeting with, 57
background of, 55-57
Caesarea deities established by, 142
Caesarea founded by, 72-75, 155
declared King of the Jews, 56
as master builder, 59-72, 105
palaces built by, 62-70, 86
Romanization of Caesarea by, 108
Samaria refounded by, 70-72
Hexapla, 159, 189
Hippodamian urban plans, 86
Hippodamus of Miletus, 86
hippodrome, 129, 131
Hissarlik (Troy), 31
History of the Expedition to Jerusalem, A (Fulcher), 219
History of the Wars (Procopius), 189
Holy Sepulcher ship, 195
Homer, 31, 133
honorific portico, 153
hookah breathing apparatus, 94
Horns of Hattin, 220, 235
horrea (warehouses), 88-89
pottery sherds found in, 134-37
Hoshaya, Rabbi, 196
human skeletal biology, 226
Humphrey, John, 131
Hyrcania, 62

Idumaea, 55, 56
Ikhshidids, 207
Iliad (Homer), 133
infrared photography, aerial, 35, 37
instrumenta domestica, 119
insulae, 86
Isaac Napha of Caesarea, Rabbi, 107, 108, 196
Ishtar (goddess), 26
Isis (goddess), 144-45, 153, 158
Islam, 202
Israel, 44
 archaeological remains in, 19
Israel Department of Antiquities and Museums (IDAM), 17, 19, 42, 165
 archaeology supervised by, 241
Israeli National Parks Authority, 17
 Caesarea cleared of modern buildings by, 241

Jaffa, *see* Joppa
Jebel Fareidis (Mountain of Herod), 66, 67, 69
Jerash (Gerasa), 124
Jericho, 31, 33
Jerome, Saint, 189
Jerusalem, 22, 33, 62, 69, 111, 112, 156, 203
 Baldwin I crowned King of, 219
 Caesarea vs., 107, 188
 David's conquest of, 26
 Hadrian's plan for rebuilding of, 124
 Helena in, 194-95
 siege of, 56
Jesus Christ, 109-10
 ministry of, 155
jewelry, Muslim, 214-15
Jewish Antiquities (Josephus), 57, 73-74, 79, 86, 90
Jewish Wars, 74, 111-12, 114, 124
 Josephus on, 75
 Romanization and, 111-12
 second, 124, 129
Jewish Wars (Josephus), 57, 72, 73, 90
Jews:
 Caesarean citizenship rights demanded by, 108
 Christian emperors on, 196
 in Crusader Caesarea, 220
 migration to Holy Land by, 238-40
"Joan of Caesarea," 226
Johannes, 188
John I Tzimisces, Byzantine Emperor, 206
John the Baptist, 62
Joint Expedition to Caesarea Maritima (JECM), 11, 16, 17, 19
 CAHEP's reconstruction disputed by, 53
 head of Dionysus found by, 143-44
 hippodrome surveyed by, 131
 Muslim bronze objects uncovered by, 210, 211
 Muslim suburb excavated by, 213
 seventh-century depopulation confirmed by, 204
 stratigraphic archaeology of, 33, 34-35
 on wall of Caesarea, 79
 warehouses discovered by, 88-89
Joppa (Tel Aviv), 22, 30, 70
 Peter's vision in, 157
Joseph, 109
Josephus, Flavius, 57, 61, 69
 CAHEP's confirmation of descriptions by, 98
 on founding of Caesarea, 72-74, 79
 Jewish War statistics reported by, 75
 on Sebaste, 72
 Sebastos described by, 90, 91, 100, 142
Judaea:
 Caesarea as capital of, 109
 renaming of, 124
 see also Palestine
Judah the Maccabee, 53
Jupiter (god), statuette of, 144, 145
Jupiter Capitolinus (god), 124
Jupiter Dolichenus (god), 145, 153, 158
Justinian I, Byzantine Emperor, 189
 Palestine construction projects of, 193
Justus, 197

Kenyon, Kathleen, 33
Kitchener, H. H., 17, 18
kurkar sandstone, 168

Lake Caesarea, 173
lamprotatos, 180
Lapp, Paul W., 33
Latin, 111, 118, 180
Levine, Lee, 17, 169
library, 189
lighthouse, 98-99
Link, Edwin A., 17, 90
list of priestly courses, 198
locus numbers, 38
locus sheets, 38
loom weights, ceramic, 117
Louis IX, King of France, 220
Luke, Gospel according to, 109

Machaeros, 62
Macrobius, 57
magnetometer, 141
Maioumas, 127
 inscription found in, 115, 118, 122
Maqdisi, al-, 207
Mark Antony, 56, 57
marketplace (*agora*), 87, 176
martyrium, 177
Mary, 109
Masada, 22, 62, 69
 palaces in, 62-65
Mask of Comedy mosaic, 121
Mask of Tragedy mosaic, 120
Maxentius, Emperor of Rome, 162
megaloprepestatos, 180
menorot, 196
millefiori glass vessels, 79, 81
Missione Archeologica Italiana, 17
 Byzantine wall discovered by, 164-65
 evidence of Pilate discovered by, 109-10
 Roman-style bath explored by, 182-85
 theater excavated by, 85, 109
 wall of Caesarea excavated by, 50, 52
Mithraea, 148
Mithraic medallion, 152
Mithras (god), cult of, 148-53, 158, 164
 bull slaughter myth in, 149-50, 152
 sun in, 150-51
Mnason of Cyprus, 156
mortuary archaeology, 224-26
mosaics:
 Byzantine, 170-71
 Mask of Comedy, 121
 Mask of Tragedy, 120
mosques, 202
 see also Great Mosque
Mountain of Herod (*Jebel Fureidis*), 66, 67, 69
Mount Carmel, 22
Mount Gerizim, 75, 196
Mount Zion, 75, 196
Mu'awiya, 203
 on Caesarea, 206
 Caesarea's fortifications rebuilt by, 206
Muhammad, 201
Mumford, Lewis, 25, 26, 107-8, 164
Munsell Soil Color Charts, 137
Muslims, 201-2
 burials of, 224
 Palestine invaded by, 203

Nabataean Arabs, 55
Nablus (Neapolis), 75, 124
Nasir-i-Khusrau, 207
National Endowment for the Humanities, 21
National Geographic Society, 21
Nazareth, 155
Neapolis (Nablus), 75, 124
Negev, Avraham, 17, 43, 44, 211, 226
 eastern quay discovered by, 46
 horde of Muslim jewelry discovered by, 214-15
 marble capital found by, 178
Nero, Emperor of Rome, 112, 143
Netanya, 75
Netzer, Ehud, 17, 62, 69, 169
 on Promontory Palace, 86
Nicolaus of Damascus, 59
"Noble Sanctuary," 59-61

Ocean (mythical being), 153
Octavian, *see* Augustus, Emperor of Rome
oil jug (*aryballos*), 93
oil lamps, 41, 116, 205
 Byzantine, 167
 Herodian, 81
 Muslim, 210, 212, 213
On the Martyrs of Palestine (Eusebius), 161
opus caementicium (concrete construction), 101
opus sectile, 184
Origen, 158-59, 161, 189
 background of, 158
 in Caesarea, 158-59
Orion, 189
Ottoman Empire, 238

Palestine:
 Muslim invasion of, 203
 Persian invasion of, 202
 see also Judaea
Palestine Jewish Colonization Association (PICA), 238
 dissolution of, 240
Pamphilus, 161
parazonium, 113
Paul, Saint, 23, 145
 Caesarea visited by, 111, 155-56
 Christianity spread by, 155-56
 letters written in Caesarea by, 158
 Philip and, 156
Paula, 194
Pausanias, 74, 79
pedion (Campus Martius), 176
peribleptos, 180
Persia, 148
 Palestine invaded by, 202
 Rome attacked by, 201
Peter, Saint, 157, 178
Petra, 55
Phasael, 56
Phasaelis, 70
Philip the Evangelist, 156, 178
 Saint Paul and, 156
Phoenicians, 27
Piganiol, André, 201

Pilate, Pontius, 22-23, 156
evidence on existence of, 109-10
temple dedicated to Tiberius by, 110-11, 143
pilgrimages, religious, 193-94, 217
Pilgrim of Bordeaux, 194
pillar, limestone, 179-80
Piraeus, Sebastos vs., 100
piscina, 184
Plain of Sharon, 30, 70, 73, 75, 134
Plutarch, 26
Poleg, Nahal, 75
Politics (Aristotle), 26
Poloner, Johannes, 238
Pompey the Great, 56
Portus Augusti, see Sebastos
pottery:
Byzantine, 166, 168
of Crusader Caesarea, 221, 222, 223
found near quay, 44
in Muslim Caesarea, 205, 213-14
sherds of, 41-42, 43-44, 78, 79, 81, 134-37
terra sigillata, 79, 80
pozzolana, 101
praefurnium, 184
praeses, 162
Praxiteles, 116
Priam, King of Troy, 31
priesthoods, 143
Procopius, Saint, 161, 177
children named after, 177-78
Procopius of Gaza, 185, 187, 189, 196
Promontory Palace, 17
as Herod's palace, 86
public festivals, 142
Pythian games, 145

Qaisariyah, *see* Caesarea
Qelt, Wadi, 69
Quirinius, 109

recording, 38
in underwater archaeology, 98
reliquary cross, 217, 28
reporting, 42-43
Reybaud, L., 238
ribatat, 206
robbing, 204-5
Roger, F. E., 238
Roma (goddess), 113, 142
Romanization, 108-21, 122
Caesarean art and, 119-21
Caesarean mint and, 112-15
Caesarea promoted to colony and, 113-14
chariot racing and, 133
Jewish War and, 111-12
Maioumas inscription and, 115, 118
Rome, Roman Empire:
census in Judaea by, 109
concrete construction in, 101
as foe of Israelite kingdom, 107-8
Herod and, 56-57
Piganiol on fall of, 201
second Temple of Jerusalem destroyed by, 59
Rostovtzeff, Michael Ivanovich, 164
Rothschild, Edmond de, 238
Royal Portico, 61

Sabbarin, 127
St. Peter, Cathedral of, 234-35
Saladin, 220, 234-35
Samaria (Sebaste), 30, 70-72, 87, 107, 133
Philip's preaching in, 156
Samaritans, 75
in Christian Palestine, 196
in Crusader Caesarea, 220
revolts of, 199
San Lorenzo Cathedral, 220
Saturn (mythical being), 153
Saturnius, C. Sentius, 109
Schliemann, Heinrich, 31
Scythopolis (Beth Shean), 124, 161
Sdot Yam kibbutz, 11, 17, 21, 23, 35, 165
founding of, 239-40
Sea Diver, 90
Sea of Galilee, 155, 220
Sebaste (Samaria), 30, 70-72, 87, 107, 133
Sebastos (god), 12, 16
Sebastos (harbor), 16, 17, 22, 112, 134
CAHEP explorations of, 91-105
CAHEP mapping of, 96, 97
concrete used in, 100-101, 102
demise of, 141-42, 185
Josephus's description of, 90, 91, 100, 142
lighthouse of, 98-99
in Muslim Caesarea, 211
Piraeus vs., 100
scenario for construction of, 105
shipwrecks in, 137-41, 185
statues at entrance of, 99
Strato's Tower harbor as inner basin of, 100
wooden frameworks used in, 101, 102, 103, 104
Secret History (Procopius), 189, 196
Senesh, Hannah, 240
Sepphoris (Diocaesarea), 124
Septimius Severus, Emperor of Rome, 133, 145
Serapis (god), 145, 153, 158
Severus Alexander, Emperor of Rome, 134
sewers, 86, 175-76
sheave bloc, 93
Shechem (Tell Balatah), 33
sherds, ceramic, 41-42, 43-44
shipwrecks, 137-41, 185
Sidon, 22, 27, 30
sigillum, 79, 80
Sindaya, Wadi, 127
site surveys, 35
solidi, 188
sophists, 189
spina, 131, 132
sportula, 188
squeezes, 115, 118
stratigraphic archaeology, 31-43, 79
destruction layers in, 203
five key concepts of, 34
at Troy, 31
underwater, 91
Wheeler-Kenyon method of, 33
Strato, King of Sidon, 22, 27-28, 30, 43-44, 207
Strato's Tower, 22, 72, 73, 112
access to foreign markets at, 30
search for, 25-53
southern harbor of, 100
strategic location of, 27
wall of, 44, 49-53
Zeno's visit to, 30-31, 34
stratum, 31
streets, 175-76
refurbishing of, 193
stylobates, 204-5
sun, in Mithras cult, 150-51
sug, 202

talmud, 107, 197
Tanninim, Nahal, 127
Taylor, J., 238
Tel Aviv (Joppa), 22, 30, 70, 157
Tell Balatah (Shechem), 33
Temple of Caesar, 73, 88, 89
Temple of the Jews, 22, 23
destruction of, 112
Herod's rebuilding of, 59, 62
tepidarium, 184
terra sigillata pottery, 79, 80
tetrapylon, 176
theater, 82, 84, 85
exotic Artemis unearthed in, 147
Theodora, Empress of Rome, 189
Theophilus, Bishop of Caesarea, 188
Thomson, W. M., 91
Thousand and One Nights, The, 202
Tiberias, 124
Tiberius, Emperor of Rome, 110
temple dedicated to, 110-11, 143
Tigris River, 202
Titus, 57, 111-12, 118, 122
Tivoli, Hadrian's villa at, 122
"To Caesarea" (Senesh), 240
Tosefta, 44
Trajan, Emperor of Rome, 114
transport amphoras, 135
Trebonianus Gallus, Emperor of Rome, 115
trenches, balks of, 33
Troy (Hissarlik), 31
Tulunids, 207
Tyche, 14

Umar, Caliph, 206
Umayyad caliphate, 202, 203
underwater archaeology, 94-98, 137-41
Urban II, Pope, 217
urinatores, 105
Uruk (Erech), 26

Vespasian, Emperor of Rome, 57, 86, 111, 112, 118, 122, 207
Caesarea promoted to colony by, 113-14
villas, 182
Virgil, 108
volunteers, 20-21

Wailing Wall, *see* Western Wall
wall of Caesarea, 79-82
Byzantine, 164-65, 179
under Muslims, *see* fortification wall
wall of Strato's Tower, 44, 49-53
wall of Caesarea and, 79, 82
warehouses (*horrea*), 88-89
pottery sherds found in, 134-37
Warren, Charles, 61
water flask, ceramic, 212
Wegman, Aharon, 17
Western Wall (*ha-kotel ha-ma'aravi*), 59, 60
Wheeler, Mortimer, 33
Wright, George Ernest, 33

Yadin, Yigael, 62, 64
Yarmuk River, battle of, 203
Yeivin, Shmuel, 17, 125, 182
mosaic floor examined by, 182

Zalouphios, 188
Zangemeister, K., 118
Zeno, 30-31, 34
Zeus, 122, 124
Zeus at Olympia, 73
Zodiac boat, 94
Zoilus, 53
Zoroastrianism, 148